DATE DUE			

MAN ON HIS PAST

THE WILES LECTURES
GIVEN AT THE QUEEN'S UNIVERSITY
BELFAST 1954

MAN ON HIS PAST

THE STUDY OF THE HISTORY OF HISTORICAL SCHOLARSHIP

BY

HERBERT BUTTERFIELD

Emeritus Professor of Modern History
in the University of Cambridge

CAMBRIDGE
AT THE UNIVERSITY PRESS
1969

PUBLISHED BY
THE SYNDICS OF THE CAMBRIDGE UNIVERSITY PRESS

Bentley House, 200 Euston Road, London, N.W.1
American Branch: 32 East 57th Street, New York, N.Y. 10022

Standard Book Numbers:
521 07265 4 *clothbound*
521 09567 0 *paperback*

First published 1955
First paperback edition 1969

*First printed in Great Britain at University Press, Cambridge
Reprinted in Great Britain by Page Bros (Norwich) Ltd.*

To

JANET D. BOYD
*Founder of the
Wiles Trust
Lectures*

FOREWORD

In 1953 the Queen's University of Belfast was given a bene-faction to be known as the Wiles Trust. Its purpose is to promote the study of the history of civilisation and to encourage the extension of historical thinking into the realm of general ideas.

The purpose of the Trust is to be fulfilled by inviting an historian each year to deliver in Belfast a series of lectures in which he relates his researches to the history of civilisation or reflects upon the wider implications of more detailed historical studies. The first lectures of the series were delivered in November 1954 by H. Butterfield, Professor of Modern History in the University of Cambridge.

E. A. ASHBY

The Vice-Chancellor of
The Queen's University,
Belfast

CONTENTS

ix

Contents

PREFACE

The Wiles Trust, while calling for work that shall be based upon serious historical enquiry, asks that the results of such enquiry shall be extended into regions of wider survey and more general reflection. It happens, however, that these are regions into which I have already made more excursions than I ever intended to make—partly in lectures delivered under other Foundations, and partly in courses which were provoked by specific needs in my own University. I had only one thing left which seemed capable of being turned to the purposes of the new Foundation, while allowing a change in the angle of approach or an opportunity for a fresh kind of commentary: and that was the interest which I had long had in the history of historiography, and the idea which for some time I had been entertaining of an attempt to write about the utility of this subject, to say something of its scope and method, and to discuss its place in historical scholarship.

It may serve a useful purpose if I make it clear in the first place that in the present lectures I am not pretending or proposing to 'set up' as an historian of historiography. I should be disqualified, I think, for the task which I am particularly trying to perform if I were not interested (and, indeed, mainly interested) in other aspects of historical scholarship. The point must be stressed that it is the general historian who, almost by definition, has the prerogative—because he is under the inescapable necessity—of relating the parts of historical study to the whole; just as it is he who, having regard to the larger lines of the story, inevitably decides in the long run what is the significant episode, the strategic factor, the pivotal event. We may say that we will lock ourselves in some local topic, or burrow in a special field, or isolate a single aspect of history; but the mere act of 'digging ourselves in' is not the thing which qualifies us to establish even our own subject in its external relations and its wider significance. Because the role of the general historian is so important, and because the decisions that we make in our capacity as general historians are liable to be the most far-reaching of all—because, also, we cannot even escape having a general history which in a certain sense must preside over the works of multiple specialists and co-ordinate them with one another—it would be a serious matter either to neglect the training or to overlook the function of the general historian. Men, like Acton, who valued this function, and who did not merely 'compile' general history but used the occasion to carry historical thinking to a higher power, are the ones who seem to have favoured and promoted also the history of historiography.

My attention was drawn to the subject when I was invited to lecture in certain German universities in 1938, and was told that readers of my *Whig Interpretation of History* were asking about the history of the Whig interpretation—a point into which it had never occurred to me to enquire. The result of my attempt to meet the demand appeared in the first half of my book on *The Englishman and his History*; but the work published in the interval (by Professor Douglas in particular) as well as the work published since, and work still to be published, induces me to omit from the present lectures the very things which drew my attention to the history of historiography in the first place. I omit the seventeenth century with regret because it illustrates so well the intimacy of the connection between historical interpretation and constitutional controversy. Also this chapter of the story reminds us of important developments which took place in historical scholarship long before the rise of the modern German school of history.

The death which the outmoded historian has to suffer is more complete and pitiful than ordinary death. A man who has written a single lyric may outlast the centuries, living on in perpetual youth; but the author of a hundredweight of heavy historical tomes has them piled upon his grave, to hold him securely down. A mere literary dressing would seem to be insufficient to defend such an author from the ravages of time.

Preface

The historian who survives seems to be the one who in some way or other has managed to break through into the realm of enduring ideas or gives hints of a deeper tide in the affairs of men. If those whom the general reader has chosen for survival are considered by the professional scholar to have been in some sense unworthy of so great an honour, it does not appear that either the verdict of the profession or the history of historiography is going to alter that august decree. Like Acton, we can only take refuge in the thesis that 'one great man may be worth several immaculate historians'.

It is not my purpose in the present lectures to resurrect those historians who have gone out of date—historians who may have their reward in heaven, but who on earth must stand fairly high in the hierarchy of the unread and unloved. I could bear to see a history of historiography somewhat like that which the original promoters of the subject seemed to envisage —one which could be narrated almost without the use of proper nouns. It is not at all my object, now, to insist that we should make an attempt to bring our useless predecessors back to life; I wish rather to see whether some advantage cannot be achieved—some fertile interaction produced, perhaps—by a more disrespectful treatment of their remains. Their books are to be handled rather in the way that the economic historian might handle the stale records of a defunct business house: so that we may learn whether there is not a history to be wrung out of them totally unlike anything that the writers of them ever had in mind.

The primary purpose of the following lectures, then, is to describe and illustrate the rise, the scope, the methods and the objectives of the history of historiography, treating this not as an account of a branch of literature but as, so to speak, a subsection in the history of science. The illustrative topics have been chosen in the hope that they will combine to give a general impression of the modern historical movement from the middle of the eighteenth century to the time of Lord Acton; and they have been taken at points at which it seemed possible perhaps to throw new light on the general course of development in that period. Their main intention, however, is to provide examples of the varied ways in which the history of historiography may be approached by those who wish to carry its study into regions of fresh discovery. Since Niebuhr and Ranke, for example, have long been taken as representing the great turning-point in the development of modern historical study, it seemed useful to show the importance of the type of enquiry which addresses itself to the period immediately preceding a great transition—useful in this case to delve into the prehistory of what we might call our 'Scientific Revolution'. And, as one of the antecedent movements appeared to have suffered neglect, but seemed at the same time to carry a story which was worth telling, this introductory phase in the rise of the German historical school has been chosen to form the subject of the second lecture. In regard to the main course of the nineteenth-century historical movement, Lord Acton has some significance for Englishmen, since this movement was the chief subject of his work as an historian of historiography; but also he could discuss it as a contemporary observer; he had developed along with it; and he stood as its most self-conscious representative in this country. His views and analyses have been illustrated largely from manuscript sources in the Cambridge University Library; and some of these are printed in appendices.

In an attempt to illustrate the variety of the approaches to which the history of historiography is susceptible, it seemed appropriate to draw attention to the rise of some of the ideas which lie behind our treatment of what we call general history, particularly modern European history. This is a kind of history which easily tends to assume a conventional shape, as writers fall into routine; and when at last somebody raises uncomfortable issues in this field, we sometimes think that the problems are novel and we fail to note that men have faced them before—faced them so directly that they could not escape being fully conscious of them. Sometimes we neglect

Preface

to discover the considerations upon which our predecessors made their decisions on the larger points of policy when they were setting the course for the future—when they were giving general history the kind of texture that is familiar to us, and placing the history of Europe in a framework which, since their time, may have remained too rigidly fixed. The world in general, when it discusses the basic ideas which are here in question, seems to find it useful to examine them as they are embodied in the work and views of Ranke; and possibly it is true that Ranke had the principal share in the development of the nineteenth-century tradition. There would be grounds for saying, however, that some of the main ideas and decisions go back behind Ranke: and this may be true even to a greater degree than is suggested below.

In order to provide samples of the way in which the history of historiography may apply itself to specific themes, I have added by kind permission of the Editor of the *Cambridge Historical Journal*, an article on 'Lord Acton and the Massacre of St Bartholomew' which appeared in that Journal in 1952; also, by kind permission of the Court of Glasgow University, my David Murray Lecture of 1951 on *The Reconstruction of an Historical Episode: The History of the Enquiry into the Origins of the Seven Years War*.

If it is primarily an examination of the history of historiography as a branch of learning, the following work is also intended to give glimpses of the modern transformation of historical scholarship and to throw new light on the famous German school. All its chapters save one are at the same time directly relevant to the labours of any student who desires to make a critical study of Lord Acton. Over and above this, I have attempted to use all the opportunities which the subject affords to discuss an issue which it is possible that we gravely neglect. I have tried to make the Wiles Lectures an essay on the whole problem of 'general history'—a problem always so important to Acton, and to Ranke, as well as to some of their predecessors.

Preface

I have never felt comfortable when research students have worked on vague and indefinite subjects; and I seem to be the last person in the world to go on believing that a precise piece of straight diplomatic history is a happy training even for the man who intends to move over into 'the history of thought'. In these days, however, when the research-student is so often allowed to wander in marshy fields of intellectual and social history, I am not clear that the history of historiography (though it has its dangers) does not lend itself to what I should call precision-work more adequately than some of the subjects which are often actually chosen for research. The real purpose of these lectures, however, is to suggest that the history of historiography has utility for students of history in general, and for those who are interested in reflecting about the past, and for those who wish to dig to the roots of historical scholarship.

Finally, I must express my deep gratitude to Mrs Boyd, whose generosity and great love of history produced the Wiles Foundation; to Dr Ashby, the Vice-Chancellor of the Queen's University, who unites the arts of management with such enviable human qualities; and to Professor Michael Roberts, whose advice and help were invaluable to me in Belfast. By the terms of the Trust a number of history teachers and research students from other universities were invited to Belfast during the delivery of the lectures and took part in the subsequent discussions. They comprised Professor Burn of Newcastle, Professor Douglas of Bristol, Professor Erdmann of Kiel, Professor Goodwin of Manchester, Professor Moody of Trinity College, Dublin, Professor Sayles of Aberdeen, Professor Williams of University College, Dublin, Miss McKisack and Mr W. H. Walsh of Oxford, Mr I. G. Jones and Mr E. Jones of the University College of Swansea, Miss Ben-Israel and Mr Nurser of Cambridge, and Mr Witcombe of Manchester. The opportunity for such discussions is a distinctive feature of the Wiles Trust Lectures; and to nobody could they possibly be so valuable as to the lecturer himself.

Preface

For the attendance and collaboration of these historians and students a special word of thanks is due; and along with them must be mentioned the members of the Department of History, as well as some from the Departments of Philosophy, Classics, etc., in the Queen's University, Belfast, who played an important part in the discussions.

H. B.

CAMBRIDGE
April 1955

I

THE HISTORY OF HISTORIOGRAPHY

I. ITS RISE AND DEVELOPMENT

The history of any science is calculated to throw considerable light on the nature of scientific enquiry and on the processes that lead to scientific discovery. It helps us to disengage those factors outside the science itself which may have affected the development of any branch of the subject—now the improvement in industrial technique; now the necessities of war; now the progress of mathematics, for example. By the use of history the scientist may become more conscious of the forces that are liable to affect his work, more alive to the nature of the methods he is using, more sensible of the direction in which he is going, more cognisant of the limitations under which he labours, more aware of the things which ought to be regarded with relativity. If to all the other perceptions of the scientist were added an internal knowledge of the history of his own subject, that combination would be capable of producing a higher state of awareness and a greater elasticity of mind.

Lord Acton, at the end of his life, set out to illustrate the new place which history had come to hold in the realm of the intellect, and the change it had produced in the structure of human thought. In this connection he pointed out more than once that there were now two ways in which every branch of science was to be studied: first by its own forms of technical procedure, and secondly by an examination of its history.[1] If all this is open to dispute in the case of the natural sciences, there are independent grounds for asserting its validity and for stressing its particular application when the science in question is actually that of the historian. Our knowledge of the past is

[1] Cambridge University Library, Add. 5011, 341: 'Each science has to be learned by a method of its own. But also by one and the same method, applicable to all, which is the historical method.' Cf. ibid. 390: 'History is not only a particular branch of knowledge, but a particular mode and method of knowledge in other branches.' See also pp. 97–8 below.

The History of Historiography

seriously affected if we learn how that knowledge came into existence and see the part which historical study itself has played in the story of the human race. Indeed, since there exists a science or a technique which we call the history of historiography, perhaps the best way to explain even this is the historical way—that is to say, by showing how the subject came to develop and what has been happening to it in recent times.

First of all we may say that the history of historiography is not merely the study of past historians. The Renaissance humanists, in their researches into classical literature, did not neglect the historical writers of the ancient world. Before the end of the sixteenth century we meet with an *Histoire des Histoires*,[1] but such books for a long time were a mere rope of sand, providing comments only on a succession of individual authors. In 1694 Edmund Bohun reissued a work, then over half a century old, on *The Method and Order of Reading both Civil and Ecclesiastical Histories*, by Degory Wheare, the first Camden Professor of History in Oxford. Bohun added a Preface in which, after describing Wheare's plan, he declared: 'I am very much tempted to alter his title and to call this Piece, *The History of the Greek and Latin Historians*.'[2] Treatises pur-

---

[1] Lancelot Voisin de la Popelinière, *Histoire des Histoires, avec l'idée de l'Histoire accomplie* (Paris, 1599). See further, Appendix 1, p. 205.

[2] See 'The Preface to the Reader'. This edition includes 'Mr Dodwell's Invitation to Gentlemen to acquaint themselves with Antient History', which, in complete contrast with La Popelinière, urges the absolute superiority of the Ancients even in the art of war. 'We improve only on the Invention of those Barbarous Nations which overran the Roman Empire upon the decay of [its] Politics and Military Skill....So far we are from superstructing, as is thought, on the Inventions of the Antients themselves. For as the Romans were decayed when they were overcome...so the Greek Commonwealth were decayed and ruined long before. Thus it comes to pass that the principal Excellencies of both the Greek and Roman Constitutions are so far from being ingredient in our modern Discipline, as that indeed they are not capable of being now retrieved otherwise than by antient Monuments.' I have discussed this whole attitude to historical study and the time-process in *The Statecraft of Machiavelli* (London, 1940), 26–41.

A. Momigliano, in 'Ancient history and the Antiquarian', *Contributo alla Storia degli Studi Classici* (Roma, 1955), 75–6, writes: 'To the best of my knowledge, the idea that one could write a history of Rome which should replace Livy and Tacitus was not yet born in the early seventeenth century. The first Camden Praelector of history in the University of Oxford had the statutory duty of commenting on Florus and other ancient historians (1622)....Both in Oxford and in Cambridge Ancient History was taught in the form of a commentary on ancient historians.'

porting to deal with historical method are older—and they were much more numerous before 1700—than one might imagine; but here again we are liable to be misled by pretentious titles. The Abbé Lenglet du Fresnoy produced his *Méthode pour étudier l'Histoire* in 1713, and prefaced it with a critique of well over a score of men who had written on this subject in the two preceding centuries; and amongst these he gave an important place to the famous Jean Bodin.[1] He closed his work with a catalogue of the principal historians and appended some critical remarks concerning their literary achievement. On the other hand, it need hardly be said that the history of historiography is not by any means to be regarded as a branch of literary criticism. Although the eighteenth century showed an increasing awareness of the importance of the history of the arts and sciences, it generally left the historical writers to annotated bibliographies or gave them fuller treatment only in the general histories of literature.

The history of historiography seemed at one time to mean—and with many people still appears to mean—something like a chronological series of encyclopaedia-articles on individual historians, with a résumé of their careers and achievements (and a grouping into 'schools' or 'movements') after the manner of old-fashioned text-books in the history of literature. It seems to be the case that, in respect of the history of natural science, this kind of encyclopaedic compilation has even seemed at times to serve an immediate purpose; and at a certain point in the proceedings it has ranked as a useful auxiliary. Things have been advanced a stage when some scholar, examining the masses of obscure books and minor treatises, many of which may have been unopened for centuries, has produced a comprehensive survey of a considerable field—a guide to the vast literature which is available for the research

---

[1] Lists of early works on historical method are to be found also in J. G. Meusel's edition of Struvius, *Bibliotheca Historica*, I, i (Lipsiæ, 1782), 2–11; and J. C. Gatterer, *Handbuch der Universalhistorie*, I (Göttingen, 1761), 58–60.

student. Even in the history of natural science, however, it is not clear that, if there had been a more conscious control of policy, this cumbrous intermediate process could not have been eliminated. When the history of historiography is conceived in this primitive manner, it is very easy, and very proper, to say that students would do better to read a few of the great historical works themselves—read Gibbon, Ranke and Macaulay, for example—than to wade through another book about books, spoon-feeding themselves with second-hand knowledge. In reality, the protest against the encyclopaedic and biographical treatment of the history of historiography is as old as the demand for the subject itself, and goes back to the eighteenth century.

It was important that the men of the eighteenth-century Enlightenment set their face against the older kind of rambling chronicle-histories, and against the kind of compilations which merely accumulated disjointed facts. They even went to the opposite extreme, so that narrative itself came to be at a discount and required the Romantic movement to give it a new stimulus at a later time. The apostles of the Age of Reason hankered after a kind of history which both they and we would call analytical—the kind which subjects the movements of the past or the processes of change to scientific examination, as though they were phenomena in astronomy or physics. It is just at some such stage of conscious transition that the student, sensible of his conflict with his predecessors, and highly aware of the fact that he represents something new, will begin to take stock of the general position, and to see in the contrast between the past and the present something which requires to be explained. As Srbik has pointed out, the historian himself is an historical creature, and in the latter part of the eighteenth century he was beginning to take a more detached view of himself as existing within history.[1] Out of these two things—the new view of historical study and the new consciousness in the

---

[1] Heinrich Ritter von Srbik, *Geist und Geschichte vom deutschen Humanismus bis zur Gegenwart*, 1 (München und Salzburg, 1950), 1.

historian himself—the demand for a genuine history of historiography arose.

In fact the need for such a thing was being felt, and the call for it was repeatedly made, before anybody ever set out to supply the article itself. The whole story centres around the university of Göttingen in the decades immediately before and immediately after the year 1800. ·It goes back to the time when what we call the 'academic historians' were beginning to take command of the ship, and the famous German school of history was just coming into existence. The Göttingen professors reflected on the aims and methods of history; they surveyed the state of the whole study as though it were a science; they measured the progress taking place in Germany and in other countries; and they developed a whole group of auxiliary techniques.[1] The demand for a history of historiography emerged in a natural way out of the discussion of just these problems, which themselves were close to the practical world. The cry came as soon as the movement towards a more technical kind of history—the movement which was to achieve such great victories in the nineteenth century—had secured a firm kind of base, namely a foothold in a university.

The first of this series of Göttingen history professors, J. C. Gatterer, wrote in 1760, that is to say, at the very beginning of the German movement:

I do not know why this branch of learning has suffered the unfortunate fate of not having admirers and practitioners who up to now ever thought of producing a HISTORY OF HISTORY worth reading.

He mentioned the names of one or two people who had seen the necessity for such a work and had made an attempt to meet the case; but these experiments had been so inadequate that they only magnified the urgency of what he described as one of the greatest needs of historical science at this time.[2] Gatterer was moved in all this partly by utilitarian motives, though

---

[1] See Chapter II, below.   [2] *Handbuch der Universalhistorie*, I (1761), 1.

he does not appear to have left us an explanation of all that was in his mind. He thought, for example, that the planning of an historical work—the lay-out of a treatise on universal history in particular—would be improved if one made a methodical comparison of the policies followed by historians in the past.[1] He was interested also in the general problem of historical criticism, and deprecated the casual ways of reviewers. In 1772 he declared that from the very beginning of journalism the critics had been making a serious mistake in their general treatment of historical literature. Confronted with a new work on some specific subject they ought to have stated first what the ancient writers had achieved in this field of study, then what had been added to knowledge since 'the reinstatement of the sciences' (that is to say, since what we call 'the Renaissance'). Finally they ought to have pointed out whether the new book had made any further contribution to this body of knowledge or whether indeed it did not come short of what somebody somewhere had previously achieved. Journalists had gone wrong on this point from the very beginning, however, and what they had failed to achieve would be made good now, said Gatterer, if there were a proper history of historiography. In fact, every branch of science ought to be supplied with its history in the way that had happened so fortunately already in the case of physiology.[2]

In 1785 his colleague, Schlözer, called attention to the same need; and, in attempting a brief sketch of the History of World-History, he noted that the subject had not been adequately worked up as yet; though he hoped that a more

[1] *Versuch einer allgemeinen Weltgeschichte* (Göttingen, 1792), Vorrede. H. Wesendonck, *Die Begründung der neueren deutschen Geschichtsschreibung durch Gatterer und Schlözer* (Leipzig, 1876), 209. Cf. ibid. 63–4, 104; F. X. von Wegele, *Geschichte der deutschen Historiographie* (München und Leipzig, 1885), 762, 787, n. 2.

[2] 'Allgemeine Uebersicht der ganzen teutschen Litteratur in den lezten 3 Jahren' in *Historisches Journal*, I (Göttingen, 1772), 269–70. 'Ihren Mangel, was das Vergangene anbetrifft, könnten ausführliche Geschichten jeder einzelnen Wissenschaft ersezen, wenn wir sie nur über alle Wissenschaften so hätten, wie über die Physiologie von dem Herr^n. von Haller. Also ist auch von dieser Seite überall nichts als Mangel und Dürftigkeit.'

comprehensive survey would be carried out by somebody or other, sooner or later.[1] In his edition of the Russian chronicle of Nestor in the early years of the nineteenth century, this man, Schlözer, provided a remarkable illustration of the way in which the exposition of a subject could be bound up with the history of the historiography of that subject. In 1811, Schlözer's pupil, Friedrich Rühs, said that there was a palpable need for an intelligent history of historical study—'not a mere enumeration of the various historical writers and their books', but a work of a genuinely fundamental character, which should show 'the development and the shaping of historical research and historical writing' amongst the various peoples. Such a work, he said, must make constant reference to the way in which outside factors and external events influence the historian; it must point out the relations between history and the other sciences; and it must show the effect which historical study itself has had on the course of human history. He added:

Not for a moment has any attempt ever been made to carry out such a work as this; for, in particular, the compilations on the history of literature are too paltry and too far from meeting the case.[2]

It was amongst the men who were devoted to what they called 'universal history' that the demand for a history of historiography arose. These Göttingen scholars produced highly-documented work in specialised fields, but when they discussed the issues of larger policy they functioned as what we should call 'general historians', bringing the whole range

[1] *Weltgeschichte nach ihren Haupt-Theilen*, I (Göttingen, 1785), 120, sect. VII, 'Geschichte der Weltgeschichte'.
[2] Friedrich Rühs, *Entwurf einer Propädeutik des historischen Studiums* (Berlin, 1811), 261. In the field of ancient history, however, Friedrich Creuzer had already published, in 1803, *Die historische Kunst der Griechen in ihrer Entstehung und Fortbildung*. A. Momigliano, in 'Friedrich Creuzer and Greek Historiography', *Contributo alla Storia degli Studi Classici*, 234, describes it as 'nothing more nor less than the first modern history of Greek historiography', and calls attention to the *Göttingische gelehrte Anzeigen* (which on 27 February 1804 devotes particular attention to this book), as well as pointing out, p. 242, Heyne's 'memoir on the origin of Greek historiography in the Göttingen *Commentationes* of 1799'.

of the study under consideration. Rarely—and perhaps hardly even in the case of Ranke—have the higher strategies of the historian, and the relations of the parts of the study to the whole, been so consciously and comprehensively considered by directing minds. Furthermore, like Ranke and Acton, who are their lineal descendants, these men (though they had inadequate material to work upon) believed in 'historical thinking' as something like the counterpart of 'scientific thought'. On the one hand they were in reaction against the superficialities of the Enlightenment, but on the other hand they were its disciples in that (like Ranke once more) they believed in the possibility of carrying history to higher levels of generalisation. Like Ranke, they were particularly interested in what they called 'the interconnectedness of events' and one of the books of Schlözer contains an essay under this very title.[1] As the case of Lord Acton would suggest, if the history of historiography is a hobby-horse, it is the hobby-horse of the general historian—even the 'generalising' historian. If it is a specialisation it is so not in the way that the microscopic study of a diplomatic episode is specialised, but rather after the manner of biochemistry, which employs particular techniques but has a wide range of subject-matter.

Even at this early stage in the story it was further realised that the man who studies the history of history must avoid the disjointed chronicle, the temptation to give a straggling, meaningless string of names. He must examine the internal development of historical scholarship, always relating it to movements in general history, to the progress of other sciences and to the conditioning circumstances which affect its fortunes. He must see, for example, how historical study corresponds to the form of a country's constitution, to the state of public opinion, to the availability of evidence, and to the activity of universities, learned societies and periodicals. Some of the

---

[1] *Vorstellung der Universal-Historie*, 2nd ed. (Göttingen, 1755), 255, ch. ii, 'Vom Zusammenhange des Begebenheiten'. Cf. Schlözer, *Weltgeschichte*, 73–7, on the 'Verbindung der welthistorischen Materie'; and L. Wachler, *Geschichte der historischen Forschung und Kunst*, I (Göttingen, 1812), Vorrede, VI.

early attempts to show what the history of historiography ought to be like are little essays in general history which try to seize on the strategic factors in the story and are very sparing even in the use of proper names. And, though it is true that in this period the vision of the historian's objective had considerably outrun the ability to assemble the materials requisite for the proper execution of the design, the earliest samples (in essay form) of what the history of historiography might be like are interesting demonstrations of the way in which the idea of the mere 'chronicle' comes to be transformed into the idea of 'general history'.[1] Where once there had been a mere succession of names, a discussion of historians in sequence, we now find, for example, rough sketches of the way in which the Reformation affected historiography. We are shown the way in which it altered the place of historical study in German education and the way in which its controversies (because they were to a considerable degree historical) helped the development of a more scientific method. Since each religious group had necessarily driven the other to more intensive criticism, it was soon possible to reach the paradoxical conclusion that the most violent partisanship may serve the cause of impartial history itself.[2] Even in the eighteenth century, in fact, there is

[1] In his *Entwurf*, 261 ff., Friedrich Rühs has a chapter entitled 'Allgemeine Geschichte des historischen Studiums' in which he points out that the higher kind of historical writing depends on constitutional and political relationships and is impossible in despotic states. He quotes Johann von Müller for the view that great historians flourished in the ancient world only so long as the feeling of liberty prevailed, and that only in the Italian struggle for independence and in Great Britain had they found any worthy successors. By far the greatest majority of Arabian manuscripts, he says, are historical in their contents, but they display not the slightest notion of criticism. Luther helped history by making it more important in German education, and by setting the example in the use of the vernacular; but the Protestants were uncritical and it was the Catholics who set the example of criticism, especially the Jesuit, G. Henschen, in his profound researches into various of the old French kings. Already in the sixteenth century the mania for the collection, of historical materials had started in France and Germany. Bodin increased the importance of history by showing how necessary it was for the study of law. Finally, the rise of political science contributed to the development of history, and here the works of Montesquieu and of various English writers were of special significance.

[2] See Friedrich Rehm, *Lehrbuch der historischen Propädeutik und Grundriss der allgemeinen Geschichte*, 2nd ed. (Marburg, 1850), 88–100, 'Geschichte der historischen

a clear idea that the history of historiography is more than a chronicle and that it can be treated in the 'analytical' way that 'general history' requires.

In 1812 and 1820 another Göttingen student, Ludwig Wachler (inspired and assisted by still another Göttingen professor, Heeren), produced a two-volume work on the history of historical scholarship since the beginning of the sixteenth century. The volumes were part of a considerable series, also associated with Göttingen, which set out to provide a large-scale history of the arts and sciences.[1] Wachler was concerned to relate the historical writing of a given period to the general intellectual climate of the age, which he would describe in the introduction to the successive sections of his book. He saw that the history of universities, historical societies and periodicals was relevant to his theme.[2] At the same time he did not escape the tendency to encyclopaedic compilation and he, too, fell into the habit of setting out strings of names. This may explain why it was still possible for men to go on demanding a history of historiography which should be more than a study of successive individual authors.[3]

After this there was a pause, and perhaps there came a period when historians were sufficiently occupied in other fields; for at the next stage in the story it seemed to be the whole of the past that was requiring to be retraversed by the

Forschung und Kunst'. Rehm wrote in 1830, and seems to follow the Göttingen writers of the eighteenth century in his appeal for a history of historiography.

The Prague professor, K. J. Vietz, in *Das Studium der allgemeinen Geschichte nach dem gegenwärtigen Stand der historischen Wissenschaft und Literatur* (Prag, 1844), gives on pp. 170–211 what he calls 'Andeutungen zu einer Geschichte der Welthistorie und ihrer Literatur'. He, too, is influenced by the Göttingen school, and insists that the history of historiography must be more than a recapitulation of book-titles. On pp. 193–4 he sketches the history of the Four-Monarchy system which for some time had provided the basis for the periodisation of world-history.

[1] Ludwig Wachler, *Geschichte der historischen Forschung und Kunst seit der Wiederherstellung der litterärischen Cultur in Europa*, 2 vols. (Göttingen, 1812–20), in the series 'Geschichte der Künste und Wissenschaften'. See the Dedication to Professor Heeren. Hallam calls attention to this series on pp. vi–vii of his *Introduction to the Literature of Europe*, 1 (London, 1837), and says: 'So vast a scheme was not fully executed; but we owe to it some standard works, to which I have been considerably indebted'. On Wachler, see also p. 178, below.

[2] E.g. op. cit. II, 771–3.   [3] See Rehm and Vietz, p. 9, n. 2, above.

research student.[1] At the close of the Preface to his *Introduction to the Literature of Europe in the fifteenth, sixteenth and seventeenth centuries*, Hallam wrote in 1837 that 'unless where history has been written with peculiar beauty of language, or philosophical spirit, I have generally omitted all mention of it'. From the fourth chapter of the second book of Bacon's *Advancement of Learning*, however, he extracted a summary of the things which the student of this kind of subject ought to set out to discover: 'the origin and antiquities of every science, the methods by which it has been taught, the sects and controversies it has occasioned, the colleges and academies in which it has been cultivated, its relation to civil government and common society, the physical or temporary causes which have influenced its condition. . . .'

It is possible that after this time new motives had to be generated before another impulse could be given to the history of historiography, and a further development could be achieved. By the end of the 1850's the papers of the youthful Acton suggest that the subject—at least so far as it related to the story of what had been happening in the previous half-century—was already a familiar thing. What is chiefly notable at this time, however, is the fact that—whether it had any influence or not—the famous *History of Civilization in England* by Thomas Buckle, in 1857, gave a remarkable proportion of its space to the history of history. It also provided a new argument for the subject itself, though I do not know that the argument has ever had much weight in the academic world. Buckle took the line that the history of history ought to be given an important place in the study of the development of society and civilisation. He tells us that it is his object

to incorporate into an inquiry into the progress of Man, another inquiry into the progress of History itself. By this means [he says]

[1] Johann Samuel Ersch, *Literatur der Geschichte und deren Hülfswissenschaften seit der Mitte des XVIIIten Jahrhunderts*, new ed. (Leipzig, 1827), is merely a bibliography. In 1830 Rehm and in 1844 Vietz were calling for a history of historiography, see p. 9, n. 2 above. In 1852 there appeared at Tübingen F. Ch. Baur, *Die Epochen der kirchlichen Geschichtschreibung*.

great light will be thrown on the movement of society; since there must always be a connexion between the way in which men contemplate the past, and the way in which they contemplate the present.

He adds that 'it is important for the student of any particular science to be acquainted with its history'; and he urges us 'to observe the way in which, during successive ages, historians have shifted their ground'.[1]

It was in the next two decades, however, that the whole subject made an appreciable advance. This took place in Germany and was partly due to the great interest which scholars in that country had come to have in the sources of their medieval history, including the chroniclers. In 1858 W. Wattenbach published a study of the sources of German history down to the middle of the thirteenth century; and this was continued by Ottokar Lorenz in 1870 to the end of the fourteenth century, and in 1876 to the end of the fifteenth century.[2] The real dynamic, however, came from a different aspect of the study altogether, and for some time now the effect of this had already been making itself felt. The historical movement, that had been so remarkable in Germany since the earliest decades of the century, had by this time arched itself into a wave more powerful and portentous than anything which historical scholarship had hitherto seen. It not only transformed the methods of study and loaded the world of knowledge with mountains of new matter; it was making itself felt

---

[1] Henry Thomas Buckle, *History of Civilization in England*, 1 (London, 1857), 266–7. Acton says of Buckle (C.U.L. Add. 4931, 75): 'Il a introduit les sciences dans l'histoire générale. Elles n'en sont plus sorties. La tendance lui a survécu de regarder la vie des peuples comme une partie de l'histoire naturelle.' Concerning one of the points raised in the passages quoted from Buckle, Acton himself seems to have similar views, e.g. C.U.L. Add. 5002, 262, 'As each age, so is its view of the Past'; Add. 4930, 136; 'False notion of history gives a false colour to [the] present time.'

[2] W. Wattenbach, *Deutschlands Geschichtsquellen im Mittelalter bis zur Mitte des dreizehnten Jahrhunderts* (Berlin, 1858). In the preface to his new edition of this work (Bd. 1, Heft 1; Berlin, 1938), Robert Holtzmann states, p. vi, that the Wedekindstiftung in Göttingen in 1853 had declared 'the history of German historiography down to the middle of the thirteenth century' the subject of a prize-essay. O. Lorenz continued Wattenbach's work in two stages in *Deutschlands Geschichtsquellen im Mittelalter von der Mitte des dreizehnten...Jahrhunderts* (Berlin, 1870, 1876).

even in other regions of intellectual life, and it was beginning to revolutionise the place of history in human thought. Now there existed reasons for having a history of historiography—and a possibility of turning this into an organic theme—which must have been entirely beyond the vision of the early Göttingen professors. In 1865 A. H. Horawitz published in Vienna an outline-history of the development of German historiography in the nineteenth century.[1] In 1876 H. Wesendonck published a study of the Göttingen movements which in the closing decades of the eighteenth century were laying the foundations for the later German school.[2] Wesendonck was inspired by his teacher, Heinrich Wuttke, who was an enthusiast for the history of historiography, and who in 1879 intervened in the controversy concerning the massacre of St Bartholomew with an outline of the whole literature of this subject.[3] In the same period, Friedrich Jodl introduced a discussion of the problem of *Culturgeschichte* with an interesting account of the rise and development of this branch of scholarship.[4] And here is a further function for the history of historiography—it is apparently the appointed way in which to set out the issues in a controversy concerning the nature or the methods of historical study. At the next stage again, Franz von Wegele, in 1885, bridged the gap between the Middle Ages and the most recent period with a large-scale study of German historiography since the Renaissance.[5] This work

[1] A. H. Horawitz, *Zur Entwickelungsgeschichte der deutschen Historiographie* (Wien, 1865).

[2] H. Wesendonck, *Die Begründung der neueren deutschen Geschichtsschreibung durch Gatterer und Schlözer* (Leipzig, 1876). Cf. H. Wesendonck, *Der Stand der neueren deutschen Geschichtsschreibung vor Gatterer und Schlözer* (Leipzig, 1875), which was reproduced as the introductory chapter of the *Begründung*.

[3] H. Wuttke, *Zur Vorgeschichte der Bartholomäusnacht* (Leipzig, 1879). Cf. pp. 19, 171, 192 below.

[4] F. Jodl, *Die Culturgeschichtschreibung, ihre Entwicklung und ihr Problem* (Halle, 1878). Cf. the reason given by La Popelinière for his excursion into *L'Histoire des Histoires*, App. I, p. 205 below.

[5] F. X. von Wegele, *Geschichte der Deutschen Historiographie seit dem Auftreten des Humanismus* (München und Leipzig, 1885). Ottokar Lorenz (see p. 12, n. 2) gave a quite different treatment to the subject in the following year, in *Die Geschichtswissenschaft in Hauptrichtungen und Aufgaben* (Berlin, 1886).

was to have a significance in England; for it provided the occasion for Acton's famous essay on 'German Schools of History'.[1]

In the meantime the need for a history of historiography had continued to be felt and on occasion the call for it had still been heard. On 22 June 1867 *The Chronicle* printed a review by Lord Acton of the *Storia Generale della Storie* which Gabriele Rosa had published in Milan. Acton declared that 'Signor Rosa had overrated his powers and failed grievously'. He added, however:

> But he is almost the only man who has yet attempted to explain the progress, the means, and the purposes of historical science, and to supply information which would be of infinite assistance in many branches of study.

2. ITS SUBJECT-MATTER AND ITS SCOPE

The history of historiography would have a very limited interest if it resolved itself into a mere compendium—just another 'book about books'—or threaded a long line of historians into a loose form of chronicle. Once we have decided that we will imitate the scientist and examine a single thread in the tapestry of history, it may be a mistake to stop in the middle of the course, as though the policy were one to be undertaken with misgiving. If from the whole past we have abstracted certain kinds of data—those which concern the history of historical study, for example—there is not necessarily much point in reproducing these as they first emerge in a chronological chain, which may only be a rope of sand. The truth is that the whole series requires to be thrown back into the crucible for further analysis. Only then does the mind really begin to mix with the matter, and the shape of the main problems become apparent.

Within the history of historiography, therefore, we carry the

[1] Lord Acton, *Historical Essays and Studies* (London, 1919), 344-92.

analytical procedure to a further degree of specialisation and concentrate our attention upon certain strategic topics. Indeed it would appear that in this field the primary object of study has always been the development of a more technical form of scholarship, the rise of a more scientific history, and the progress in the critical treatment of sources. One of the advantages of the historical study of anything (and the very point of the empirical method) lies in the fact that it brings out paradoxes and surprises—things which would never be suspected or imagined by the arm-chair theorist, attempting to work out by inference what is likely to have happened, what in fact he thinks *must* have happened. And one of the paradoxes in the history of historical method is the fact that sometimes the world learns a lesson and then forgets it, so that the same experience has to be gone through more than once—sometimes the human race has to make the same discovery at least twice over. Some of the achievements of both English and German historiography in the latter part of the seventeenth century, for example, would seem to have quickly gone underground; and of these there are some which stayed underground for a long time; for this is a story in which relapses have occurred on occasion. And perhaps there is something in historical method which, like poetic inspiration, does not run in a straight historical series—something which is never gained by mere inheritance, but which each generation of historians has to bring home to itself afresh in direct experience. Another paradox in the story is the fact that the critical method in historical study goes behind the story of the German school in the nineteenth century, behind even the history of historiography as we usually understand it. Much of it was taken over from the classical and biblical scholarship which had hitherto been progressing at a quicker pace. Lord Acton once suggested that the truth of religion was so momentous an issue, and the controversies about it were so intense, that the critical methods were developing in ecclesiastical research before anybody thought of transposing them into the field of modern history.[1] As we pursue our enquiries backwards in the quest for origins, therefore, we find that historical scholarship sends back its roots into wider fields—into neighbouring and associated branches of learning. The topic which we had isolated for study carries us outside itself, and that very process of specialisation with which we began soon comes to be reversed. In the end it is not only classical and biblical scholarship but a fantastic miscellany of strange and unexpected things which, after being kicked out by the door, are summoned back by the window—all of them to be absorbed into the history of historiography.

On the other hand, while the men who talked of scientific history in the nineteenth century often had in mind only the critical handling of the documentary sources, the eighteenth-century Enlightenment was interested in a further aspect of the matter: the question of seeing how the historical data, once established, could be made amenable to scientific treatment. Here, once again, the problem sends its roots into regions outside the realm of history. It carries us back to the exponents of the seventeenth-century Scientific Revolution who claimed that they were in possession of a method capable of transfer even to human studies.[2] History, for example, instead of regarding itself as essentially a record of people—of lives which one could only narrate—might seize on a society

[1] 'The Study of History', *Lectures on Modern History*, p. 3: 'It is our function...even to allow some priority to ecclesiastical history over civil, since by reason of the graver issues concerned, and the vital consequences of error, it opened the way in research, and was the first to be treated by close reasoners and scholars of the higher rank.' Cf. 'Mabillon', *Historical Essays and Studies*, 460: 'Historical criticism was reduced to an art for the sake and honour of the Benedictines'; 465: 'In the seventeenth century the purposes of controversy were dominant; ecclesiastical history was more developed than civil.'

Cf. C.U.L. Add. 4931, 21: '15 Dec. Kritik grew up on the lives of Saints. Henschen, Lannoy, Mabillon, Hermant, Ruinart, Tillemont.'

Ibid. 22: '15 Dec. Papebroch says, Vita Boll., that criticism is more necessary in the lives of saints, because there error is injurious to religion.'

[2] I have discussed this in 'The Role of the Individual in History', which is about to appear in *History*. See Frederick J. Teggart, *Rome and China, A Study of Correlations in Historical Events* (Berkeley, Calif., 1939) which asks 'whether historical data might not be utilised for other ends than the composition of historical narratives'. Cf. p. 34 below.

or a civilisation as its basic unit, and set out to examine more impersonally the interactions within it. Taking the religions of the world, and making a comparative study of these, one might seek to elicit certain forms of generalisation which should be valid irrespective of the truth of any particular religion. The ideas which Professor Toynbee presents in his *Study of History*, and his notion of the scientific use to which historical data can be put, may be right or wrong, but they have a long chain of predecessors. The ingredients of the communist theory of history are to be traced far behind Marx; while the policy of organising the whole human drama on the basis of the class-conflict has antecedents of considerable antiquity. But the study of the varied attempts to make a scientific use of historical data is possibly one of the more neglected aspects of the history of historiography. And if the nineteenth century carried to a high degree the microscopic examination of evidence and the critical use of sources, there has not always been the same conscious attempt to develop the scientific method in respect of our wider constructions and interpretations.

A further subject of enquiry has been the way in which the study of the past came to gain in depth through the development of the right imaginative approach—the cultivation of what we call historical-mindedness.[1] One is tempted to feel that this is almost a new dimension added to our thinking—there is such a remarkable lack of it in the Renaissance and even in much of the eighteenth century. We can see signs of it (in certain English writers, for example) already in the seventeenth century; while Vico in Italy and Herder in Germany foreshadow important developments. Even the eighteenth century, especially in its treatment of the early stages of

[1] E.g. Friedrich Meinecke, *Die Entstehung des Historismus* (München und Berlin, 1936) and *Vom geschichtlichen Sinn und vom Sinn der Geschichte* (Leipzig, 1939). Hans Proesler, *Das Problem einer Entwicklungsgeschichte des historischen Sinnes* (Historische Studien, Heft 142; Berlin, 1920). Cf. the interesting essay by G. Buchholz, 'Ursprung und Wesen der modernen Geschichtsauffassung', *Deutsche Zeitschrift für Geschichtswissenschaft*, II (1889), 17–37.

society and civilisation, made a contribution which has sometimes been overlooked. But it was Edmund Burke who—having recovered contact with the historical achievements of Restoration England—exerted the presiding influence over the historical movement of the nineteenth century, at least in respect of the point that we are now considering; though some of the historians in the first half of this century claimed that the novels of Sir Walter Scott had influenced their attitude and affected their feeling for the past. In the whole general phenomenon of Romanticism we can in fact watch human beings coming to fresh terms with their past after the shock of the French Revolution. At this point the history of historiography touches more intimately a significant phase of general human experience.

And because it can be said that all this may be carried too far—that the Romantic movement, for one thing, had its unfortunate side—let us by all means study the perversions of history, and in particular hunt out their origin. Even the development of historicism in the bad sense of the word, the rise of the various kinds of obsession with history, the abuses and exaggerations of the historical point of view—the reduction of everything to mere flux, for example, and the dissolving of all values into mere relativism—all this has been examined and requires more analysis.

It is important if we can discover, furthermore, how far men tend to become intellectual victims of the technical procedures which they habitually follow—procedures developed perhaps in the first place for avowedly limited objects. The historian, like other specialists, easily imagines that his own pocket of thinking is the whole universe of thought, and easily assumes a sovereign finality or ascendancy for his own branch of study. Yet intellectual aberrations and intellectual conflicts do in fact have an aspect that is likely to be amenable to historical treatment; and when they reach the stage at which they are only exacerbated by the continuance of general discussion, they may at least be clarified if we can focus the microscope more and more closely on the point where men originally diverged.

One of the developments which have taken place at a later stage has been a different way of stratifying the history of historiography, a different way of subdividing the subject-matter. What has happened has been that students interested in a particular historical theme have set out to discover how that single theme has fared at the hands of successive historians throughout the generations. All this has arisen in a natural way out of the practical needs of academic enquirers. One might imagine it to be a methodical extension of the practice of some historians who preface their work with a critical appreciation of their immediate predecessors. We have seen, for example, how in 1879 the German historian, Heinrich Wuttke, gave an account of what had been written on the massacre of St Bartholomew, though this was rather a survey of the literature than a history of the historiography.[1] In 1930 there appeared a study of the speculation which has been appearing for century after century in western Europe on the subject of the fall of the Roman Empire. This carries the history of historiography to the point where we almost see the human race reflecting from age to age on one of its great experiences.[2] The study of the way in which Magna Carta has been interpreted in one generation after another opens up a field which concerns not merely our historiography but also our constitutional history.[3] When we examine all the stages in the historical reconstruction and interpretation of a single theme—taking note of all the factors which affect the case, the appearance of new documents, innovations in historical

---

[1] See p. 13, n. 3, above.

[2] W. Rehm, *Der Untergang Roms in abendländischen Denken* (Leipzig, 1930). The works of Friedrich Gundolf (Gundelfinger), *Caesar in der deutschen Literatur* (Palaestra, XXXIII; Berlin, 1904) and *Caesar: Geschichte seines Ruhms* (1924), translated as *The Mantle of Caesar* (London [1929]), concern the student of literature, not the student of the history of historiography as such.

[3] See, for example, Faith Thompson, *Magna Carta, its role in the making of the English Constitution, 1300–1692* (Minneapolis, 1948). Cf. my book on *The Englishman and his History* (Cambridge, 1944), Part I.

technique, the influence of changing intellectual outlooks, for example—we meet more surprises and paradoxes than anywhere else in the history of historiography. An inexperienced person would hardly have deduced that memoirs and correspondence, flooding upon the world around the middle of the nineteenth century, would have taken the historians of George III's reign further away from the truth than they were before.[1] Sitting in an arm-chair we should not have guessed that the real violence of the Whig historians' attack on George III as the perverter of the constitution—the real follies of anachronistic reconstruction—would come only at a later date still, a century after that king's accession, at a time when history was supposed to have become more scientific.[2] If we study the history of the historian's attempt to elucidate the origins of the Seven Years War, we can see how the opening of archives—if the opening is only a partial one, so that the essential secrets are still concealed—may again have the effect of misleading the historian. And even when fuller materials are available it appears that the historian who has built up a rigid framework out of his studies of the Diplomatic Revolution, may still go on pushing the new materials into the old framework, so that it may be a long time before the truth is achieved.[3]

A great amount of research has been devoted to the history of the various concepts which the historian has to handle, and the concepts which govern his reconstruction of the past. For fifty years the controversy concerning the idea of the Renaissance has been carried on in one language and another until a colossal literature has been accumulated, though it is one in which English historians have hardly had any part. If on the

[1] There is a slight, and perhaps in some ways misleading, reference to this in Gerda Richards Crosby, 'George III: Historians and a Royal Reputation', *Essays in Modern English History in Honour of W. C. Abbott* (Cambridge, Mass., 1941), 303.

[2] Sir Thomas Erskine May, *The Constitutional History of England since the Accession of George III, 1760–1860* (London, 1861). The significances of the fallacies in the early pages of this work seem to have been overlooked by the author of the article mentioned in n. 1 above, who therefore exaggerates the role of Lecky.

[3] See pp. 146–9, 151–2, 155–6 159, 162, Chapter v, below.

one hand few people realise how many ingredients, how much propaganda, how many prejudices and prepossessions, have gone to the making of the conception of the Renaissance as this has been handed down to us, it is true on the other hand that the history of the way in which it developed—and even the reading of those writers on the period who never used the word Renaissance—is calculated to emancipate us from the tyranny of those superimposed concepts which so often control our historical reconstructions.[1] There has been some interest, I gather, in the history of the idea of *renovatio* or *reformatio* in the period between St Augustine and the sixteenth century; and this would seem to have some relevance to the parallel problem of the Reformation. Some time ago a German historian opened an enquiry into the history of the famous idea of Primitive Teutonic Freedom—a notion which long governed historical reconstruction in our part of the world, and which also has some significance in political and constitutional history.[2]

It is precisely when work has been done in the general history of historiography that a new dimension can be given to that aspect of the subject which still attracts the greatest interest—namely, the treatment of individual historians. Since the Second World War, three men in particular have been repeatedly examined, both in Europe and in America. They are the German, Ranke, the Swiss, Jacob Burckhardt, and the cosmopolitan Englishman, Lord Acton. It is clear that they have provoked more discussion and research than other people, not because of actual discoveries which they made from manuscript sources, but because of their historical ideas, their

---

[1] See bibliography in Wallace K. Ferguson, *The Renaissance in Historical Thought* (Cambridge, Mass., 1948), 398–407, and see below, Chapter IV, sect. 4.

[2] Erwin Hoelzle, *Die Idee einer altgermanischen Freiheit vor Montesquieu; Fragmente aus der Geschichte politischer Freiheitsbestrebungen in Deutschland, England und Frankreich vom 16.–18. Jahrhundert* (Historische Zeitschrift, Beiheft 5; München, 1925). Cf. Horst Kirchner, *Das germanische Altertum in der deutschen Geschichtsschreibung des achtzehnten Jahrhunderts* (Historische Studien, Heft 333, Berlin, 1938). Friedrich Gotthelf, *Das deutsche Altertum in den Auschauung des 16. und 17. Jahrhunderts* (Berlin, 1900) is of interest to the student of literature rather than the student of the history of historiography.

principles of interpretation and their comments on the process of things in time. In fact, they became of special interest to us after the Second World War because of a prophetic element which made their teaching more arresting than it had been in their own lifetime. The principles which they put forward have been relevant in one way or another to the diagnosis of our position today.

3. ITS UTILITY FOR THE STUDENT OF HISTORY

The study of history certainly owes much of its remarkable nineteenth-century development to the Germans, who long held the leadership over a number of extensive fields of thought. A fairly recent book on the introduction of German historicism into England shows that English historians down to the time of Acton and Maitland—that is to say, down to the beginning of the twentieth century—made repeated confession of our indebtedness.[1] It was in the nature of things, therefore, that the Germans should have been the pioneers in the study of the history of historiography also; and if we think that in this field they either follow a mistaken path or talk too much about themselves, this would be an additional reason for seeing that they were not left with the monopoly of the subject. Lord Acton and Dr G. P. Gooch concerned themselves with it a long time ago, and they clearly owed their interest in it to our earlier connections with German scholarship.[2] The last generation of Englishmen almost completely neglected it; and during this period, next to the Germans, it has been the Americans who have proved the most eager students in this field.

The English have long been notorious for their antipathy to the theoretical or philosophical treatment of the problems of

[1] Klaus Dockhorn, *Der deutsche Historismus in England* (Göttingen, 1950), e.g. 212–13 (Stubbs), 217 (Seeley and Acton), 218–19 (Maitland).
[2] G. P. Gooch, *History and Historians in the Nineteenth Century* (London, 1913; 2nd rev. ed. 1952).

history.[1] Here, however, we have a subject which is not doctrinaire, and which calls for concrete enquiry and detailed research. One would have thought that for Englishmen it would be more congenial than the more speculative studies and yet could be used for the achievement of an equivalent effect. By this route—on this country lane in which one never loses sight of the landscape—even the Englishman might be seduced into examining his assumptions. For the truth is that the very people who think that they are writing history without any assumptions easily recognise either aberration or constriction in those men who write from a different platform and have other things which they take for granted. And, if we can never remove the subjective element from our narratives and expositions, we can neutralise it somewhat by realising how men are conditioned, and seeing that some of the hidden things are brought up into our consciousness. It is something to have a glimpse of the subtle and manifold ways in which a whole miscellany of unexpected conditioning circumstances have helped to mould the historical mind in one period and another. It is through the neglect of this self-discipline that in one age after another history operates to confirm the prevailing fallacies and ratify the favourite errors of the time—even magnifying prejudices at each stage of the story by projecting them back upon the canvas of all the centuries.

Since historians do in fact talk about their predecessors— one of them blithely praising Stubbs to the skies and another wiping out Ranke with a phrase—the case for the history of historiography in a sense comprises the claim that such a thing shall at least be done methodically. In almost the first appeal that was made on behalf of the subject in Göttingen nearly two hundred years ago, the suggestion was put forward that it would provide a firmer basis for the establishment of critical standards in respect of historical writings; and I do not think that this problem of criteria has been sufficiently examined. Furthermore, as Acton said when he urged the study of this

[1] There is a comment on this in *Historische Zeitschrift*, CLXXVI (Aug. 1953), p. 93.

subject, it is important not to sit receptive before the history that one reads in books—it is important even that people should acquire the habit of trying to get 'behind the historian'.

There would be a case for saying that a research-student is better equipped if he not only reads the preceding literature but technically works out the history of the historiography of the main subject within which his special problem lies. And certainly if an author has compiled his history out of the recent books only, it lacks those deeper bass notes which come from contact with the whole accumulated tradition of scholarship. It is even possible that some subjects, like the Renaissance or the French Revolution, could be profitably taught to students by something in the way of a history of the historiography of the subject. In a wild dream one could imagine a *Cambridge Modern History* which, instead of presenting a hard piece of narrative, took subjects like the French Wars of Religion or the Origins of the War of 1914, and gave a critical analysis of the whole course of their study and interpretation. When many researches piled on one another have had the effect of producing a bewildering entanglement in certain fields (as perhaps nowadays on the subject of Luther or on parts of the seventeenth-century history of England) a methodical analysis of the whole course of writing upon the subject, or upon a significant section of it, might do much towards the unravelling of the complexities. There are some such fields where the researches have been abundant but one could wish that the whole were surveyed and remapped by a presidential mind. An analytical study of the whole historiography of Martin Luther might even be calculated to precipitate something new about Martin Luther himself; especially as the theologians, writing to persuade Protestants of the present-day, have to be disentangled from the historians who are more definitely interested in the reconstruction of the sixteenth century. The great controversy concerning Protestantism and the rise of Capitalism is an excellent training in the kind of fallacies to which historians are liable, and shows the immense amount of meticulous research which can be concentrated on pivotal points. An analytical survey of the literature—a survey of the kind which gets behind the historian in every case—and a history of the controversy itself, could be the most satisfactory way of expounding the subject. Perhaps the biggest controversy that ever took place between technical historians since the study came to its modern state— always excepting the age-long controversy concerning the downfall of the ancient Roman Empire—is the debate which divided the German historians for nearly a century on a strategic subject in the history of their own country. It concerned the question whether the identification of the German medieval monarchy with the concept of Roman Empire had been a benefit or a colossal tragedy from the point of view of the modern German nation. The debate was naturally entangled with the nineteenth-century political dispute between the pro-Austrians who supported the policy of a Greater Germany and the pro-Prussians who supported unification on a smaller scale, with the capital in Berlin. As a result of this, problems of German medieval history were staged against the background of the nineteenth-century struggle between Prussia and Austria, even though this involved a gigantic anachronism.[1] In the same way, English historians tended to imagine that the ancient Athenians were like modern Whigs; or they would interpret Magna Carta in terms of their own more recent constitutional controversies. Every age likes its historians to place events in a framework that corresponds with contemporary prejudices and answers to contemporary political desires.

At the same time it seems clear that it is not the whole of our historical knowledge which is built in this way on shifting sands. One man may write a study of Luther with his mind

---

[1] For accounts of this controversy, see Heinrich Hostenkamp, *Die mittelalterliche Kaiserpolitik in der deutschen Historiographie seit v. Sybel und Ficker* (Historische Studien, Heft 255; Berlin, 1934). As early as 1886, Ottokar Lorenz in *Die Geschichtswissenschaft in Hauptrichtungen und Aufgaben*, I, 77 n., said that this controversy was 'one of the most important and most epoch-making events in the history of modern historiography'.

fixed on the present day, so that he merely sets out to show how Luther led to the Germany of the twentieth century. A more serious study incorporates a mass of thought and material which is the deposit from centuries of research and centuries of perpetual reinterpretation. A work of this kind, though written in 1955 may embody some of the accumulated results of insights and appreciations which belonged to 1855 and 1755—to other ages altogether. Behind a serious picture of Luther there is a solid core of hard scholarship which is being built up and enlarged as the generations pass, and which is above the play of wind and weather.

4. ITS MORE GENERAL SIGNIFICANCE

It would appear that German intellectual and public life in the nineteenth century succumbed to the leadership of academic thought and bowed before the professorial mind to a greater degree than was the case at that time in England. For their interpretation of human destiny and of the role which their country had to play in the world, the intelligentsia were less guided by religion or tradition—or even perhaps by common-sense—than ours; and they depended more on the picture which the academic historian provided. The historian in fact played an important part in the German national story in that period; for in effect it was he who said to the country: 'See, *this* is your tradition, this is the line which the past has set for you to follow.' And now it is dawning on the Germans that their historians may have made the wrong diagnosis. In their function of eliciting or discerning the essential traditions of their country they may have led their contemporaries astray. In Bismarck's time one historian, Gervinus, pointed out that the militarism of Prussia was only a comparatively recent appendix to the story. It was limited to a couple of hundred years and superimposed upon a much longer tradition of federalism, local autonomy, free cities, and lax government. Gervinus thought that Hamburg would have provided

Germany with a capital more congenial to her essential traditions than Berlin. But he was dismissed as an historian of small-state psychology, too hostile to the Hohenzollern dynasty. Historians cannot prevent their work from having an effect in the world; and it seems that they perform a function which they do not always desire to exercise. They help to elicit or to diagnose their country's traditions; or rather, perhaps, as we have seen, they give added leverage or confirmation to the decision which their contemporaries are already making on this point. Whatever we may feel about the defects of our own Whig interpretation of history, we have reason to be thankful for its influence on our political tradition; for it was to prove of the greatest moment to us that by the early seventeenth century our antiquarians had formulated our history as a history of liberty.[1]

Apart from the discovery or the underlining of a tradition there seems to be a sense in which the historian may represent the thoughts of a nation as it reflects on its own triumphs or vicissitudes. And perhaps it was significant that the English, remembering the seventeenth-century civil wars, decided that revolution was a thing which must not be allowed ever to happen again; while the French, recalling the events of the 1790's, tended rather to idealise revolution as such, and to feel that it was a good thing to have.[2] The German historians in recent years have not neglected the function of representing their nation in its reflections on its tragic experiences. And, curiously enough, it transpires that their attempt to review the past, to discover their mistakes, to correct their traditions and to revise their ideas about their position in the world—all this came to its critical stage in the form of a controversy in the history of historiography. The problem: 'What is wrong with Germany?' has really culminated in the question: 'What has been wrong with the German historical school?'

[1] On the fallacies of the Whig Interpretation, see my *Whig Interpretation of History* (1929). On its function at a certain stage in the history of our historiography, and on its value for our political tradition, see my *Englishman and his History* (1944).

[2] This is discussed ibid. Part II, especially 103–17.

After the First World War the German historians, who were interested in the problems of their contemporary life, either concentrated their attention on the War Guilt question or set out to rescue Bismarck from the over-Machiavellian interpretations which the Prussian school had seemed content to place upon his career. One of the greatest of the German scholars, Meinecke, attempted to re-examine the bases of German historical science, but he was a man who stood above most of his contemporaries, and as such was not likely to represent a general tendency. It is the Second World War which has led to the questioning of one of Germany's most central traditions—namely the basic principles of the leading historical school. Partly this has arisen from an anxiety to meet the allegation that German thought—and particularly German historical and political thought—had really been preparing the way for Hitler, and pointing necessarily to him, for many generations. Partly some Germans came to feel that their country had been becoming even culturally separated from the other regions of western Europe—a paradoxical thing, if one considers the intimacy of the connection between German and English historical thought down to the very end of the nineteenth century. So there have been attempts to build up again the broken bridges, or at least to discover the point at which German thought and the rest of Western civilisation began to diverge. For Germans this has meant rolling back their modern tradition of historical writing and enquiring more deeply into the basis of it. In particular it has meant a re-examination of the fundamental principles established by the greatest of the nineteenth-century historians, Ranke.[1]

[1] See, for example, Hans Kohn, *German History: Some New German Views* (London, 1954) with Bibliography, pp. 213–20. The editors of *Geschichte in Wissenschaft und Unterricht* make it clear in their first number, April 1950, pp. 1–2, that the discussion of this problem is one of their main purposes. See, for example, Erich Weniger, 'Zur Frage der Richtlinien für den Geschichtsunterricht', ibid. 32–6. An important aspect of the German historical revision has been the attempt to reassess Bismarck, as in the essay by Franz Schnabel from *Hochland*, October 1949, translated as 'The Bismarck Problem' in H. Kohn, op. cit. 65–93; Gerhard Ritter, 'Das Bismarck-Problem', *Merkur*, June

The Aberrations of National Historiography

But if it can be argued for a moment that German historiography was at fault through some national aberration, this gives us no reason to assume that our own is central and normative—that because the one is wrong the other must be right. The very contrary is more likely to be the case; and the fact that Germany erred in her own way rather favours the presumption that something in the national mentality is liable to deflect the historiography of every country—each people making its own peculiar kind of mistakes. If a single nation can go wrong in this manner, we must enquire whether there is not a considerable tract of unredeemed territory in the historical thinking of all countries, which still needs to be explored. There are hidden factors behind any national tradition of historical interpretation, and these need to be raised as far as possible to the level of consciousness, so that they can be neutralised or brought under control. A committee of historians, when once approached on the subject of the history of science, greeted the overture with a stony silence, save that one man said: 'Thank God the scientists are waking up at last'; and, in this way, the 'other party'—whether now it is the Germans or now it is the scientists—always seems to be subnormal if we take ourselves as being the norm. The history of historiography, surveying everything from a higher altitude,

1950; cf. Hans Rothfels, 'Problems of a Bismarck Biography', *Review of Politics*, July 1947. Another aspect is dealt with, e.g. in G. Ritter, 'Grossdeutsch und Kleindeutsch im 19. Jahrhundert' in *Schicksalswege Deutscher Vergangenheit* (ed. W. Hubatsch), Essays presented to Professor S. Kaehler, 177–201. On this whole process of historical revision Ritter has written, e.g. *Geschichte als Bildungsmacht, Ein Beitrag zur historisch-politischen Neubesinnung* (Stuttgart, 1947); 'Deutsche Geschichtswissenschaft im 20. Jahrhundert' in *Geschichte in Wissenschaft und Unterricht*, May 1950; and 'Gegenwärtige Lage und Zukunftsaufgaben deutscher Geschichtswissenschaft', *Historische Zeitschrift*, June 1950. For the deeper purposes of the historian of historiography the most important contributions to this process of revision are the ones in which representatives of the central tradition enquire into the roots of that tradition, and seek to grapple with fundamental problems of historiography or trace the remoter origins of intellectual divergences. Irrespective of agreement or disagreement with Ritter, one can hardly deny his power as an historian or quarrel with the view of Jules Menken, in 'German Historical Writing, 1939–1945', III (*Times Literary Supplement*, 22 August 1952, p. 554), that he writes 'with characteristic honesty and courage (and with great anguish of spirit)'. Cf. however, J. A. von Rantzau, 'Individualitätsprinzip, Staatsverherrlichung und deutsche Geschichtsschreibung', *Die Sammlung*, May 1950.

and subjecting all parties to the same kind of analysis, has a profounder significance in that it operates also to bring our own sins home to ourselves.

At this stage in the argument it becomes clear that the problems of historiography are at certain points closely connected with the problems of life. They touch the question of the way in which human beings are to take their vicissitudes on the earth—the way in which nations are to reflect on their corporate experience. A people that lived without any knowledge of its past—without any serious attempt to organise its memory—would hardly be calculated to make much progress in its civilisation. Over and over again we discover to what a degree, in politics for example, men do their thinking and form their attitudes by reference to some presumed picture of the procession of the centuries. The framework which people give to their general history—the notion they have of man in time and of the processes of time—may do much to determine the rest of their outlook. Yet we, who can lavish vast areas of print on researches into some minute episode may come to our fundamental ideas in the most casual manner possible, and may devote to them only the kind of thinking that is done in asides. It is possible for historians to mislead a nation in respect of what it might regard as its historic mission. It is possible for them to give men a wrong notion of what they can do with their destiny. An aspect of the history of historiography which has been somewhat neglected is the examination of the part which historical study and historical thinking have played in the development of the European nations during the last one hundred and fifty years. The nineteenth-century myth of romantic nationalism would appear to have been born of historical study—it could hardly have come into existence if men had not been so interested in delving into the past, while so unschooled in their attitude to bygone things. It would seem that the decline of religion gives undue power to history in the shaping of men's minds—undue power to historical over-simplifications; and multitudes of young students have even come to the study of technical history in the expectation that it would help them to shape their fundamental views about life. It is an expectation that is often disappointed.

In our own day writers have been studying the changes that have taken place in men's attitude to time and to the time-process—the cyclic view of history in the world of classical antiquity, for example, the very different Biblical assumptions, and the transition to the idea of progress. In this field of study a considerable part has been played by theological writers, interested in the development of man's religious consciousness.[1] The history of historiography comes to points at which it carries us beyond its own domain, and breaks into a realm of profounder questioning.

[1] Oscar Cullmann, *Christus und die Zeit, Die urchristliche Zeit- und Geschichtsauffassung* (Zürich, 1946), Engl. transl. *Christ and Time: the Primitive Christian Conception of Time and History* (London, 1951). Reinhold Niebuhr, *Faith and History: a comparison of Christian and modern views of history* (London, 1949). Cf. John F. Callahan, *Four Views of Time in ancient philosophy* (Cambridge, Mass., 1948).

II

THE RISE OF THE
GERMAN HISTORICAL SCHOOL

I. BEGINNINGS

The history of science could never be adequately reconstructed by a student who confined his attention to the few men of supreme genius. We should produce a misleading diagram of the whole course of things if we merely drew direct lines from one of these mighty peaks to another. The great books are undoubtedly preferable to the reader, more serviceable in education, and more enriching to the mind; but, if we restrict ourselves to these, the result is likely to be a rope of sand; and in any case this is not the way in which to make discoveries in the history of any science. In reality, the technical historian, bent on discovery—proceeding therefore from the known to the unknown—tends to find himself drawn rather in the opposite direction. Aware of the importance of Sir Isaac Newton, he strains to see what was the state of science in the period before Newton took hold of his problems. He follows the history of gravitation—not excluding the mistakes and misfires—down to the moment when the famous apple fell. And, in reality, only in this way can anybody take the measure of what Newton himself achieved.

We are in a similar position when we learn that Leopold von Ranke, and, behind him, the classical historian, Niebuhr, established the modern method and inaugurated a new epoch in historical study. We have to ask ourselves whether it would not be worth while to dig deeper, in our quest for 'origins', and this means that we must turn our attention to the preceding period. Keeping Niebuhr and Ranke as giants in the background of the story, I propose in the present lecture to enquire into some of the antecedents of that revolution in historical study with which their names have been particularly associated. Amongst these there are some which have been neglected and they seem to me to present a story that is still worth telling. The narrative introduces us to an academic scene which I think is interesting in itself and it enables us to observe a significant phase of university history. It makes it possible for us to see what historians have neglected so greatly—the spectacle of the world as it stands on the brink of a great intellectual change; and it exposes some of the processes by which a revolution is accomplished. I choose it particularly because it seems to me to illustrate the importance of carrying an historical enquiry perpetually a stage further back; and it shows that, apart from the well-known writers, the smaller men make an appreciable contribution to the changes that take place in the world. Also it reminds us that the history of historiography is more than a mere branch of the history of thought, more than the mere study of individual thinkers. It comprises the story of establishments and institutions, the policies of governments and teaching bodies, and the results of co-operative endeavour.

The historical writers of the eighteenth-century 'philosophic' school have long been regarded as essentially unhistorical in their outlook. They were so sure of being right on the subject of life and the universe that they quickly judged all other ages by their own standard. When they were dealing with alien peoples and unfamiliar systems they failed to see that any great effort of understanding might be called for. Perhaps men so intent on their own propaganda would hardly realise that historical understanding should be promoted as an end in itself. This may help to explain why the eighteenth century proved so unsatisfactory in what we should regard as in a sense a test case. It came short in its reconstruction of the Middle Ages, and dismissed the period as one of intellectual eclipse. For this reason it was left for the nineteenth century to carry out what perhaps still remains as the greatest creative achievement of historical understanding—the recovery and exposition of the medieval world.

Even the 'philosophic' writers, however, had their contribution to make to the recovery and the comprehension of the past. They had a vision of a general history of society and culture which should supersede mere calendars of marvels, disasters, battles and political events. They sought to examine movements, states of society and transitions; and, as in the case of Voltaire's *Age of Louis XIV*, they were prepared to break with the chronological order in their presentation of the result. Since they did not merely recover the past but asked for explanations, they produced a kind of historical writing which was more expository in its form. As Fueter has shown, they were concerned to bring out the connections between events, to track down lines of development, to discover 'general causes' and to achieve types of historical synthesis.[1]

On the other hand, the idea that the historian must imaginatively transpose himself and make intellectual adjustments when he confronts an earlier age of history is not the mere product of the sentiments and sympathies of the Romantic movement. We find the germs of it amid the rationalism of even the 'philosophic' writers, who realised that primitive societies and 'the state of nature' required to be studied on their own terms.[2] There is, moreover, an intermediate group of pre-Romantic writers who, just after the middle of the eighteenth century, were travelling further in the same direction. One man would attempt to recover the flavour of the heroic and patriarchal society that lies behind the work of Homer. Another would see the world of the Old Testament not merely as the setting for sacred drama, but also as a piece of history, possessing a character of its own. Now there would be a sympathetic attempt to describe the

[1] Eduard Fueter, *Geschichte der Neueren Historiographie* (München und Berlin, 1936), 334–49.
[2] Ibid. 341. On the view that the development of the historical sense owes more to the eighteenth century and less to the Romantic movement than once imagined, see R. Wittram, 'Das Interesse an der Geschichte', *Die Welt als Geschichte* XII (1952), 1, with reference to R. Stadelmann, 'Die Romantik, und die Geschichte', *Romantik, Ein Zyklus Tübinger Vorlesungen* (Tübingen und Stuttgart, 1948), 161. See also pp. 60–1 and 72–5 below.

knights of the Middle Ages. Now the atmosphere of Scandi-navian saga would give colour to an historical reconstruction. The question was raised: Whether Gothic architecture, in-stead of being mere corruption or barbarism, did not possess style in its own right—a style which it would be wrong to condemn merely because it failed to conform to the standards of classical Greece. Here was a movement which in the 1750's and 1760's seems to have progressed further in England than in any other country. It emerges not exactly perhaps as a movement within historical study as such, but in certain associated fields.[1]

Soon after the middle of the eighteenth century, therefore, we can see something of rationalism on the one side and some-thing of romanticism on the other side when men are writing about the past. In the one case the historian is a scientific enquirer; in the other case there seems to be a suggestion of the historian as poet. But the two blur into one another and even in a later period of conscious conflict there were men whose position has been a matter of controversy. If both of these schools proved inadequate, this was not because they were imperfectly combined, but because each of them equally suffered from a paucity of knowledge—each had a vision of something better than the materials could as yet provide. And that is why there is a third factor which it is important to bring forward at this point in the story—the straight development of history as a form of scholarship.

From this point of view it is clear that the later decades of the eighteenth century have a considerable interest for us. Up to this time the history of historiography had been somewhat broken and inconsequent, and even in respect of critical method an exceptional achievement might be followed by a relapse, so that it failed to be caught into the stream of general tendency.[2] Some discoveries had even been made and then allowed to be

---

[1] Friedrich Meinecke on 'Klassizismus, Romantizismus und historisches Denken im 18 Jahrhundert', in *Vom geschichtlichen Sinn*, 46–67.
[2] See, for example, H. Wesendonck, *Begründung*, pp. 18–19 on Cellarius and pp. 19–21 on Puffendorf.

buried—in some cases they were not to reappear for centuries. It is in the 1760's that there opens a new chapter in the history of historical scholarship; and it embraces something broader than isolated individual achievements—henceforward the whole story becomes more continuous and organic. The movement takes its rise in Germany, and now, on a wider front, we see the development of that intellectual world which was to form the essential background for Niebuhr and Ranke. This is where we shall find the effective origin of the German historical school.

Up to the 1760's historical study in Germany had lagged behind that of France and England, and behind some other branches of learning at home. It had remained subservient to theology or philosophy;[1] or students had concerned themselves with local history and *minutiæ*; and the chief advances had been made in auxiliary sciences like genealogy.[2] The historical scholars of the new generation, in a surprising number of cases, were men who had originally intended to be clergymen, and had been converted to history by their theological studies.[3] When they talked about their debts to their precursors, they did not mention historians but named specific teachers of philology, classical literature and the Bible. Already in the 1760's we find them speaking as men who are conscious that they are living in a new age of historical scholarship— they imagine that history is established as a science at last. One professor in 1768 described Russia as fortunate; her historical studies were only beginning now, at a time when men had just learned how to hunt out, examine and purify the sources; Russia could start off, therefore, on the right foot. This writer continues:

For a couple of centuries we have been producing histories of the Germans and of Germany. But where do we stand now? We are

[1] H. Wesendonck, *Begründung*, ix.   [2] Ibid. 142.
[3] Schlözer, for example, addressing the Russian clergy in *Nestor*, III, iv, points out that there seems to be a natural transition from theology to history, and that a number of the most famous German historical scholars had been settled students of theology in the first place.

36

only at the very beginning.... Something of the same is true of the study of general world-history in our time.[1]

Even in the 1790's it was still customary to talk of the great change that had taken place in the position of historical scholarship during the previous thirty years. Through German influence, Bohemian history and Slavonic history were being transformed and the change once again was referred back to the 1760's.[2] The multiplication of learned societies and historical journals, particularly from the same decade, shows that there is movement and that it is taking place on a wide front.[3] Indeed, the number of predominantly historical periodicals in Germany is calculated to have risen from three in 1700 to one hundred and thirty-one in 1790.[4] Certainly by the year 1772 one can begin to see why it should have been in Germany that historical study began to make a general advance. In that year, a German scholar calculated that, out of nearly five thousand writings which had appeared in the country in the three years from 1769 to 1771, nearly a fifth, that is to say, nearly a thousand, were in the field of history.[5] In France the number of equivalent items came to only a quarter of this figure.[6] No other country in Europe at this time approached either Germany or France in the number of its historical writings; while in England the proportion of the historical to the total output, far from being one-fifth, was only a ninth.[7] The same German scholar explained in

---

[1] Heyne's review of Schlözer's *Probe russischer Annalen* in *Göttingische gelehrte Anzeigen*, 3 March 1769, p. 308. This article actually refers to the fact that an age has arrived in which 'history is beginning to be studied in a more critical manner than hitherto'. Cf. *Historisches Journal*, VI (Göttingen, 1776), 193: 'It is a great disadvantage for the history of most of the German states that the writing of it was begun too early, before people knew properly how to collect the material from the sources and to handle it in a critical manner.' Cf. ibid. V (1775), 2, which describes how much of world-history needs to be examined 'mit dem Scharfsinn der neuern Critik'.

[2] E.g. Schlözer, *Nestor*, II, 297, 299. Cf. ibid. II, 69.

[3] L. Wachler, *Gesch. der hist. Wissenschaften*, II, 771-3.

[4] R. Wittram, 'Das Interesse an der Geschichte', *Die Welt als Geschichte*, XII (1952), I.

[5] *Historisches Journal*, I (Göttingen, 1772), 266-301. Gatterer calculated that there were 3000 writers of books in Germany.

[6] Ibid. I, 45-66.   [7] Ibid. I, 159-70.

another place that the legal and constitutional controversies in Germany—those between the various sectional interests within the Empire, as well as those between the individual members and the imperial authority above them—had necessitated the critical and documentary study of the nation's history, the technical enquiry into rights and precedents. This kind of scholarship had been more common amongst the Germans, therefore, than, for example, amongst the French.[1]

The scholar who tells us all this is far from showing a disposition to flatter his fellow-countrymen; and in still another place he makes it clear that he has no illusions about German men of learning. Already, he sketches out for us the figure of 'Dryasdust', who seems to have appeared in German historical scholarship much earlier than Lord Acton believed. The Germans were feverish collectors of data, this man tells us, and many of their historical writers were mere compilers, utterly devoid of taste.[2] There never had existed on this earth a nation so eager for foreign languages; and certainly they knew more about the books of other countries than the others ever knew of theirs. Over and above this, they were passionately eager to have such books translated; though sometimes the head gave little help to the hand in the execution of this work. Occasionally, however, the original book, when it appeared in German, would be corrected or amplified by the addition of footnotes. The industrious Germans, in this man's opinion, were a people exactly suited to the production of learned footnotes.[3]

On the one hand, therefore, it would not seem necessary to go back earlier than this for the opening of the new chapter in the story. On the other hand, considering the character of much of the material, one would hardly expect that the next general advance would take place amongst the dusty pedagogues themselves. When it is a university teacher who

---

[1] *Historisches Journal*, 1, 90. Cf. ibid. 1, Vorrede: 'die sonst so gründlichen und ernsthaften Teutschen, die von Natur eine so gute Anlage zur Geschichte haben.'

[2] Ibid. 1, 48. Cf. the later comments on German scholarship in K. J. Vietz, *Das Studium der allgemeinen Geschichte* (Prag, 1844), 159.   [3] Ibid. 1, 274–5.

suggests such a thing it is necessary to keep all the police-dogs on the alert, as he may be suspected of partiality for the career he has made his own. To be sure, in some of the centuries of modern history the academic profession seems to cut no very glorious figure in the world; and though sometimes all its members seem to draw together in the defence of a vested interest, there are occasions when it is only the few who have been brave, though the heroism of the few, by a curious transfer, will come to be imputed retrospectively to the whole body. It is notorious that the Scientific Revolution of the seventeenth century had to by-pass the universities and found it necessary to supplement these with new establishments of its own. And even the scientists cannot escape the constitution of things which seems to decree that teaching-bodies are more fitted to continue the globe in its existing course than to guide it into new regions of the sky. But, though the lower humorists reduce us to caricature throughout the ages, we who are in the academic line will look a little fondly on our predecessors, who gain humanity when seen at close quarters, and whose function is never quite so derisory as it can be made to seem. In the field of historical study it is perhaps not too much to say that, in the period we are now considering, a university, in a system of combined operations, achieved what amounts to a creative act.

2. THE UNIVERSITY OF GÖTTINGEN

Nestling in the folds of a moderate range of hills, south of Hanover and north of Cassel, lies the small town of Göttingen, the seat of a university to which Englishmen have reason to be particularly attached. Baron Münchhausen, the cousin of the famous inventor of fables who bore the same name, secured its foundation in 1734, under the auspices of the Elector of Hanover, who was then George II of England. The connection with England is in itself not irrelevant to our story, for as a result of this the freedom allowed for the publication of ideas was the envy of scholars elsewhere in Germany, though offensive to the rulers of some of the other states.[1] And the scholars of Göttingen were able to move more easily than those of other universities to Great Britain or to the Netherlands.[2]

The Hanoverian rulers of the eighteenth century showed particular favour to their university. Treitschke tells us that some professors there enjoyed special postal privileges for anything connected with their work.[3] A lecturer on contemporary affairs would benefit from permission to travel abroad and from the provision of periodical literature.[4] One of the greatest assets of the university was the library, which then had the reputation of being the biggest and the best arranged in the whole country.[5] Apparently it was so good that it discouraged teachers from accepting calls elsewhere. Provided they were Protestants, the professors would be drawn by a wise and careful administration from the best scholars in the country, irrespective of the principality to which they belonged.[6] Napoleon said at a later date that Göttingen did not belong to any particular state or to Germany alone, but stood as a European university.[7]

Government policy favoured philological studies, for which Göttingen soon became the chief centre in Germany. In theology, first Mosheim, and then Semler and Michaelis, formed a strong tradition which leaned to the philological and historical treatment of the Bible. In classical philology, Gesner and Heyne gained parallel distinction, and made themselves the foremost teachers of the history, the language

[1] H. Wesendonck, *Begründung*, 55–6. Cf. F. Frensdorff, *Von und über Schlözer*, Abhandlungen der Königlichen Gesellschaft der Wissenschaften zu Göttingen, Philol.-Hist. Klasse. Neue Folge Bd. xi, no. 4 (Berlin, 1909), 51, 77–8.

[2] F. Fürst, *August Ludwig v. Schlözer, ein deutscher Aufklärer im 18 Jahrhundert* (Heidelberger Abh., 56, Heidelberg, 1928), 12.

[3] Treitschke on Maskow in Ad. Schmidt's *Zeitschrift für Geschichte* quoted in H. Wesendonck, *Begründung*, 56.

[4] Frensdorff, op. cit. 32–44; and pp. 51–2, below.

[5] L. Wachler, *Gesch. der hist. Wissenschaften*, ii, 783. F. Fürst, op. cit. 12. See the comparison with Vienna in *Historisches Journal*, iii (Göttingen, 1774), 167.

[6] F. Fürst, op. cit. 12.

[7] M. Wischnitzer, *Die Universität Göttingen und die Entwicklung der liberalen Ideen in Russland im ersten Viertel des 19 Jahrhunderts* (Historische Studien, Heft 58, Berlin, 1907), 24.

and the culture of Greece. These departments of study were so directed, therefore, as to inspire many students with a passion for history.[1] From the point of view of many who came to be taught there, however, the great attraction of Göttingen lay in the fields of law and political science. Students came for the sake of these subjects irrespective of the principality in which they had been born—came sometimes for a short period merely to take these courses—until this gave the university a special character.[2] Here was a further factor which had considerable effect on the development of a definitely historical school. And, long before Seeley said that 'History without Politics descends to mere Literature', a Göttingen professor said at the very opening of the nineteenth century that 'History without Politics is mere monkish chronicles'.[3] The field which was allowed to be neglected was that of philosophy. From the time of the French Revolution the university set itself up as the enemy of the revolutionary cause, the enemy of rationalism and doctrinairism. Göttingen supported that more concrete treatment of politics which was congenial also to the Englishman. It gave itself, not to speculative adventures, but to the study of history.[4]

[1] F. Fürst, op. cit. 11–12. Fürst also points out, p. 13, that 'even in the field of juristic and theological studies, the investigation of the process of historical development is the characteristic of the work done in Göttingen'. On p. 21 he notes the influence of Montesquieu on Michaelis, whose treatment of Moses as a legislator and statesman is discussed in Christian von Schlözer, *A. L. von Schlözers öffentliches und Privatleben, aus Originalurkunden* (Leipzig, 1828), I, 22 (cf. Fürst, op. cit. 20–1). See Wesendonck, *Begründung*, 182, where the more liberal views of Michaelis are regarded as the effect of his stay in England. F. Fürst, op. cit. 172, notes the debt of a great part of the new historians to classical philology and especially to Professor Heyne in Göttingen.

[2] See p. 51, n. 4, below. Cf. Wesendonck, *Begründung*, 94, where it is stated that at this date Göttingen (like Bonn, and to a certain degree Berlin, in the 1870's) was the university attended by all who wanted 'die höhere Staatscarriere' as well as by those who in the manner of the higher aristocracy only studied *pro forma*.

[3] Schlözer, *Weltgeschichte nach ihren Haupttheilen*, 3rd ed. (Göttingen, 1785), Einleitung, p. 2, n. 4.

[4] F. Fürst, op. cit. 13. Cf. ibid. 171: 'In contrast to the speculative tendency of other German universities, here [in Göttingen] is the seat of historical thinking.' The *Historisches Journal*, III (1774), 158, quotes Io. Matth. Gesneri *Primæ Lineæ Isagoges in eruditionem universalem*, I (Lips. 1774), to show that Göttingen is known abroad as an historical university. Cf. *Historisches Journal*, III, 170, which shows the comparatively poor condition of history in Vienna.

The Rise of the German Historical School

In spite of the case which historians of science have made against the seventeenth-century universities, it is hard to deny the distinguished place which the university of Padua holds as the main seat of scientific development in the pre-revolutionary era. It is equally true that the university of Göttingen prepared the way for what was to be the Scientific Revolution in historical study. In the closing decades of the eighteenth century it built itself up as the leading German historical school, seeking to give the subject a scientific character, and making itself the centre for the study of method. It retained its imposing character and maintained its influence until well into the nineteenth century.

A convenient starting-point[1] is the nomination to the chair of history in 1759 of Johann Christoph Gatterer, whom a Prague professor in 1844 described as 'the ideal example of an eighteenth-century German scholar'.[2] He is the man whom we have just seen taking stock of the condition of historical study at a slightly later period; and it was he who at this early stage in the story called for a history of historiography. Those who have praised him and those who have criticised seem to me to have overlooked a remarkable feature of his thinking, namely, its programmatic character—its attempt to map out the future development of historiography. He was responsible for the editing and for much of the production of two successive historical journals, and he established for a time an Historical Institute which was apparently something like the precursor of the seminar.[3] He did much to promote the sciences which were then auxiliary to history—geography, genealogy, heraldry, numismatics, etc.—and was regarded as having made original contributions to some of these, as well as having given a great impulse to the study of diplomatic.[4]

[1] For Göttingen before 1760, see H. Wesendonck, *Begründung*, 50–3.

[2] K. J. Vietz, *Das Studium der allgemeinen Geschichte*, 200.

[3] Wesendonck, *Begründung*, 90, says that the Institute came into conflict with the Königl. Societät der Wissenschaften at Göttingen which had an historical *Klasse*. See also L. Wachler, *Gesch. der hist. Wissenschaften*, II, 778, and F.X. von Wegele, *Gesch. der Deutschen Historiographie seit dem Auftreten des Humanismus*, 761.

[4] F. X. v. Wegele, op. cit. 760–1, 763–4.

What is more interesting to us, however, is the fact that he ranged over the whole historical field, trying to show what was needed to establish history as a serious form of scholarship— trying in fact to create a strategy and to draw up a plan of campaign.

In his view, the earlier history of Germany, for example, was being held back by a defective knowledge of medieval geography and chronology. The history of imperial Germany was crippled by the fact that it was treated in a routine manner as a mere auxiliary to the study of public law.[1] Gatterer foreshadows Ranke in his argument that the mere history of the Emperors was not enough—that, just as Hume had concentrated on the English Parliament, the Germans should turn their attention to the proceedings of the Reichstag.[2] By 1768 he was proposing to produce (apparently through his Historical Institute) a critical edition of the sources of German history. For a long time, he said, it had been a Frenchman, Rapin, who had held the field in English history, while another Frenchman, Barre, had been the leading writer on the history of Germany. The English now had their David Hume; but 'we Germans—ah! we Germans—we still have to wait for our Hume, if we can expect him at all in this romanticising, dramatising, Voltairean age, which is so blustering in its windbag-history'.[3] Surveying the whole scene and marking out what was required to establish history on a firmer footing as a form of scholarship, he anticipates a number of the ideas

[1] Gatterer's 'Zufällige Gedanken über die deutsche Geschichte' in H. Wesendonck, *Begründung*, 107. F. Fürst, op. cit. 170–1, says that only nobles and jurists listened to the famous Pütter on the history of the German *Reich* and that the lectures were of no interest to anybody else because of the juristic mode of treatment which they gave to the subject-matter. Monarchs were enumerated, elections, partitions, wars and peace-treaties were noted—'a dry stringing-together of facts without any attempt to establish any inner connection between the individual events'. Cf. J. S. Pütter, *Vollständigerer Handbuch des Teutschen Reichshistorie*, 2nd ed. (Göttingen, 1772), Vorrede.

[2] 'Zufällige Gedanken' in Wesendonck, *Begründung*, 107.

[3] *Historisches Journal*, I, 170. Gatterer's reference to Rapin points to his *Histoire d'Angleterre*, 8 vols. (La Haye, 1724) while Joseph Barre (1692–1764) wrote the *Histoire générale de l'Allemagne*, 11 vols. (Paris, 1748). On the fashion for affecting the manner of Voltaire, Hume and Robertson, see *Historisches Journal*, I, Vorrede. Cf. C. F. Rühs, *Geschichte Schwedens*, I (Halle, 1803), viii and ix.

of the future. One of his views was to be significant in the nineteenth century and touched on a point that gave Acton great exhilaration in his youth. He urged the importance of medieval history for the study of the constitutions of the modern European states; and he noted that this applied to France (where the notion was less familiar at this time) as well as to Germany.[1]

3. THE PROBLEM OF UNIVERSAL HISTORY

The strategic and programmatic schemes of Gatterer were not confined to the field of German studies. He attached great importance to what was called Universal History, and his career draws attention to the problems which this aspect of historical study provokes. Universal history has ceased to hold a prominent place in our interests, presumably because it spreads the mind over so wide an area that the knowledge can hardly avoid becoming too thin. The subject became a living issue for a considerable period,[2] however, partly owing to the commotion produced by Gatterer, who here starts a course of development that culminates in Ranke. For to Ranke Universal History was the supreme objective, and he kept it in his mind even when he was working in limited and local fields. He hoped to crown the labours of a lifetime with the famous *Weltgeschichte*, which in fact he never completed. From 1760 the whole problem had been reopened. How ought the history of the world to be laid out? What ought to be put into it? How should the various parts of it be spaced and proportioned; and what should be the relations between the parts? How also should time be marked, and the division into periods arranged if the history was to be really 'universal'?

[1] *Historisches Journal*, I, 60–1. Cf. ibid. I, 152.
[2] R. Fester, 'Die Säkularisation der Historie', *Historische Vierteljahrschrift*, XI (1908), 441 ff. W. Dilthey, *Gesammelte Schriften* (Leipzig und Berlin, 1927), III, 223. H. Wesendonck, *Begründung*, 89 (where we are told that Gatterer and Schlözer were the first in Germany to make general or universal history a successful subject of university lectures). Cf. ibid. 218.

The Periods of Universal History

The importance which Luther and Melanchthon had attached to the study of the past had resulted in the establishment of universal history in the schools of sixteenth-century Germany.[1] It had produced also a reversion to the system under which the whole course of the story was subdivided into periods corresponding to four World-Empires, the Assyrian, the Persian, the Greek, and finally the Roman, which was to last till the end of the world. This system, which had reference to the book of Daniel, had appeared in ancient times, and is sometimes described as 'Hellenistic'; though for a long period in the eighteenth and nineteenth centuries Melanchthon's friend, Carion, was regarded as having actually devised it.[2] The Catholics were content to accept it, however; and the system appears to have established itself in Germany. From the time of the Renaissance some such term as 'the middle ages' would occasionally appear, but it did not occur to people to follow out the logical consequence of this and to divide world-history into three great periods. This triple division, when it does emerge, makes its appearance first of all in anomalous experimental forms. It seems to take its start in 1644, but on this occasion it was applied purely to the history of the Church, so that the entire scheme had reference only to the Christian era.[3] In another case a writer who favoured the idea of having a middle period made that period run merely from the first century A.D. to the fifteenth. It was the philologists who decided the issue, for it was they who had come to use the term 'medieval' to denote the kind of Latin which they met with after the fall of Rome. And Christopher Cellarius, who in the period around 1685 was dividing history into ancient,

[1] Srbik, *Geist und Geschichte*, I, 70: 'Melanchthon...is the creator of the teaching of world-history in the Protestant universities.' F. X. v. Wegele, *Geschichte der deutschen Historiographie*, 178–338, 'Die deutsche Geschichtschreibung unter den Einwirkungen der Reformation'. A. Momigliano, in 'Ancient History and the Antiquarian' in *Contributa alla Storie degli Studi Classici*, 75, writes: 'Ancient history was still written as part of universal history (a tradition especially cherished by Protestant universities).'

[2] K. J. Vietz, *Das Studium der allgemeinen Geschichte*, 193.

[3] See H. Spangenberg, 'Die Perioden der Weltgeschichte', *Historische Zeitschrift*, CXXVII (1923), 11.

medieval and modern in the manner that is still current, may have set an example which was to be significant for future historians, but acted confessedly under the influence of his preoccupations as a philologist.[1] His work did not result in the immediate abandonment of the Four-Monarchy system, which had its defenders early in the eighteenth century; and indeed, when that system was dropped, the adoption of our modern threefold division was not a foregone conclusion. The Renaissance humanists had suggested the Barbarian Invasions as the great dividing line; and down to the middle of the nineteenth century some historians preferred to take this date as the beginning of what was called 'modern' history.[2] This is the view embodied in the Regius Chairs of Modern History in Oxford and Cambridge, which were established in the eighteenth century and which assume that modern history starts where ancient history ends. In the first half of the nineteenth century some historians held that a totally new period should be opened at the year 1789. Vietz, a professor of history in Prague, declared in 1844 that the end of the Seven Years war was a preferable starting-point, since it signalised the rise of the British Empire and the Prussian monarchy. He put forward the view that the year 1783, marking the achievement of American independence, was bound to prove an important date in world-history.[3]

This last example is sufficient to illustrate the point that the mode of dating and subdividing general history depends on one's conception of the subject as a whole, and also on one's way of estimating the importance of particular events. It was these larger points of policy in fact which attracted the attention of the Göttingen historians; and because they involved what we call 'historical thinking' there is probably some truth in the suggestion which somebody once made, to the effect that it was the interest in universal history which saved German

[1] See H. Spangenberg, 'Die Perioden der Weltgeschichte', *Historische Zeitschrift*, CXXVII (1923), 11–12.
[2] See, for example, Vietz, op. cit. 163.   [3] Ibid. 164–5.

scholarship at this time from the tendency to bury itself in the *minutiæ* of local history, whether of family or of town or of church. In the sixteenth century the programme of universal history had been narrowly conceived and conventionally planned. The subject soon froze into routine in a way that is only too common with a teaching syllabus. It was claimed in Göttingen that universal history had degenerated into a mere succession of dates which were to provide a basis of reference for classical and biblical students;[1] though it was admitted that certain French writers in recent generations—particularly Bossuet and Rollin—had done something to redeem the subject by literary elegance; and Rollin, who was still followed to a certain degree, had a considerable influence on both writers and schools during much of the eighteenth century.[2] For a short period it seemed that the English held the leadership in historical scholarship, especially as from 1736 they had begun the publication of a colossal co-operative universal history.[3] The work was translated into many languages but it was a rambling and discursive compilation, needing much annotation and amendment when it made its appearance on the continent.[4] Severe criticism from Göttingen helped to bring about the decision to abandon the German translation and to make up the remainder of the series with volumes of independent work.[5] By this time the Göttingen historians

[1] A. L. von Schlözer, *Weltgeschichte*, I (Göttingen, 1785), 1 and 4. Cf. J. C. Gatterer, *Universalhistorie*, I, 60. Schlözer complains, op. cit. 4 n., that universal history died out for a period in the universities and that from the beginning of the eighteenth century its name and place had been taken by the history of the modern European states.

[2] J. C. Gatterer, op. cit. Vorrede. K. J. Vietz, op. cit. 197.

[3] *An universal history from the earliest account of time to the present compiled from the original authors* (38 vols. London, 1736–65). Gatterer, in the Preface to his *Universalhistorie*, says that the authors of this book had made great use of Rollin though they had not made sufficient recognition of the fact.

[4] J. G. Meusel, *Bibliotheca Historica*, I, i, 117.

[5] The German translation was edited at first by J. Baumgarten under the title *Übersetzung der allgemeinen Welthistorie, die in England durch eine Gesellschaft von Gelehrten ausgefertiget worden*, and began to appear in Halle in 1744, vol. XXX being printed in 1765. Schlözer's criticisms in the *Göttingische gelehrte Anzeigen* brought about a replanning of the German production, which in 1771 became the *Fortsetzung der allgemeinen Welthistorie, durch eine Gesellschaft von Gelehrten in Teutschland und England ausgefertiget*. Schlözer himself inaugurated this development with vol. XXXI which embodied his

were interesting themselves in universal history, and they made a complete break with the English conception of the subject.

Bolingbroke in his *Letters on History* in 1735 had pressed the importance of modern history, as against the ancient;[1] but the Göttingen professors set out to counteract the growing tendency to adopt this view.[2] On the other hand they were ready to keep the study of universal history within moderate bounds, and not to let it pile itself up into an accumulation of detailed national histories. They brought out in fact a more definite idea of a world-history in contradistinction to the English kind of universal compendium. In any case, their works were not of the colossal type, and they were interested rather in the plan of campaign, interested in showing how the programme of a world-history should be arranged. Though they hoped to appeal to the general reader,[3] they wrote initially for the university student, and their short books were designed to be supplemented by oral teaching. They were experimenting and Gatterer himself produced eight versions of universal history, each of which was different from the last. Even the first of these, in 1760, was considered to be 'epoch-making' and to represent a 'giant stride'. We hear a little later that 'the better handling of universal history in Germany goes

famous *Allgemeine Nordische Geschichte*. See J. G. Meusel, *Bibl. Hist.* I, i, 120. Gatterer's *Historisches Journal*, III (Göttingen, 1774), after giving (41–52) some remarks on the *Übersetzung*, discusses (53–104) the *Fortsetzung*. Gatterer himself, in the Introduction to his *Universalhistorie*, vol. II (1764), had severely criticised the Chinese section of the English work. The shorter English production, *A General History of the World*, by W. Guthrie, J. Gray etc. appeared in London in twelve volumes (1764–7); and the German translation, under the editorship of Heyne appeared in Leipzig from 1765 under the title *Allgemeine Weltgeschichte...aus dem Englischen übersetzt. Aus den Originalschriftstellern berichtiget und mit...verschiedenen Anmerkungen versehen.* The *Historisches Journal*, III, (1774), 225, points out that since the work has been taken over by German scholars it has become epoch-making, while the subsequent pages of the same journal, to p. 283, show something of the way in which the German edition was transformed. J. G. Meusel, *Bibl. Hist.* I, i, 125, shows how when the history of Poland was reached in 1775 the great weakness of the English scholars in the field of Northern European history was exposed. See also p. 53 below.

[1] Bolingbroke, *Works*, III (London, 1809), 440–2.

[2] A. L. von Schlözer, Vorbericht to 3rd ed. of *Welt-Geschichte*. J. C. Gatterer, *Universalhistorie*, Vorrede.   [3] Ibid. 1.

back to this date'.[1] He widened the horizon of a subject which had hitherto kept close to Europe; he introduced an unprecedented amount of cultural history; and he showed skill in his diagnosis and discussion of the turning-points in the story, such as the Barbarian Invasions and the discovery of America. In his attempts to make his whole narrative more organic he laid himself open to the charge of finding connections between things that ought to have been kept separate.

Yet J. G. Schlözer who became his professorial colleague in 1769 carried all this so much further that he in turn has also been called 'the father of universal history'.[2] He rejected the idea of a co-operative work, with one expert writing on France, another on Venice, and so forth; for such a system resulted only in an aggregate of national histories.[3] World-history, he said, must be distinguished from the plan of the great English compendium—it was 'the history of mankind, a new sort of history, hitherto only written by philosophers'.[4] Its real purpose was to show how the earth and humanity as a whole had come to the state in which they now stood;[5] and an important feature of this kind of history, according to Schlözer, ought to be an account of inventions and discoveries.[6] Like Acton over a hundred years later, he insisted that such a history was not to be a mere burden on the memory;[7] in fact, he said, it was not addressed to the memory at all—it was 'philosophy, perpetually connecting results with their causes'.[8] Mankind was a unity, and world-history, provided there was unity in its plan, was capable of ranking as an epic.[9] At the

---

[1] Quoted in Wesendonck, *Begründung*, 207, from Heeren. J. C. Gatterer, in *Universalhistorie*, Vorrede, claims that he is producing universal history on quite a new plan.

[2] K. J. Vietz, writing in 1844, op. cit. 199. Vietz adds that Schlözer's work is still indispensable.

[3] *Weltgeschichte*, 77. *Vorstellung*, 'Vorrede zur zwoten Ausgabe', 5.

[4] *Vorstellung*, 244. Cf. ibid., Vorrede and also 'Vorrede zur zwoten Ausgabe' which speaks of 'an entirely new work'. *Weltgeschichte*, 6, makes the distinction between world-history and universal history. Cf. *Vorstellung*, 237–8. See also Schlözer's *Weltgeschichte*, I, 71 ff.: 'Begriff der Weltgeschichte.'   [5] *Weltgeschichte*, 4.

[6] Ibid. 67; *Vorstellung*, 245; F. Fürst, *A. L. v. Schlözer*, 196–7.

[7] *Vorstellung*, 250.   [8] *Weltgeschichte*, 8.

[9] *Vorstellung*, 256; *Weltgeschichte*, 90.

same time he was prepared to argue that history did not begin to take on a genuinely universal character until the time of the Persian Empire;[1] and, possibly, he was prepared to drop world-history after the discovery of America, leaving the rest of the story for separate national studies.[2] Whereas Gatterer counted the years from the Creation or the Flood, Schlözer numbered them backwards from the birth of Christ, on the ground that on this latter system the student would be less hampered with big figures.[3] For some time both he and his Göttingen successors, when they followed this policy (which they borrowed from foreign writers)[4] regarded it as needing an explanation.[5] Schlözer, moreover, introduced into world-history still more peoples which had hitherto been neglected in such surveys; and he was masterly in his classification of these, declaring that their relationships were not to be decided by their names, their religion or their own literary accounts, but simply by their speech. It was he who grouped together the peoples we call 'semitic' and gave them the composite name by which they are still designated.[6]

The world moves forward, however; and, curiously enough, it was Schlözer's pupil, Johann von Müller, whom Lord Acton regarded as the first universal historian.[7] It is significant that three historians who were connected with Göttingen should have successively been regarded as pioneers in this field.

[1] F. X. v. Wegele, *Gesch. der Deutschen Historiographie*, 793.

[2] Ibid.

[3] A. L. von Schlözer, *Vorstellung*, I, 51 ff.; *Weltgeschichte*, 87; cf. F. Fürst, *A. L. v. Schlözer*, 200; H. Wesendonck, *Begründung*, 156.

[4] Schlözer, *Weltgeschichte*, 87n., says that he follows the 'berümtesten, besonders auswärtiger Historiker'.

[5] A. H. L. Heeren, *A Manual of Ancient History*, Engl. transl. (London, 1847). 'Preface [of 1799] to the First German Edition', p. viii.

[6] H. Wesendonck, *Begründung*, 214, shows that the originator of the term was Schlözer, not Eichhorn, as had previously been believed. See also F. Fürst, op. cit. 200.

[7] See p. 78 and Appendix VI, below.

4. THE DEVELOPMENT OF CRITICISM

At an early point in the story, Gatterer tells us in his *Historical Journal* that the university of Göttingen allowed an historian to devote himself to his chosen field.[1] From the 1850's, one of the professors was building up a famous course which was called *Statistik*[2] and which was a study of contemporary countries—their population, their conditions, their internal relations, their legislative policy and the physical and moral forces at work in them.[3] The course took its rise in the legal faculty, where it seems to have been realised that constitutions were not the only features of contemporary states which were worth studying; but it was transferred to an historian in the early 1770's, and was a great attraction to students from the other German principalities.[4] It was recognised that the professor in question ought to be released on occasion to visit the countries on which he lectured;[5] so that one is reminded of the Cambridge Chair of Political Science, which was founded in 1927 and was designed to allow leave of absence for purposes of travel. The story has a modern ring when we read of the Göttingen professor taking leave in order to go to France, collecting in one office there all the recent legislative enactments, making connections with writers, historians and public officials, and hob-nobbing with a man who had been at the

[1] *Historisches Journal*, i, 265: 'J. C. Gatterers Räsonnement über die jezige Verfassung der Geschichtkunde in Teutschland.'

[2] From the late 1740's G. Achenwall had been establishing the teaching of this subject in Göttingen. See J. S. Pütter, *Selbstbiographie* (Göttingen, 1798), i, 187; and F. Frensdorff, *Von und über Schlözer*, 32 ff. A Dissertation produced by Achenwall in 1748, *Notitia rerum publicarum academiis vindicata* suggests one way of describing the subject. Cf. F. Frensdorff, op. cit. 40, on the use of the term *Staatsmerkwürdigkeiten*.

[3] H. Wesendonck, *Begründung*, 94, says that in other universities 'scarcely the name was known' of the two courses on *Statistik* and *allgemeine Politik*.

[4] Wesendonck says, ibid. 94, that the two courses on *Statistik* and general politics were for practical purposes the decisive factor in the choice of Göttingen by many of the students. Schlözer, writing 9 September 1773 (F. Frensdorff, op. cit. 34–6) says that many of the *noblesse*, particularly from outside Hanover, who either did not take the *Cursum juridicum* or had already taken it at another university, came to Göttingen 'bloss der Cursus politici wegen'.

[5] See Frensdorff, op. cit. 32; Achenwall had leave of absence for the summer semester of 1751 and 1759 and his travels were assisted from public funds.

Foreign Office under Choiseul—a man who had known better than the minister himself what was going on, besides being now in a position to show less reserve in his communications.[1] The same professor established a wide system of correspondence with useful people abroad;[2] and it would appear to have been for the sake of this branch of teaching that the government facilitated the rapid transmission to Göttingen of periodical literature.[3] The fruits of such topical researches would appear in published articles[4] or in lectures on the contemporary scene for the students in the university.[5]

The history professor who distinguished himself in this field of contemporary studies was Schlözer,[6] who has already been noticed in a number of connections. He has since been remembered chiefly as a publicist; but there can be no doubt that he is more important today for his part in the development of technical history.[7] Having spent some years in Sweden, he studied the available resources for the history of northern Europe; and he gave this branch of scholarship a drastic revision which was to have no parallel until the famous

---

[1] Schlözer to J. D. Michaelis, 23 November 1773, F. Frensdorff, op. cit. 47.

[2] Frensdorff, op. cit. 36, shows how Schlözer attempted in 1773 to secure elevation to the dignity of *Hofrat* (like his predecessor Achenwall) so as to have a better standing with the people with whom he desired to make contact.

[3] Ibid. 32.

[4] E.g. A. L. v. Schlözer, *Briefwechsel meist statistischen Inhalts* (Göttingen, 1775), beginning July 1774. Cf. Frensdorff, op. cit. 50.

[5] H. Wesendonck, *Begründung*, 94–7. Wesendonck also notes the existence of the *Zeitungscollegium* in universities from before 1700 and into the early part of the nineteenth century.

[6] F. Fürst, op. cit. 49, says that Schlözer began teaching Politics alternately with Achenwall, and adds, p. 55, that when Achenwall died in 1772 Schlözer took over the course. Frensdorff, op. cit. 32–40. F. X. v. Wegele, *Gesch. der Deutschen Historiographie*, 771. Schlözer succeeded so well in his interim conduct of the *Statistik* course after the death of Achenwall that a successor to the latter was not appointed in the juridical faculty and he himself was given charge of this teaching. H. Wesendonck, *Begründung*, 96, says that Stein and Count Münster were influenced by Schlözer, who in 1787 held the *Nominalprofessur der Politik*. L. Wachler, *Gesch. der hist. Wissenschaften*, II, 786, says that Schlözer raised *Statistik* to greater maturity and brought it into closer connection with *Staatswissenschaft*.

[7] F. Fürst, op. cit. 170, says that if Göttingen, after having the lead in jurisprudence and ancient philology, was transformed into the seat of historical science, and if it had a great influence on history as a whole, this was due in great part to Schlözer.

Niebuhr carried the argument a stage further by a still more remarkable revision of the history of ancient Rome. At the same time it was Schlözer's exposure of the weakness of the English historians in the field of northern European studies which precipitated the decision to abandon the German translation of the famous *Universal History*.[1] That work, as we have seen, had come to be regarded as a collection of separate regional and national histories; and when it was decided to complete the German series by new and independent productions Schlözer himself was commissioned to write on northern Europe, while he secured that his pupil, Johann von Müller, should be asked to undertake the history of Switzerland. The moment was an exhilarating one; for, even in the field of national history, the English, who had been greatly admired, were seen to have fallen short of the new German standards.[2] The Göttingen historians had in mind the revising of the history of foreign nations after all the available sources had been reconsidered and the new critical methods had been brought to bear on them. It is clear that they conceived such an overhauling of a national history to be within the power of a single scholar.[3] The assumption reminds us that historical scholarship was still at an early stage in its development; but we must remember that Ranke himself, when young, is to be regarded as representing a stage only slightly more advanced. He rewrote considerable parts of the modern history of successive European nations, and, though he drew on some

[1] H. Wesendonck, *Begründung*, 112–13, tells us that in 1766 many sheets of Part II of the German translation of the Swedish section of the work had already been printed but were destroyed as a result of the condemnation of Part I by Schlözer. Cf. F. X. v. Wegele, op. cit. 798.

[2] A. Momigliano, in 'Gibbon's Contribution to Historical Method', *Contributo alla Storia degli Studi Classici*, 195, notes that 'The reviewer [of the *Decline and Fall*] in the *Göttingische gelehrte Anzeiger* of 1788, though full of admiration for Gibbon, immediately emphasised the superiority of German source-criticism.'

[3] *Historisches Journal*, IV (Göttingen, 1775), 51–2, where it is admitted, however, that it is not within the compass of a single man to establish in a critical manner the history of every people and 'der Forscher aller Geschichte zu seyn'. In a review of Häberlin's German History in the *Allgemeine Welthistorie*, ibid. 3, it is noted as a matter for surprise that no individual had hitherto made a documentary study which extended to the whole of German history.

additional manuscript sources which greatly assisted him, he developed only gradually the scientific use of these.

The German authors who produced the continuation of the *Universal History* were not always as diligent as Schlözer in his work on northern Europe. But if we have doubts about the modern turn which scholarship was taking, a glance at the further labours of Schlözer in the field of Russian studies will do much to clear them away. He moved from Sweden to St Petersburg and in this capital he served for some years (like a number of other Germans) at the Academy of Science.[1] He inaugurated the first really serious development in Russian historiography, mapping out a great programme of research which was only partially put into execution.[2] Already in the 1760's he was securing one friend to publish the Byzantine sources of Russian history, while another was to deal with the Arabian evidence, he himself working on the native chronicles.[3] Having discovered thirty different peoples living on Russian soil he called for an expert to deal with the Finns, another to work on the Mongols, etc., and contemplated a division of labour between men from varied sciences or branches of scholarship.[4] When he took up his chair in Göttingen in

[1] F. Fürst. *A. L. v. Schlözer*, 31. Few of the foreigners at the St Petersburg Academy understood the Russian language, which Schlözer had studied so much.

[2] F. Fürst, op. cit. 191, notes that Karamsin's history of Russia (which appeared in 1820 with many references to Schlözer and, which passed as the best in existence throughout the nineteenth century) is closely connected with Schlözer, with whom Karamsin was in correspondence. L. Wachler, *Gesch. der hist. Wissenschaften*, II, 785, says that Russian history owes to Schlözer its establishment on a scientific basis. H. Wesendonck, *Begründung*, describes him, p. 77, as the father and creator of Russian history and, p. 83, as the man who laid the foundations of Slavonic history as a whole. F. X. v. Wegele, *Gesch. der deutschen Historiographie*, 801, calls Schlözer one of the founders of Russian historical research.

[3] Schlözer to Köhler, 7 Oct. 1767, in F. Frensdorff, op. cit. 19. H. Stritter (a pupil of Michaelis) produced the Byzantine sources in 4 vols. (1771–9). Schlözer wanted Köhler to undertake the Oriental sources. See F. Fürst, op. cit. 43, on Stritter's Byzantine sources and Köhler's Arabian sources. Fürst tells us that Schlözer intended also to edit the Icelandic sagas. Cf. ibid. 174, where it appears that Semler was to do the German sources of Russian history.

[4] A. L. v. Schlözer, *Nestor*, II, pp. xxiv–xxvi. See also Schlözer to Köhler, 2 Oct. 1767, in F. Frensdorff, op. cit. p. 18, which asks for a medieval geography of Northern Europe, to be based on the oriental sources. See also *Nestor*, I, 20, where Schlözer calls for a Russian Brunet or Pütter who will describe the particular histories of all the great

1769, there was an idea that he should continue this work and build up a school of Russian studies, just as previously Göttingen had made itself a centre for English literature and scholarship. Arrangements were made with the Academy in St Petersburg, and for year after year Russian students were sent to Göttingen, and Russian books were dispatched, so that a remarkable section was built up in the University Library. Owing partly to professional rivalries and personal animosities in Göttingen and partly to the death of Münchhausen, who had favoured the whole policy, the plan was for the most part abandoned; and for a long time the great collection of books remained unused, and Schlözer dropped his idea of keeping Germany in touch with Russian literature by reviews and articles.[1] In the earliest years of the nineteenth century, however, he returned to the work which had represented the principal preoccupation and the greatest ambition of his life—his critical edition of the so-called Russian 'Chronicle of Nestor'.[2]

At this point, where we come to the very edge of the modern scientific movement, it is necessary to remember the law which must govern our assessments in the history of any science. If we were to judge some of the works of William Harvey or Robert Boyle—or indeed of Francis Bacon—by the standard of our present-day knowledge, we could hardly fail to decide that the ideas of these men were wrong-headed. A twentieth-century schoolboy could make some of the founders of modern

and small principalities into which Russia was divided, from the time of their establishment to the date of their union with Moscow. The work of Brunet to which he refers is the *Abrégé chronologique des grands fiefs de la couronne* (Paris, 1759), while the corresponding work by Pütter is the *Historisch-politisches Handbuch von den besonderen teutschen Staaten*, 1 Th. (Göttingen, 1758).

[1] F. Fürst, op. cit. 50–3, discusses the professional jealousies. Cf. F. Frensdorff, op. cit. 28–31, 99. Schlözer himself, when he tells the story in *Nestor*, 1, 99–101, describes the death of Münchhausen in 1770 as the reason for the collapse of the scheme. On Münchhausen, see p. 39, above.

[2] A. L. v. Schlözer, *Nestor. Russische Annalen in ihrer Slavonischen Grundsprache verglichen, übersetzt, und erklärt*, 5 Thle. (Göttingen, 1802–9). In the dedication of vol. 1 to the Tsar Alexander I he says that he hopes that as a result of his work there will be produced a history of Russia with the *Gründlichkeit* of Maskow, the *Geschmack* of Robertson, the *Unbefangenheit* of Giannone and the *Anmuth* of Voltaire.

science look foolish; and this is the point in the argument at which the greatest fallacies may result from an unhistorical approach to the question. The Göttingen historians of the eighteenth century stand in the same position as the early natural scientists; and even the earlier works of Ranke come to appear inadequate if we judge them from our modern point of view. It is necessary that we should always measure such thinkers against the state of things which preceded them—not against the twentieth century. It is useful even to learn something of the views which were held about them by their own contemporaries and by their immediate successors; for though such views are not in any sense infallible they may serve to check our own anachronistic fallacies, and at least they can properly enter—along with many other considerations, of course—into the estimate that we form.

Schlözer's edition of the 'Chronicle of Nestor' is not a work which one would recommend to a present-day student of Russian history; but it seems to me to be one of the remarkable documents in the history of historiography. It was the more remarkable at the time in that nobody as yet had ever set out to produce a comparable edition of any German chronicle. In 1761 the ecclesiastical historian Semler had complained of the uncritical nature of the many existing publications of German source-material, and had indicated some of the forms of criticism that were required.[1] Before the end of the same decade Gatterer, as we have seen, had planned a more scholarly edition of the German sources. Schlözer in turn called for a more methodical treatment of the problem of editing the German chroniclers. Europe possessed excellent editions of classical writers which showed how the work should be done, he said; but the editions of the early German writers showed only how it ought not to be done—'as though Einhard, Liutprand and Ditmar were not incomparably more important to us than Sallustius, Eutropius and Am-

---

[1] J. S. Semler, *Versuch den Gebrauch der Quellen in der Staats- und Kirchengeschichte der mitlern Zeiten zu erleichtern* (Halle, 1761).

mianus'.[1] He complains of the amount of his own time that has been wasted because a critical edition of these German chronicles did not exist. This is significant, because amongst his pupils were some of the founders of the famous *Monumenta Germaniæ Historica*.[2]

In spite of the fact that nobody has really attempted the task for a German text, Schlözer, as he tries to produce a model edition of the Russian chronicler,[3] insists that he is not being original. In this he writes as a man who is concerned to clear himself of the possible charge of novelty. The plan which he follows is not his own, he says; it has been recognised by scholars in all countries.[4] But the precedents which he quotes are always from biblical or classical scholarship; the ideal examples are the critical editions of the New Testament.[5] In so far as the methods are subject to rules, the biblical scholars have expounded the rules; though even those scholars would be baffled by the transpositions which are required to meet the peculiarities of the older Slavonic history;[6] and, he says, there is something in criticism which cannot be subjected to rule, because there is a sense in which every case is a special

---

[1] Nestor, II, 291. In H. Wesendonck, *Begründung*, 116–17, is Schlözer's Preface to Mably, 'Von der Art die Geschichte zu schreiben' (Strasburg, 1784), which states what would be the requirements for the time of Charlemagne.

[2] F. Fürst, op. cit. 169, mentions W. von Humboldt, Freiherr von Stein, J. von Müller, K. F. Eichhorn and Schlosser as the great pupils of Schlözer, and he tells us that when Stein at the end of his life turned to history again his work went back to some stimulus which he owed to Schlözer. Of the eight signatories of the Berlin memorial asking for the establishment of a society for German historical research, K. F. Eichhorn and Rüss were strongly influenced by Schlözer, while Altenstein and Savigny were similarly influenced by Schlözer's younger colleague, Spittler.

[3] On the importance of the *Nestor* as a model, see L. Wachler, op. cit. II, 785, H. Wesendonck, *Begründung*, 118, 197–8; F. X. v. Wegele, op. cit. 801; L. T. Spittler, *Entwurf der Geschichte der europäischen Staaten* (Berlin, 1794), II, 368; *Sämmtliche Werke*, IV (1828), 323.

[4] *Nestor*, Dedication to Bk. II, and ibid. Vorbericht, p. xx. Cf. ibid. II, 284.

[5] Ibid. II, 294: 'Griesbach's edition of the Greek Testament, 1774 and 1796.' Cf. ibid. II, p. xxxii, on the importance of the critics in the field of classics. Cf. H. Wesendonck, *Begründung*, 73: 'The school of the famous exegete, Michaelis, led him to history and laid within him the foundations of a critical method in historical study.'

[6] *Nestor*, II, pp. viii–ix; F. Fürst, op. cit. 175. See ibid. 175–7 for a commentary on Schlözer as a follower of the critical method in general. Cf. H. Wesendonck, *Begründung*, 196.

case. The collation of manuscripts; the recovery of a purified text; the diagnosis of interpolations and corruptions; the discovery of the earlier sources which the writer has used—all these are techniques which Schlözer avowedly takes over from the classical scholars and the theologians. At the same time, throughout his historical thinking he shows the common sense of a man who as he looks at the past sees it as his own present, and handles its problems as matters of contemporary experience. He would believe a story told by his grandmother about the Thirty Years War, he says, because she learned it from her own grandmother who lived through the war. But he will not take his grandmother's authority for an event in the reign of Charles V—still less in the reign of Charlemagne. Yet historians are continually asking him to accept the equivalent of this.[1] Herodotus learns, presumably through an interpreter, what some ancient tribe have to say about their ancestors of a thousand years earlier still; and the modern world, which would know what to do with traveller's reports of the parallel legends of Kamtchatkans or Red Indians, takes such records seriously instead of treating all the barbarians alike.[2] Schlözer perpetually asks 'Where does our knowledge come from and how has it reached us?' And he examines the sources which the medieval chronicler used even when he has to divine those sources and has no extant independent version of them to help him.[3] He is not satisfied to show that medieval chroniclers and ancient writers must have been wrong—he sets out to prove that in one case and another they could not possibly have known the truth.[4] If his principles were consistently applied he says that they would overthrow the ancient history of all peoples, and would wipe out the current version of the first five centuries of Roman history.[5] He brings to his

---

[1] *Nestor*, I, 34. Cf. II, Dedication.   [2] Ibid. I, 33 n.

[3] E.g. *Nestor*, I, 13.   [4] Ibid. I, 25, 34; and II, Dedication.

[5] Ibid. I, 33 n. Cf. ibid. II, 34–5. H. Wesendonck, *Begründung*, 195; cf. ibid, 84, which also refers to Schlözer's view that ancient world-history would require complete revision if the sources for the history of Egypt, Persia, etc., were completed, assembled and subjected to critical treatment. See also F. X. v. Wegele, *Gesch. der deutschen Historiographie*, 797, with reference to Louis de Beaufort, *Dissertation sur l'incertitude des cinq*

work a tremendous knowledge of languages and a conviction that, when literary sources fail, the study of language-relationships will throw some light on early history.[1] He says that the natural scientist rather than the historian is the man who is going to dispel something of the darkness of prehistory.[2] He asks the right questions. Who were the earliest discoverable inhabitants of Russia? Who were the Slavs? Who were the Warangians? Who were the people called 'Russians'?[3] Entangled all the time with his treatment of Russian history is his discussion of the history of our knowledge of Russia and its past; for he sees the importance of the history of historiography.[4] Included in this is the history of our geographical knowledge; for only in the last one hundred and forty years have the western peoples possessed any real idea of the shape of northern Europe on the map; and this fact in itself affects our reliance on the ancient and medieval writings about Russia.[5]

There are defects in his critical practice; and in certain regions it does not occur to him to apply his principles or he fails to give them the extension of which they are capable. A hostile reader who, in judging him, makes concealed cross-reference to the state of historical science at the present-day,

premiers siècles de l'histoire romaine (Engl. transl. London, 1740). The *Historisches Journal*, v (Göttingen, 1775), 2, also mentions the fact that there could be no more certainty about the early centuries of Roman history than about the history of Mexico. Schlözer is no merely destructive doubter, however, and in *Nestor*, II, xvi, he quotes what he had said against such sceptics in his *Allgemeine Nordische Geschichte*, 259.

[1] F. Fürst, op. cit. 180–90. Cf. ibid. 183, where we are shown how Schlözer interested himself in the reports of scholarly people in the Russian service who had journeyed through Siberia and observed the populations there.

[2] For Schlözer's attitude to natural phenomena, see F. Fürst, op. cit. 178–9. *Nestor*, III, 261–2, shows him consulting the professor of physics, Mayer, on the possibility of closing the Bosphorus to shipping by means of a chain. H. Wesendonck, *Begründung*, 74, points out that Michaelis had already used medical, natural and other sciences to throw light on ancient Hebrew history.

[3] This is pointed out by Heyne in a review of earlier work on Russian history by Schlözer. See p. 37, n. 1, above.

[4] This is seen throughout the work rather than in I, 83 ff. where there is a section entitled 'Geschichte der russischen Geschichte von ihrem Aufang an bis nun in 60 Numern'.

[5] *Nestor*, I, 23–5. On p. 24 Schlözer says that Einhard gives the first correct news of the Baltic, and that everything before him is fable. F. X. v. Wegele, *Gesch. der deutschen Historiographie*, 798, refers to Schlözer's examination of Pliny's reports concerning northern Europe.

could therefore easily expose him, so that he would appear naive and uncritical. It is not even true to say of him that he was a mind of the first rank; though he is certainly the most interesting figure in the Göttingen story, and the range of his activities is astonishing. Apart from the various aspects of his life which we have been discussing, he developed the study of German eastern colonisation and his work on the history of Leipzig provoked admiration from Wuttke, who worked on the same subject almost a century later. And he has his place in the history of serious German studies on the subject of the United States.[1]

It is true that more remarkable individuals appeared elsewhere in Germany in the latter half of the eighteenth century.[2] Winckelmann and Herder are well known to students of the history of historiography; and they are certainly more powerful figures than the men of the Göttingen school. It is Göttingen, however, which offers us the spectacle of a broadly based movement and a continuous development. It is here that historical scholarship, in its collective progress, comes most close to the system established by the nineteenth-century school. At this university, in fact, the conflicts between the *philosophes* and the *érudits*, and those between the Enlightenment and the Romantic Movement were already being resolved. The ideas that belonged to the Age of Reason had a powerful effect; but they were sifted, and brought into conformity with the demands of scholarship, so that there is antagonism as well as acceptance. And some of the attacks on

[1] Friedrich Kapp in 'Zur deutschen wissenschaftlichen Literatur über die Vereinigten Staaten von Amerika', *Historische Zeitschrift*, XXXI (1874), 242. Schlözer also worked on Turkish history and showed its importance to the student of modern Europe. F. Fürst, op. cit. 192, points out that Schlözer's pupil, Müller, passed on his influence to his own pupil, von Hammer-Purgstall, who in 1827 produced at Müller's instigation a famous history of the Turkish Empire.

[2] Wesendonck, in the *Begründung*, to which reference has been made in various places above, laid himself open to criticism in that he ascribed too much genius and modernity to Gatterer and Schlözer as individuals, when their books are in many respects so defective. His case would have been stronger if he had kept in mind rather the collective achievement and the general tradition at Göttingen, and the stimulus which Gatterer and Schlözer gave.

the superficialities of the *philosophes* are strangely similar to the attacks on Lytton-Strachey-ism in the decades between our two World Wars. Similarly, one finds in Göttingen some of the ideas that are associated with the Romantic Movement; but at the same time there is generally a love of scholarship which saves the writers of this university from the aberrations of that movement. The dynamic ideas which helped to transform historical study may have arisen outside the universities; but in Göttingen we see them critically considered and carefully combined so as to form a system of historical scholarship. Whether we envisage the attitude adopted to this kind of scholarship, or the treatment of universal history, or the revision of national and regional studies, or the teaching of contemporary politics, or the development of historical method and the editing of texts, the school of Göttingen seems to bring us to the very brink of the modern world.[1] In the case of some of these things, the very next step is Niebuhr, or Ranke, or the *Monumenta Germaniæ Historica*. Niebuhr and Ranke used the new methods with greater flair and reached a wider world because they excelled the Göttingen writers in the production of books. But the intellectual revolution with which their names are associated resolves itself into a process much more gradual and slow than many of us once imagined. Even before Ranke transposed something of the method of Niebuhr into more modern historical fields, there were other intermediate writers (like Stenzel in his medieval work) who had already set out on the same course. A more detailed historical study need take nothing from the stature of the great men, though sometimes it induces us to locate their genius in a different place. It does show us, however, that a real importance belongs also to the smaller people, working faithfully in their little world.

[1] D. F. S. Scott, however, in 'An English Impression of the University of Göttingen in the year 1823', *Durham University Journal*, March 1955, p. 74, notes that 'in 1831 we find Professor C. O. Müller, the classical scholar, complaining about the quality of the students and of their academic attainments, which he held were in a state of decline. The American historian John Motley...complained in 1832 that it was no longer worth while studying in Göttingen, as all the former ornaments of the University were either dead or too old to be of use....'

III

LORD ACTON
AND THE NINETEENTH-CENTURY
HISTORICAL MOVEMENT

1. LORD ACTON AND THE HISTORY OF
HISTORIOGRAPHY

Lord Acton had the reputation of being the greatest man of learning in England in the closing decades of the nineteenth century. He was the type of historian who is primarily the omnivorous reader, at home in many centuries, and familiar with the older literature as well as the new. He reflected much on this knowledge, perpetually turning it this way and that, and constantly working on it to bring it to a higher state of organisation. Often he would do such thinking on paper, so that we can see how he would correlate the data or how a famous epigram gradually took shape.[1] When his notes are of this reflective kind they are sometimes written in pencil; and sometimes his hand becomes jerky as though he were writing in the train.

In a sense we can say that all his knowledge, when put in order and shaken down, would assemble itself into something like a panorama—it constituted, so to speak, Acton's view of modern history. He did not stop there, however, but gave it a further shaking, marshalling all the parts of it into a more elaborate system; so that, when he considered Mary Queen of Scots, for example, the subject itself seemed to acquire a new dimension—it emerged stereoscopically, with all kinds of unexpected depths and folds. And what he saw now was not merely a certain Mary Queen of Scots as depicted by historians, but the history of the historiography of the whole subject, with Mary herself more completely disengaged from

---

[1] E.g. Add. 5015, 53: 'Power, the greater it is, the more it demoralises.' The references to Add. MSS. in this chapter are to the Acton Papers in the Cambridge University Library.

any single writer's picture of her. This enabled him to decide
more clearly his own strategy as an enquirer or a writer—it
helped him on occasion to see what was the next step to take
in the study of a given subject. Above all, it provided him
with another way of piercing through the curtain—another
way of getting behind the historian.

He was only a little over the age of an undergraduate when
he decided in Munich that it should be his function to communicate to England the continental scholarship of the 1850's,
and particularly the new history. The German historical movement—whether he diagnosed it properly or not in the first
place—entered deeply into his consciousness, and his mind
was particularly sensitive to anything which might throw
light on its development. The earliest notebooks of his which
we possess contain a surprising amount of material about the
history of historiography. And, still, in the last decades of his
life, this is the subject which appears to have been in the very
forefront of his interests. To this field belong his important
later essays and much of his famous Inaugural Lecture at
Cambridge in 1895. The massive notes produced at the end of
the year 1900 for a Romanes Lecture which he never delivered
must constitute his last significant piece of work;[1] and they are
largely devoted to the same theme.

In the boxes of cards which he left, and which are now in
the Cambridge University Library, there will always be one
extract transcribed or a single personal reflection recorded on
each card. On one of these we read the solitary assertion:
'the great point is, the history of history.'[2] Another is headed

---

[1] Add. 5002, 263: 'Nov. 24, 1900. Agreed to deliver the Romanes lecture early in June.
Gladstone, Huxley, Morley: First ideas. History in the 20th century. History of modern
history.'
   Ibid. 98: 'Nov. 24. make this an opportunity to speak of what is collected in my Historik
[Add. 5436 and 5437]. Append a bibliography.'
   Add. 4931, 159: 'Nov. 28. How to prepare the Romanes. All the books on Historik.
The articles in reviews. My extracts. Give a bibliography of Historik.'
   Ibid.: 'Romanes. Bibliographie der Historik. Notes and quotations under the text.'
[2] Add. 5438, 38. Cf. Add. 4931, 169: 'On n'y connaît pas l'histoire de l'histoire.'
On Acton's use of cards or slips see pp. 64, 209, 217 below.

'Romanes', and it merely says: 'Teach to look behind historians, especially famous historians.'[1] On another we read: 'History—modern—begins by getting behind historians. No use to learn it exclusively from Ranke, Macaulay, Thiers.'[2] More than once Acton says that we must read the letters of historians, so that we can have a better insight into their minds and their mode of work.[3]

Acton's boxes of cards form a curious kind of quarry and at times they leave one with the impression that here is a man who has a mania for making lists. Often these consist of swift bibliographical notes on some historical point that has occurred to him, but often also they carry a collection of historical examples. He will even repeatedly bring out new lists of the same things when he remembers new instances, or when he appears to have forgotten that he has dealt with the matter already. Archives themselves are not always reliable, he says; there are no documents about the battle of Marengo at the French Dépôt de la Guerre; a year of the pontificate of Pope Clement XIV is missing at the Vatican archives; and so forth.[4] In preparing his Romanes Lecture, he lists those historians whose work does not come straight from the archives, because first of all they have the papers digested by humbler hands.[5] He lists the historians whose correspondence is particularly useful for the insight which it gives into the historical mind.[6] He lists the historians whose works, he thinks, are equivalent to sources;[7] also those who were forces in the making of modern Germany—'the Phalanx of historians at Berlin'.[8] He has an imposing list of what he calls 'especial historians', which includes Macaulay, Mommsen, Gierke, Lecky, and Harnack;[9] another which enumerates the 'solid, but dull historians',[10] and

---

[1] Add. 5002, 7.

[2] Add. 4931, 127. Acton adds: 'The use of history depends on independent study.'

[3] Add. 5002, 56: 'Dec. 14', mentioning particularly the letters of R. Simon, Muratori, Leibniz, Mabillon, J. Müller, Niebuhr, Boehmer, Agustin.

Cf. ibid. 209: 'Dec. 5...J. Müller known to us best from the letters in which he describes his studies. Letters invaluable to students of history—like R. Simon's.'

[4] Add. 4929, 121.   [5] Add. 4931, 51.   [6] See n. 3, above.

[7] Add. 5436, 94. Cf. 4931, f. 79.   [8] Add. 4929, 130.   [9] Add. 5438, 95.   [10] Add. 4930, 188.

another giving what he calls 'the sufficient historians'—this last including Roscoe, Hallam and Stubbs.[1] Yet, amongst all this grit, there will appear on occasion quite a delicate flower—one of those flashes of intuition which, like some single lines of poetry, seem to carry us higher than mountains of our usual prose. And, though I never cease asking myself if I am not being bewitched, I find myself constantly saying (with renewed surprise) as I read his notes, 'What a wonderful jewel this toad has got in its forehead!' In recent years quite a number of us have criticised Lord Acton because he seemed too partial to what I might call the 'sensational' side of history —too inclined to be on the watch for the hint of melodrama. One is reminded of this when he draws up his lists of the great historical riddles—the Casket Letters, the problem of the treachery of Wallenstein, the question of premeditation in the massacre of St Bartholomew, for example. Acton, however, puts a footnote to the list, and here he writes, 'But this is not the reality'—this does not constitute for him the essential aspect of the study of the past. The parts of history which really need light, he says, are the 'clearest parts' where the untrained eye does not see that there is any problem at all.[2]

As an historian of historiography Lord Acton has some curious personal characteristics. In spite of his enormous reading and knowledge, it is not clear that he had mastered the course of development before the rise of the German school. He refers to Laurentius Valla who in the fifteenth century had shown the Donation of Constantine to be a forgery. He writes ably of the critical progress achieved by Mabillon and his successors, but he is chiefly interested in the ecclesiastical implications of their teaching, and in his notes he constantly returns to the question of the attitude of the Church.[3] He knows some of the English seventeenth-century writers, but he does not seem to mention Robert Brady and the achieve-

[1] Add. 5438, 96.
[2] Add. 4929, 319. Cf. Add. 5002, 289: 'Dec. 5. Long Controversies.'
[3] 'Mabillon', in *Historical Essays and Studies*, 459 ff. and e.g. Add. 4931, 23, 142.

ments of our Restoration historiography. At the same time, it would not be true to say that he ascribes to the Germans the sole merit for the development of a more critical kind of historical scholarship. When he blames the Germans for assuming too much of the credit, what he has in mind is the work done in Italy in the latter half of the eighteenth century, particularly the ecclesiastical historians there—a literature which he says has been too greatly neglected. He does not enlarge very much upon this, and if at one point he says that the Germans stood on the shoulders of the Italians, he writes in a manuscript note that this Italian work was little known beyond the Alps, and he mentions it as the most neglected part of literature. He also says that Raumer in the nineteenth century introduced the Germans to the achievements of the Italians.[1]

On the other hand, he tells us that 'the glory departed from the French after 1712';[2] and here he is speaking of a glory in the field of strict scholarship. He regarded the eighteenth-century *philosophes* as essentially unhistorical, but he held that, through this very fact, they were able to contribute to the development of historical science. He said it was like the case of a person who, precisely because he is ill and incapacitated, is driven to 'devise ingenious contrivances'.[3] Similarly, having once shown great impatience at the work of Thomas Buckle, he came to look more kindly even on the methods of the Positivists. Those who discovered regularities in history and elicited laws, he said, were achieving more than Bossuet, who thought that he could tell where the hand of God was moving.[4] To Acton, however, the 'unexpected truth, stranger than fiction', lay in the fact that the French Revolution, instead of being the ruin, proved to be 'the renovation of history'. It was

---

[1] In *Historische Journal*, v (1775), 241 and 295 are surveys of current Italian historical literature. See also Appendix II, p. 207.   [2] Ibid.

[3] Add. 5528, 70: 'The eighteenth century, poor of character, neglected individuals and dealt with laws &c in history. Its incapacity made it make an advance in the science as an invalid may devise ingenious contrivances.'

[4] 'M. Littré on the Middle Ages' in *The Chronicle*, 3 August 1867, p. 444.

this upheaval, and men's reactions to it, which, he said, made historical study 'infinitely more effectual as a factor of civilisation than ever before'. A movement now 'began in the world of minds' which in his view 'was deeper and more serious than the revival of ancient learning'.[1] Behind the unprecedented development of historical writing in the nineteenth century he sees the French Revolution which confronts men with the whole great issue of their relations with the past. It stands for him as a profound human drama. 'Those who lived through it with intelligence', he writes, 'had a larger experience, and more intense, than other men have ever had.'[2]

It was natural that, both in his private notes and in his published work, the nineteenth-century German movement should occupy the principal place, and should stand for the movement which really turned history into a science. Yet at first neither Acton nor his teacher, Döllinger, was a scientific historian of the modern kind; and, in spite of the arrogance of the younger of these, perhaps both were a little slow in getting into step with the new movement. Acton's later manuscripts explicitly recognise that Döllinger himself—who trusted to hunches and did not even know how to take notes—could never have taught anybody historical method.[3] In a sense, however, both men entered the movement and both of them— but particularly Acton—then continued to develop along with it. Acton's reconstruction of the whole story would often be coloured by his own experience. He tells us further, in one of his later notes:

I have had the privilege of knowing most of the German writers from the group of Niebuhr's friends to Harnack and Stieve, the masters of the gen[eration] to come.[4]

---

[1] 'The Study of History' in *Lectures on Modern History* (London, 1906), 14. Cf. Add. 5609, 36b: 'The French Revolution made an epoch in history as much as in politics.'
[2] Add. 5436, 77.   [3] See Appendix III, p. 209.
[4] Add. 4929, 332. Acton adds: 'but at 8 universities I met no man with whom it was so interesting to talk, or so difficult to agree, as Gfrörer.'
Cf. ibid. 317: 'I knew nearly all.' Gfrörer talked the ablest. From Philo to Maria Theresa, he was fully informed. He had read more than Böhmer. An eye for doctrines,

He could embrace, therefore, practically the whole movement and practically the whole century with the kind of personal and backstairs knowledge which he always so greatly prized.

It happened that Acton, in his youth, was greatly interested not only in the rise of the German historical school but also in the general revival of Catholicism and Catholic scholarship, especially in Munich in the time of Döllinger. The two movements were connected of course, and at the end of his life, when he was preparing to write a biography of Döllinger, he again devoted much of his reflection to both. The historical renaissance and the Catholic renaissance were more closely linked in his mind in that there was an important piece of ground which was common to the two, or perhaps rather an important source from which both of them drew strength. This was the Romantic movement—an intellectual reaction on a European scale against the eighteenth-century rationalists and the French Revolution. Much of Acton's interest came to be directed to this particular chapter in the history of western thought.

From first to last he seems to have recognised that, behind this whole aspect of the historical movement, there stands the figure of Edmund Burke; and if, in his youth he found Burke the ideal political teacher (especially for a Catholic) and the ideal expositor of the British constitution, he was equally prepared to say that 'he would have been the first of our historians'. The student of the history of historiography who reads Burke's early work entitled *The Abridgement of English History* can hardly fail to realise the significance it possesses in view of its place in the chronological series; and it is doubtful whether the student of the general thought of Burke has paid sufficient attention to this work, when one

for institutions, for politics, for literature, for policy. In grasp and vivid perception of past ages, he was, I think, beyond any other man. The imagination that realised, transformed. He rang as many changes on a text as a Talmudist. It grew in his hands like the seed under the manipulations of an Egyptian juggler.'

Add. 5591 is a Diary, containing his engagements, and some notes on conversations with historians in Berlin, 1877.

considers to what a degree the historical views which it embodies must actually entail the characteristic features of the man's political outlook. Acton, in one of his earliest writings describes this *Abridgement* as his 'most remarkable literary production', and quotes Lappenberg for the view that 'if Burke had devoted himself continuously to historical pursuits, England might have possessed a history worthy to rank with the masterpieces of the Attic and Tuscan historians'. He refers to the story that Burke altered his intention when he saw that Hume had taken up the subject; and his comment is that 'it must ever be regretted that the reverse did not occur'.

In that part of the work which he completed, he speaks of medieval institutions with an intelligence and appreciation which in his time were almost equally rare among Catholics, Protestants and infidels. The great ecclesiastical writers of the preceding age, such as Bossuet and Fleury, had about as little sympathy with the Middle Ages as Mosheim or Voltaire. Leibniz alone had written about them in a tone which would not now be contemptible. The vast compilations of great scholars, of Ducange, Mabillon and Muratori, had not yet borne fruit on the Continent; and in England the rise of a better school of historians was still remote. Several generations of men were still to follow, who were to derive their knowledge of the Middle Ages from the Introduction to Robertson's *Charles V*, to study ecclesiastical history in the pages of Gibbon, and to admire Hume as the prince of historians. At the age of thirty, Burke proved himself superior to that system of prejudice and ignorance which was then universal, and which is not yet completely dissipated.[1]

Because Romanticism had the effect of producing sympathy for the Catholic cause and a desire for a medieval revival, Acton found it significant that it took its rise in the Protestant world. Late in life he copied out, for use in a lecture, a passage which described it as emerging out of North German Protestantism; and he noted that the Catholics themselves were for

---

[1] *The Rambler*, April 1858, p. 270: reprinted in Acton, *Essays on Church and State*, edited by Douglas Woodruff (London, 1952) 455. Cf. Add. 5643, 69b: 'He [Burke] was the originator of Savigny.'

some time inactive and indifferent.[1] In his view, the leaders of the movement began by admiring and defending the Middle Ages—in other words they were moved merely by partisan-ship—and the real attempt to understand the medieval world came only at a later stage in the story.[2] On the other hand, says Acton, the Romantics were wanting to supply 'the missing ingredient of imagination'. They were moved by the idea that 'men's minds were darkened by the narrowness of mechanical studies'.[3] It was their virtue, in his opinion, that they sought to study the past, not in order to arrive at laws, or even to benefit themselves in any way, but because the past deserved to be studied—had a right to be studied—for its own sake.[4] So, in a note, written at the end of his life, he tells us:

> History issues from the Romantic School. Piecing together what the Rev[olution] snapped. It hails from Burke, as Education from Helvetius, or Emancipation from the Quakers.[5]

The Romantic approach to the past, he said, particularly directed itself to 'phenomena of the spontaneous sort'. It set men looking 'for origins, for mythology, language, legend, for popular poetry'.[6] He saw less than we should be prepared to see of the strange stirrings that had been going on behind the eighteenth-century 'philosophic movement'; and he thought that it was because of Romanticism that the Germans acquired their love for what was remote—their interest in Far Eastern languages and in the early literature of their own country.[7] The rationalists of the eighteenth century, he said, had looked on the predominance of Christianity as the prolonged and tedious reign of a mere lie. Now, men set about to discover the good not only in Christianity but even in Islam and Brahminism.[8]

---

[1] Add. 5478. Cf. ibid.: 'N.B. Romantik all favourable to Catholicism.' Ibid.: 'Specially agreeable to Catholic ideas.' Add. 5437, 26: '...But a dozen went over, and the Converts weakened the impression—by suspicion of Crypto-Catholicism. It produced some reaction; some discredit to men like Creuzer and Menzel....'

[2] Add. 5011, 84. [3] Add. 5437, 9.

[4] Add. 4929, 161, referring to the influence of Wolf.

[5] Add. 5437, 18. [6] Add. 5437, 9.

[7] Add. 5437, 19. Cf. ibid. 12, 20. [8] Add. 4929, 156.

A point of special significance to Acton is the attitude of the legal historian, Savigny, who, he says, at a certain moment took a step that gave an important impulse to the Romantic movement in historiography. Savigny opposed the idea of creating a commission to provide Germany with a legal code, on the ground that the policy was too artificial and savoured too much of eighteenth-century rationalism. He taught that law emerged—and ought to emerge—more spontaneously from the life of a country; that custom was more powerful and authentic than legislative decree; and that there was a natural organic growth in nation-states which one ought not to attempt to override. Acton came to see that such a doctrine had its sinister aspects; it led to the view that a nation only had to be true to itself—had only to follow the law of its own being—instead of conforming to a universal law discoverable by reason.[1] Acton would not have denied, furthermore, that the cult of legend and folk-lore might lead nations to idealise their primitive literature and their early mythology overmuch—so helping to feed the dangerous myth of romantic nationalism.

At the end of his life Acton regarded the Romantic movement as having contributed much to the development of the historical mentality;[2] and repeatedly he says in his notes that it did not necessarily work in favour of conservatism.[3] What he condemns in the Romanticists is the fact that, studying an age for its own sake, they tended at the same time to try to judge it on its own terms. They imagined that allowances should be made for the standards of the distant past, the

[1] Add. 5609, f. 46a. Cf. Add. 5437, 12: 'The beginning is Savigny, then Grimm.' Add. 5478: 'Romantik. The notion of constructing society anew, with laws not its own produce, but imposed by external wisdom, seemed to them unscientific confusion of organic and inorganic, of the mechanical with physiology. As if a man should think that you can construct a feather or an apple as you do a button or a pen.'

[2] E.g. Add. 5478: 'Romantik. Its services to history. The alternate sympathy and detachment by which we understand and are able to judge times, ideas and men.' Ibid.: 'Romantik enlarged the horizon of culture. Everything was brought into it, Antiquity, Middle Ages, the East, Literature, Language.'

[3] Add. 5478. Cf. 5437, 20: '...So, very conservative—fond of tradition, of authority, of religion. But national, progressive. Example: Baader and the Holy Alliance. His notion of Evolution compared to Savigny and Hegel.'

influence of custom and the pressure of authoritarian systems.[1]
They thought that men are not entirely responsible for the
making of their own characters.[2] They were indulgent 'to
those who were ignorant, badly trained, ill surrounded—to
those, in short, who were wrong'.[3] And, of course, says Acton,
the Church prefers this system—prefers that its own past
should not be judged by the standards of the nineteenth
century.[4] He notes also that the Romanticists, whatever they
may have done to foster the historical imagination, were utterly
lacking in criticism.[5] As a general movement they came to an
end, he says, on the death of Frederick William IV of Prussia
in 1860—at the time when a number of their leaders passed off
the stage.

> With these men, the Romantic School went out. The preference
> for the M[iddle] A[ges] remained as a tendency but it was no more a
> danger to literature.[6]

Acton is himself entangled, however, in the intellectual
history which he has set out to describe; and if his thought is
worth taking seriously, it too must be viewed from the standpoint of the historian of historiography. Those who take his

---

[1] Add. 5609, f. 27 a: 'The Romantic school was feeble as to morals. Schlegel ran away
with another man's wife....Their tendency was to debase the currency, to bend the
standard of morality. They established the theory that every age must be understood
and judged on its own terms.'

Ibid. f. 27 b: 'Because it would be wrong today/ to torture a prisoner / to slaughter a
garrison / to try a witch by water / to disembowel a Jesuit / or crop the ears of a Puritan /
to hang a forger, to draw the teeth of a Jew / to set a price on a head / it by no means
follows that the men who did these things did wrong according to the codes by which
they must be severally tried / obeying the authorities above and the light that was in
them....' Add. 5437, 53: 'Rom. Sch. No morality.' Ibid. 55: 'Abstinence from moral
judgments was a note of Romantics.' Ibid. 72: 'The signatur of the Rom. School. To
divest oneself of one's own environment and enter thoroughly into the lives described.'
Add. 5478: 'Romantik taught to understand the past. Comprendre, c'est pardonner....'

[2] Add. 5478.   [3] Add. 5609, f. 28 a.   [4] Add. 5478.

[5] E.g. Add. 5437, 73: 'It is the note of the Rom. School that it put imagination and
constructiveness before analysis and criticism and that it was always wrong.'

[6] Add. 4929, 336. The men referred to were Eichendorff, Lasaulx, Grimm and Böhmer.
Cf. Add. 5437, 54. H. Liebeschütz, *Medieval Humanism in...John of Salisbury*
(London, 1950), p. 2, says that Schaarschmidt in his *Johannes Saresberiensis* (Leipzig,
1862) already describes 'the period of romantic enthusiasm which served to recall the
Middle Ages to the mind of Europe', as 'now over'.

published works and his manuscript notes and try to dovetail them into a connected system, are forgetting that his outlook did not remain the same throughout his life. If the later Acton sees the end of Romanticism in 1860, the younger Acton, emerging in 1857, had not escaped its influence; for he had been greatly inspired by Lasaulx, one of the men whose death he came to regard as signalizing the end of the movement.[1] The first outlines of his own programme of propaganda called explicitly for a 'medieval revival';[2] and in his earliest published writings he himself insists that the historian shall withhold moral judgement even when religious persecution is in question.[3] His romantic attitude affected from the very start his whole view of the origins of the German historical school. In his first account of this, written in his twenty-third year, he dismisses the eighteenth century outright—he merely thinks that Germany in that period had fewer historians than any other country.[4] He was a great reader of books, as we have seen; and he had a particular respect and affection for good books; but this even had the effect of limiting him as an historian of historiography. Because, in his opinion, the German writers about the past produced no good books before 1800, he begins by wiping out everything that they had achieved before the nineteenth century. Yet in other aspects of the history of thought he showed himself aware of a different policy which it

[1] On the young Acton's relations with Lasaulx see my communication, 'Journal of Lord Acton: Rome 1857', *Cambridge Historical Journal*, VIII, 3 (1946), 188–9 and n. 11.

[2] See Appendix v.

[3] E.g. Acton's review of Goldwin Smith's Irish History in *History of Freedom*, 252. In his Roman Journal of 1857 [Add. 5751, p. 29, *Cambridge Historical Journal*, VIII, 3 (1946), 203 and n. 37], Acton may be taking over the views of Döllinger when he writes: 'Superfluity of moral standard in history. We are no wiser when we know that one is good or bad, but what are the causes and effects of his life. It is the business only of Him to judge who can carry his judgments into effect.' Possibly he is merely making a debating-point when in the draft of a letter to Lord Clifford in Add. 4863 he writes: 'One of the things people learn from history is to abstain from unnecessary judgments, and it was not relevant to my purpose to determine the guilt of Fénelon.' In Add. 5009, 384, however, there is a slip which reads: 'Therefore history liberalises. It teaches not to interfere, to do justice to the other side, to leave men to their own judgments.' Cf. Add. 5010, 175: 'The morality of historians consists of those things which affect veracity.' See also pp. 92–4, below. [4] See Appendix IV below.

was possible to pursue, namely the tracing-out of the history of certain ideas not only through good books and bad, but even irrespective of books. In the essay on 'German Schools of History' he tells us that until the nineteenth century 'the Germans had scarcely reached the common level even in the storage of erudition'. A story which would be 'worth telling', he remarks would be the emancipation of German historical study from its subordination to 'divinity, philosophy and law'. He does not see that this was one of the most characteristic of the achievements of the Göttingen school, and on this subject he merely writes: 'The beginning was made by Niebuhr.'[1]

Down to the end of his life, therefore, Acton starts his first chapter in the history of the German school at the point where we should begin the second. Partly because he failed to appreciate all that the eighteenth century had achieved for historical scholarship, partly because his mind was first shaped to these questions at a time when he was himself influenced by Romanticism, and partly because his attention was fixed on finished literary works, he holds a view which overemphasises the importance of the French Revolution, and exaggerates the role of the Romantic movement in the whole story. He never achieves complete detachment in his treatment of the Romantic movement, but measures its importance in history by the vividness of the impression which it made on his own youth. He never asks himself whether the Romantic attitude to the past (though undoubtedly it had been a great stimulus to historians) had not been an effect as well as a cause of the historical movement—in a certain sense, perhaps, even an aberration within it. In his latest as well as his earliest writings on the German school, the first name which he discusses is that of an historian who inspired the age of the Romanticists but has fared badly at the hands of more modern critics—namely, Johann von Müller, the pupil of Gatterer and Schlözer in Göttingen. At twenty-three, he begins the story, in fact, with Müller, who, he says, 'had very great influence indeed,

[1] *Historical Essays and Studies*, 344. Cf. p. 109 n. below.

especially by the publication of his letters'. He adds, with a certain *naïveté*, that 'Müller and Niebuhr are the chief points' in the origin of the German historical movement.[1] Even at the end of his life he is still preoccupied with Müller, whom he values now for different reasons, however—values now as the first universal historian. And this preoccupation is perhaps the most curious feature in his attitude to the history of historiography.[2]

2. CRITICISM AND THE OPENING OF THE ARCHIVES

In his notes on the historiography of the nineteenth century, Acton sees the critical movement as coming hard on the heels of Romanticism; and this, though not true in any absolute sense, certainly represents the way in which it touched him in his own life. It was natural that a man of his general outlook, when discussing the more scientific treatment of evidence, should primarily be impressed by its destructive effects, and interested in the impact of the nineteenth-century movement on religious belief.[3] Scepticism, he says, ran riot for a time, and at first it seemed that everything was shaken. The new criticism produced greater displacements as one went further back in history—the second century was more seriously affected than the third, and fifty apocryphal gospels were exposed.[4] Acton notes that Niebuhr, after he had produced his revision of ancient Roman history, challenged the divines to apply the same critical methods to the Gospels.[5] He is interested in a remark by Laplace to the effect that when a report passes from one person to another the probability of error increases every time, until finally one reaches the stage at which it is greater than the probability of truth.[6] A thing

[1] See Appendix IV below. Cf. Add. 5527, p. 71: 'The first period of German literature, less historical, more philosophical, prepared, by higher, general Anschauungen, the way for better history—at that time there was only Müller as historian.'
[2] See Appendix VI below.   [3] See p. 15 and p. 16 n. 1, above.
[4] Add. 4929, 404.
[5] Add. 4931, 146. Cf. Add. 5609, f. 40b, and Add. 4997, 80.   [6] Add. 4929, 52.

which always had a peculiar fascination for Acton was the deliberate fabrication of false documents. 'Forgery', he says, 'is a vice very common amongst zealous Christians, and also with zealous Liberals'; and he adds that 'almost all societies begin with forged charters, etc.'[1] He sees the tide of criticism mount higher and higher as the nineteenth century proceeds, and it seems to him that new waves are for ever sweeping in to destroy what the last had left unbroken. Niebuhr, he says, produced a second edition of his Roman History in which hardly a stone of the first edition was left standing. Even so, the whole work of Niebuhr went out of date with unprecedented speed.[2] Elsewhere he points out that 'a short string of bare documents replaces all the legend, nearly all the narrative, of Swiss independence'.[3] 'And in the general overturn', he says, 'the Gospels went the way of Sir Walter [Ralegh]'s History of the World.'[4]

'Some gave it up and rejected history', he adds. 'Others believed that, by very hard work indeed, history might be reduced to certainty.' History lay at the basis of European religion; the urgent need of humanity therefore was 'to make sure of it'. All the work which had hitherto been done required to be done over again now; but men had to be prepared for shocks, as 'they had been [living] in a fool's Paradise'.[5] So, on the one hand, he shows us how, for a season, there was 'impatient, restless, storming scepticism'. On the other hand, a tremendous effort was being made to see whether there was anything which could be conclusively established. In his

---

[1] Add. 4929, 185. In this box Acton gives some lists of forgeries, together with notes on controversies, e.g. 'Dove, 1, 162. Ranke, Hegel, Grünhagen, believe in the scene at Vienna, 1742 Feb. 3. Rejected by Arneth, Droysen, Dove. La paix, M., à quelque prix que ce soit. P.V. of Fleury to Belle-Isle, defended by Droysen, I, 475, rejected by Broglie.' Cf. Add. 4984, 247: 'The Duke of Richelieu assured Voltaire that the Testament Politique was genuine and existed in the original. Mais à tout cela Voltaire avait répondu qu'à cette occasion la vérité était si peu vraisemblable qu'il ne se retracterait point. Mme d'Egmont, Richelieu's daughter, said this to Mme de Genlis. *Souvenirs de Félicie*, 1806, I, 42.'

[2] Add. 4930, 13 (in German, quoting Gervinus). Add. 5571, 27. Cf. Add. 5011, 269: 'Very little indeed remains of books which were classics a generation ago.'

[3] Add. 5011, 339.   [4] Add. 4929, 424.   [5] Ibid. 423.

view, this latter tendency was quite as strong as the former, quite as honest, and quite as scientific.[1]

In fact, Acton realised that mere scepticism, as such, was a thing which had existed before the rise of the recent critical movement. Men had declared their disbelief in the current versions of the first five centuries of Roman history long before Niebuhr had produced his revision of the story.[2] What distinguished Niebuhr was the way in which he was able to establish something new and something more reliable out of the old materials, out of the very rubble left over from the discredited system.[3] Niebuhr in certain realms was prepared to accept conclusions which others doubted; he had 'prophesied the discovery of Nineveh six years before Lassen'.[4] More significant than the doubts of the sceptics was the fact that criticism might operate to a conservative effect—might reach behind both credulity and scepticism by establishing the truth more firmly than before. Acton was naturally interested in this aspect of the matter, and loved to note where a later and more scientific historian found himself able to accept the genuineness of a document which his predecessors had condemned. He writes significantly in one place therefore: 'Correct the excess of criticism by aid of Sickel, the prince of critics.'[5]

Nobody, however, was in a better position than Acton for realising that the development of criticism was not the only reason for the transformation of historical scholarship in the

---

[1] Ibid. 423; cf. 409.

[2] Ibid. 402: 'Scepticism not introduced by Niebuhr. Beaufort. Bentley. Semler. Schleiermacher. So that Strauss etc. did not come from these.' See also p. 58, n. 5, below.

[3] 'German Schools of History', *Historical Essays and Studies*, 348–9. Cf. ibid. 364–5.

[4] Add. 4929, 402. Cf. ibid. 48: 'Clearly, Niebuhr was right that there must be divination.' Add. 5011, 329: 'Niebuhr had no exact method.'

[5] Add. 4929, 46. Cf. ibid. 249: 'Maurenbucher 66 doubted the Commentaires de Charles V and does not use them. Exaggerated precaution....' Ibid. 285: '...Giesebrecht a conservative critic. Dictatus Papæ. He defends some docts. against Pertz, Wilmans, Dümmler, Dönniges.' Ibid. 203: 'On the other hand, conservative criticism has been made possible by the examination of MSS. So Ligurinus. Sickel on the documents rejected by Böhmer, Friedmann, Dictatus Papæ.'

nineteenth century. Once again it is necessary to remember not to treat the history of historiography as though it were concerned only with a realm of disembodied thought. A radical change in the conditions of historical study took place in the nineteenth century, and Acton was particularly interested in one aspect of this—the opening of the archives. They had been used before, and men had not been without notion of their value; but Acton puts the first stage of the modern development of archival work in the period after the year 1830.[1] He realises the importance of the part played by non-German regions at this time—the work done for example in Belgium after that country had attained independence through revolution.[2] He particularly praises an account of the diplomacy of Louis XIV, written by Mignet as an introduction to a large collection of documents on the problem of the Spanish Succession.[3] In this period after 1830 a leading rôle belonged to men who had control of the archives in capitals like Brussels, the Hague and Vienna; for they published considerable sets of correspondence, relating chiefly to the sixteenth century—to Charles V, Philip II, William of Orange, etc. Acton says that it was in the days before 1848 that one began to have the notion of the German historian as dull and plodding—'a mere man of facts, incurious about ideas and laws'.[4] If the Germans came to be so greatly moved by political purposes in their writing of history, this goes back, he thinks, only to the Revolution of 1848.[5]

[1] E.g. Add. 5002, 290: 'Dec. 5...Only active from 1830.' Add. 4931, 34: 'How it began about 1830.'

[2] Add. 4908, 88: 'Brussels began.' Cf. 'The Study of History' in *Lectures on Modern History*, 15, 'Austria leading the way. Michelet who towards 1836 claims to have been the pioneer, was preceded by such rivals as Mackintosh, Bucholtz and Mignet.'

[3] *Historical Essays and Studies*, 356. See F. A. Mignet, *Négociations relatives à la succession d'Espagne sous Louis XIV* (Paris, 1835).

[4] Add. 4929, 166: 'Such a man was Gieseler, Wachsmuth, Drumann, Rehm, Bähr, Bernhardy.'

[5] Add. 4930, 155: '1848 changed German history. It became charged with political meaning. Giesebrecht, Häusser, Sybel, Droysen, Mommsen, all culminating in Treitschke.' Cf. Add. 4929, 126: 'After 1848 books were written which were political events. There were none before—only theological events. Häusser, Gervinus, Sybel, Droysen, Giesebrecht, Treitschke.'

To him, however, it is the year 1860 which really represents the beginning of the modern period. Then, as in the twentieth century, it was the overthrow of governments which led to the opening of archives—'the Italian revolution made a great difference'. In Florence, Milan, Naples, Modena and Venice, 'the records of dispossessed dynasties' came into the hands of people who had no interest in keeping them hidden from the world.[1] And, once the ball had been set rolling, other nations could hardly continue to keep their archives closed. This would have been 'a ruinous policy' to attempt, he says; for the actions of a government wear a better appearance in the documents of that government than as they are exposed in the papers of other countries. To keep one's archives barred against the historians was tantamount to 'leaving one's history to one's enemies'.[2] He points out the services rendered by Arneth, 'then deputy keeper of the archives at Vienna, who was employed laying down the great history of Maria Theresa'. In 1864 Arneth produced letters of Marie Antoinette to her mother, in order to expose the forgeries in two collections of her correspondence which had just appeared.

It is in this way that the roguery of a very dexterous thief resulted in the opening of the imperial archives in which the authentic records of the [French] Revolution are deposited....Once opened, Arneth never afterwards allowed the door to be closed on students. He published many documents himself, he encouraged his countrymen to examine his treasures, and he welcomed, and continues to welcome, the scholars of Berlin. Thirty or forty volumes of Austrian documents, which were brought to light by the act of the felonious Frenchman, constitute our best authority for the inner and outer history of the Revolution, and of the time that preceded it.[3]

[1] Add. 5002, 265: 'Dec. 9. Revolution of 1860 opened out archives. Venice, Naples, Florence, Turin, Modena, Milan. The records of dispossessed dynasties.' Cf. *History of Freedom*, 421, 'The Italian Revolution opened tempting horizons.' 'The Study of Modern History' in *Lectures on Modern History*, 15: 'When the war of 1859 had opened the spoils of Italy.'
[2] Add. 4931, 12.
[3] *Lectures on the French Revolution* (London, 1910), 364–5.

In regard to the opening of the archives Acton points out that, in the nineteenth century, historical work was 'not only a voyage of discovery' but a 'struggle' with hostile powers. The fight was against 'men in authority' who had a 'strong desire to hide the truth'. Even the Vatican finally had to give way, however, he says;[1] and his correspondence in the middle of the 1860's shows the tremendous importance which he attached to this.

Acton's own connection with the Vatican archives in the middle of the 1860's was not without its irregularities. At the beginning of 1865 he made some kind of arrangement with Theiner, the keeper of the archives, who promised to allow him to use the most important papers relating to England. He was in fact permitted to take them to his place of residence— first of all, the papers relating to the attempt of Charles I (when Prince of Wales) to secure a Spanish bride. There was a promise that the papers concerning James II should be forwarded to Acton in a similar way; and that he should receive some others in transcript. Cardinal Manning learned of this and took offence. The rumour went round that Acton was actually buying the original documents from the archivist and that there was a conspiracy to damage the Jesuits by indiscreet exposures. For a time the arrangement had to be dropped; but Acton took Gladstone to the archives, and secured his approval for the plan of having the papers copied for the Record Office, which was not expected to be treated in Rome with the same suspicion and hostility as Acton himself. This plan was soon abandoned, however; for Acton renewed his secret agreement with the keeper of the archives; and at the end of 1866 he had on his own table all the Vatican papers relating to Cardinal Pole, and the correspondence between England and Rome during the reign of James II, as well as some other papers, and was hoping to obtain those relating to

[1] Add. 4931, 48: 'Then Rome gave way, and the Aff[aires] Etrangères and Berlin, the Austrian Kriegsarchiv.' Cf. Add. 5002, 290: 'Dec. 5. Last: Vatican.' Cf. Add. 4931, 35: 'The Vatican archives: 102,435 vols. The despatches of Nuncios are 7,786 vols.'

the divorce suit of Henry VIII. In the same period Rawdon Brown was transcribing for the Record Office the papers relating to English history in the Venetian archives; but he was exceeding his terms of reference and securing copies of many documents that had no relation to England. Acton was hoping that he might purchase these, since the British Record Office would apparently be unwilling to pay for them. Acton is still the old-fashioned historian, collecting sources in every field, and assembling materials for many big historical topics at once.[1]

His mind was not free from a tendency to sensationalism and in days when the archives might still be in a disordered state, or the officials might be unaware of what they contained, he was liable to be seized with suspicions which savoured of melodrama. In his *Roman Reminiscences*, the Austrian historian, Theodor von Sickel, describes an incident which throws considerable light upon his personality in the middle period of his life. Acton was ready to maintain in print that in the past the Papacy itself had testified against the claim to infallibility;

[1] Acton to Richard Simpson 22 Nov. [1866] and 6 Dec. 1866, printed from the originals at Downside Abbey in A. Watkins and H. Butterfield, 'Gasquet and the Acton-Simpson Correspondence', *Cambridge Historical Journal*, x, 1 (1950), 99–101. On Theiner see also Add. 5751, pp. 131–5, printed ibid. VIII, 3 (1946), 190–1 and cf. ibid. n. 15. In the Downside Abbey MSS. Acton writes to Simpson from Rome, 17 Dec. [1865]: 'the best plan will be that I should go on making the most of my advantages as long as I can....I find that only the most cautious management answers....I am positively assured that the Gesù archives have been sent out of Italy....The idea of getting the Paris papers done is a very good one; but I fear Gladstone is hardly so generously disposed yet.' See F. Gregorovius, *Römische Tagebücher* (Stuttgart, 1892), 475, on the dismissal of Theiner, who was reproached partly on the ground 'dass er...Lord Acton in das geheime Archiv eingelassen habe'. Cf. Downside Abbey MSS., Acton to Simpson, 17 Dec. [1865]. In Add. 4931, 204: Acton mentions certain archives which he had not used. 'Not Simancas because I had access to Bergenroth's transcripts, the more valuable because he had decipered many. [Access also] to Froude's [transcripts] at the Museum. Fieldmann was kind enough to supply me with many papers. Not Gesù. This was a loss; for they have since been hidden. Boris however allowed me to have certain documents on the eldest son of Charles II. Tell the story. And although the central archives are out of the way, two great collections of their papers, Cologne and Munich, were taken over by the g[overnmen]t at the suppression. How I worked at the Munich one. Both since made public.' Cf. Add. 4931, 205: 'Quantities at Rome....Importance of the lesser countries. Ferrara and Modena, Este being in close relations with the papacy, particularly initiated. Genoa, for the American War....Florence, especially for England. Venice. I even found valuable matter at Mantua, but I was driven away by mosquitoes, making sleep impossible.'

and in respect of this issue a papal document, the *Liber Diurnus* (which had more than once been printed) became a subject of mystery and controversy at the time of the Vatican Council. It was claimed that not only had Pope Honorius I been condemned for heresy by the Sixth General Council of the Church, but that in the *Liber Diurnus* the recognition of this fact had been part of the oath which Popes had had to take at the time of their election. For a long time, however, the enemies of infallibility were frustrated; for the custodians of the Vatican archives asserted that they could find no trace of the actual manuscript. In the middle of September 1870, the historian, von Sickel, met Acton and his relative, Minghetti, in a Viennese hotel. Minghetti, then the Italian ambassador in Vienna, had revealed that within a few days Italian troops would be entering Rome and would be taking possession of it in the name of King Victor Emmanuel. 'The rash and resolute Acton', as von Sickel calls him, declared his intention of breaking into the Vatican archives during the disorders and stealing the *Liber Diurnus*. 'Anybody who knew Acton', writes von Sickel, 'will understand that for such a prize he would be ready for an adventure.' And both Minghetti and von Sickel were well aware that it would be useless to try to hold him back. Acton caught the next express to Rome, excusing himself from a dinner which had been arranged to enable him to meet Ranke for the first time. But Minghetti telegraphed to the Italian capital and on 20 September the Italian troops captured Acton near Rome and held him in honourable custody until order had been restored.[1] The *Liber Diurnus* attracted adventure; for, eleven years later, von Sickel himself, in the Vatican archives, happened to ask for an example of ancient handwriting for purposes of comparison. The official told him that they had a document which would meet the case; and when this was put into his hands it was the historian who quickly realised that here was the *Liber Diurnus* itself.[2]

[1] Theodor von Sickel, *Römische Erinnerungen* (Wien, 1947), 45–6, 133–7, 170–1, 184–5.
[2] Ibid. 46–7, 171–2, 185–6.

In the two decades after the middle of the century historical study was undergoing a very considerable change. In 1851, when Ranke's pupil, Von Sybel, by the special favour of Napoleon III, was allowed to see the papers of the Committee of Public Safety, he was told that the dust which covered them was the dust of 1795, as no person had set eyes on them since. Acton tells us that this statement was not quite correct, but it did not seriously misrepresent the situation.[1] Before the 1860's Acton and his teacher had consulted manuscripts, but they had made only a casual and sporadic use of these. They had secured from them additional illustrative matter, but had not realised that the whole framework of a story might be thoroughly remodelled, if it could be reassembled from the basic materials.[2] By the latter half of the 1860's Acton understands at last that a sprinkling of selected documents is insufficient and that what is required is the study of a correspondence in its continuity. The observation of the course of business as it is transacted day by day comes to be seen as the essential prerequisite for 'the renovation of history'. And in Acton's view it is only in the same period that Ranke himself passes to a more consistent use of manuscripts. He points out at a later date, furthermore, that the merely partial opening of archives had sometimes had the effect of leading the

[1] H. v. Sybel, 'Pariser Studien' in *Vorträge und Abhandlungen* (München und Leipzig, 1897), 365. The official said to Sybel, 'Sir, you must have some respect for this dust—it is dust from the year 1795. I can assure you with absolute certainty that since that time no hand has disturbed these papers or this case.' Cf. Acton in Add. 4929, 33: 'Sybel says that he was the first to consult the papers of the C[ommittee] of P[ublic] Safety. Faris had used them before him for his MS. de l'an III.'

[2] In Add. 4905, 51 and Add. 4912, 26, Acton makes it clear that during the stay in Rome in 1857, as well as during the earlier visits to Paris, Florence and Prague, Döllinger went to manuscripts only 'for particular things', and not until 1864 (i.e. the visits to Vienna and Venice) did the habit of manuscript study begin to have a real effect on Döllinger's work. Döllinger wrote to his friend and amanuensis, Jörg, 22 May 1857, J. Friedrich, *Ignaz von Döllinger* (Munich, 1899), III, 178: 'In respect of the use of manuscripts I have been afforded great facilities [in Rome], beyond my expectations.' Cf. Add. 5609, 40: 'How late he [Döllinger] understood about MSS. At Rome in 1857 he spoke as if the C[ouncil] of Trent was known by Sarpi and Pall[avicini] rather than by Le Plat and Baluze, Mansi, Lagomarsini, Morandi.' Cf. Add. 4905: 'It was not until he had spent the summer of 1864 in the Vienna Library and at St Mark's at Venice that these studies deeply influenced his views, and he turned his closer attention to the Munich MSS.'

historian astray.[1] From the 1860's, however, the archives begin to reveal the things that had been most confidential.[2] The documents relating to the most secret parts of the secret diplomacy of former times are becoming available at last. In a sketch of the historiography of the French Revolution he says that 'the true secrets of government, diplomacy and war, remained almost intact until 1865'. And he sees between that year and 1885 or 1890 a 'change in the centre of gravity which besides directing renewed attention to international affairs, considerably reduced the value of the memoirs on which the current view of our history was founded'.[3]

Acton insists, furthermore, that it was the manuscript work from the middle of the 1860's which (for Döllinger as well as for himself) brought about the overthrow of ecclesiastical history as hitherto understood.[4] In his view the opening of the archives had still another effect on the character of historical study. In the eighteenth century, as we have seen, there had been a special interest in the cultural side of history. Now, it was the political side which came to the front; for the archives released a flood of documentation that was entirely connected with the work of government. By the year 1900 Acton was even wondering whether this vein might not soon be exhausted; and he was asking what might be expected to happen then. He conjectured that there were two likely fields which would

---

[1] Cf. p. 20 above.

[2] Add. 4931,206: 'What archives reveal is the wickedness of men.' Cf. Add. 5015,55: 'The Keeper of the Berlin archives said that Prussia had nothing to fear from publicity because the worst was already known. The worst is seldom known and the exposure of all secret history has been damaging....' Cf. ibid. 54: 'The one constant result is to show that people are worse than their reputation....'

[3] *Lectures on the French Revolution*, 365. Cf. Add. 5015, 59: 'The result is infallible at a certain level. That level was reached, in revolutionary history, towards 1860.'

[4] 'Döllinger's Historical Work' in *History of Freedom*, 421: 'The revolution in method since he began to write was partly the better use of old authorities, partly the accession of new. Döllinger had devoted himself to the one in 1863; he passed to the other in 1864. ...The ecclesiastical history of his youth went to pieces against the new criticism of 1863 and the revelation of the unknown which began on a very large scale in 1864.' Acton here mentions 'four years of transition' and says of Döllinger: 'His view of the last six centuries was made up from secret information gathered in thirty European libraries and archives.'

offer opportunities of expansion: first the treatment of history after the manner of Herbert Spencer, and secondly the History of Ideas.[1] He puts forward the interesting point that there is one documentary source which is capable of bringing the historian more close to the ultimate secrets than the more formal papers in official archives. The ultimate disclosures are likely to be produced by the more unreserved communications which ministers or diplomats may have exchanged with one another behind the scenes. The private letters of such public figures constitute their ultimate exposure, and few reputations survive the publication of these. 'The unpremeditated self-revelation of correspondence', writes Acton—'This is our great addition.' He mentioned as an example the kind of private collections which were being published by the Historical Manuscripts Commission.[2] I am reminded here of the strong views expressed on this subject by my teacher and predecessor, Professor Temperley, who, while insisting on the primary importance of official documents, was convinced of the change which a narrative was likely to suffer if the private papers also came under survey. The predominance of the ethical preoccupation in his mind had the effect of making Acton particularly interested in the decisive character of the self-exposure that was possible in totally unguarded private letters. History, now, he says, can reach final judgements based on the confessions of the actual culprits.

First, we can judge men by their own utterances. At least one thousand great men from Petrarca to Cavour have betrayed their secret souls to correspondents. We penetrate far deeper into character and motive. And the test is not one which any public character can resist without damage [to his] reputation. Seeing what men are in the full glow of Christian culture, we feel some doubt about others.[3]

---

[1] Add. 5002, 153. Cf. Add. 4931, 8: 'It is all state action. So it is all State H[istory].'
[2] Ibid. 120.   [3] Add. 4929, 339.

3. ACTON AND RANKE

Acton, who was the most self-conscious English exponent of the German historical movement, stands in a paradoxical relationship with Ranke, the recognised leader of the continental school. In his Inaugural Lecture in Cambridge in 1895 he spoke of Ranke as his own 'master', described him as 'the real originator of the heroic study of records',[1] and said that his was 'the most astonishing career in literature'. 'We meet him at every step', Acton declared, 'and he has done more for us than any other man.'[2] It could hardly have occurred to any of his Cambridge students that, until something like forty years after Ranke had published his first book, Acton's remarks about him were always somewhat hostile, always slighting in tone.

The Acton manuscripts supply us with the key to the problem; for they tell us that Döllinger 'was long afraid of reading Ranke'.[3] The Munich circle, in which Acton lived at his most impressionable period, found Ranke uncongenial, in fact, and preferred another Protestant writer, Leo, whose books were better suited to their Catholic taste. One member of the circle Jörg, considered Ranke 'not honest in his [History of the] Reformation'. Döllinger himself once expressed the opinion that the theology of that book was 'slack and trivial'.[4] Acton may be quoting Döllinger when he writes at the age of twenty-three that 'there is a want of breadth' in Ranke's pictures and narrative 'and a want of a comprehensiveness in his intelligence of history'. Leo, we are told was 'far wider'.[5] Ranke's mind, furthermore, says Acton, is fitted to deal only with the Machiavellian politics of the period after 1500. 'Richelieu's

---

[1] Cf. Add. 5002, 119: '"The heroic study of records", says Prynne.'

[2] 'The Study of History' in *Lectures on Modern History*, 7, 11, 17, 19.

[3] Add. 4908, 87. Cf. Add. 5609, f. 51a: 'He shrank from Ranke's Popes [1834–6]....
When he came to the [Ranke's] Ref[ormation, 1839–47] this caution faded.'

[4] Add. 5527, f. 92; 'Döllinger's Historical Work', *History of Freedom*, 396.

[5] Add. 5528, f. 69b. Cf. Add. 5645, 4: 'Döllinger...admired Leo.' When Acton wrote on 'German Schools of History', *Historical Essays and Studies*, 358, he described how other people resisted Ranke for some time, and how 'in very early days it seemed that philosophy possessed an adept [namely Leo] who would surpass Ranke.'

policy [is] the best thing he has ever done, but he has not perceived the importance of the religious movement in France at
that time.'[1] Ranke had 'too little seriousness and dignity, and
gives only esprit but does not try to relate things as they actually
occurred'. Acton once quoted Leo's description of the man as
nothing more than a 'vase-painter';[2] and he appears to have
been influenced by this.

Ranke must have been well advanced in the sixties when
Acton wrote of him in a note-book:

> His history is all plums and no suet. It is all garnish, but no beef.
> He is a great historical decorator, and avoids whatever is dull or
> unpleasant, whatever cannot be told in a lively way, or cannot help to
> his end. He is an epicure and likes only tit-bits. He is the staff-
> officer, who leaves all the rough work to the regimental officers. He
> appears always in pumps and kid gloves.

What was worse: Ranke, according to Acton, sinned most
darkly where his art was greatest, that is to say, in selection, in
proportion and in perspective. He was 'not guided by the
importance of events' themselves; and, because he committed
falsification, 'his art becomes artifice and his ingenuity
treachery'. Every detail that he gives is likely to be correct—
'no historian has told fewer untruths, few have committed so
few mistakes'. Yet 'none is a more unsafe guide. The whole is
untrue, but the element of untruth is most difficult to detect'.[3]

When Acton was writing these remarks he knew that Ranke
had turned his attention to English history, and if he thought
him capable of dealing with the Tudors he was pessimistic
about his ability to deal with the age of the Stuarts. He found
it a 'consolation' in any case to learn that 'besides this artist's
account we are soon to have a fuller and more accurate and
useful account of the sixteenth century in England'—namely,
a work by Pauli.[4] Ranke was then writing his history of England in the seventeenth century, and he told Acton later that

---

[1] Add. 5751, 218. Cf. Add. 5528, f. 70.
[2] 'German Schools of History', *Historical Essays and Studies*, 357.
[3] Add. 5528, ff. 190b–193a. See Appendix VII below.   [4] Ibid.

he was provoked to this by the 'positive narrow standpoint' which Macaulay had adopted in his famous *History*. He himself intended not to produce a tory reply to the whig version, but to transcend the whole party issue and write his narrative on 'a larger universal view'.[1] It was the publication of Ranke's *History of England* which turned Acton at last into an enthusiastic (though not an uncritical) admirer of the German historian. Even now, he was not quite sure of himself at first, especially as the successive volumes were having a cool reception in Germany; but in 1864 he wrote of the fourth volume that Ranke had never before showed so ably 'his talent for extracting new and minute information on a familiar subject', and he described it as 'a model of the art of using authorities'. The author, he said, 'has obtained so much new matter at Paris and Oxford, in the British Museum, and the Record Office, that he is entirely free from conventional influences, and presents many new points of view'. Yet, he continues, Ranke's strength 'does not lie in the history of free communities'.

He is the historian of courts and statesmen, incomparable at unravelling the web of an intrigue, and divining the hidden, changing schemes of the most expert politician; and he understands the force of convictions, the influence of literature, and the progress of theories. ...His miniature-painting preserves with a fidelity amounting to genius the features of royal and illustrious persons, but he has not the breadth of touch requisite to do justice to great popular and national movements, and to dramas in which the actors are whole classes and provinces of men.[2]

As the work proceeds, however, Acton's enthusiasm seems to increase and in 1867 a further review from his hand re-examines the whole of Ranke's career.

He explains the reason for the important place which the German historian has come to hold in the history of historiography.

[1] Add. 5011, 321. Cf. Add. 4997, 139: The Prussian king suggested the book.
[2] *Home and Foreign Review*, April 1864, 715, reprinted in Lord Acton, *Essays on Church and State*, 425–6.

The Development of Ranke

Before Ranke appeared, modern history was in the hands of Robertson and Roscoe, Coxe and Sismondi, good easy men whose merit consisted chiefly in making things more accessible which were quite well known already.

Ranke adopted the principles of Niebuhr, transferring the new, critical method into the field of general European history. He was not the first historian to attempt this, however; for already 'these principles had been applied by Stenzel to the Middle Ages'.[1] His first work had appeared in 1824, and in this he had based his narrative solely on printed sources. He had achieved a sensational success in it through his critical handling of what might be called the chroniclers, the contemporary historians of the age of the Renaissance. Acton said later that Ranke's influence had in fact 'done more for the Middle Ages than for modern times'; for his method was 'more applicable' to the medieval field—'he extracted from the chronicle its utmost kernel'. He seems to have thought that this affected Ranke's attitude to historical sources; Ranke, he said 'is ready to believe that some one knows what he wants to learn, and his object is to find him'. Ranke, in other words, thinks that there will be some historical personage who can supply the actual answer to the problem that faces the historian at a given moment. In any case, we are told, Ranke, like Waitz, discouraged everything except medieval history.[2] 'The chief promoter of medieval studies was the modern Ranke.'

At the next stage in his career, says Acton in the review of 1867, Ranke made use of manuscript sources.

It does not appear that he was induced to resort to archives by the insufficiency of printed materials. The celebrated John Müller, in

---

[1] *The Chronicle*, 20 July 1867, 393. See Appendix VII, below.

[2] Add. 4997, 2, 4, 5, 234, 237. Cf. 'The Study of History' in *Lectures on Modern History*, 19–20: 'Niebuhr had pointed out that Chroniclers who wrote before the invention of printing generally copied one predecessor at a time, and knew little about sifting or combining authorities. The suggestion became luminous in Ranke's hands, and with his light and dexterous touch he scrutinised and dissected the principal historians, from Machiavelli to the *Mémoires d'un Homme d'Etat*, with a rigour never before applied by moderns.'

his dreamy way, had called attention to a collection of Italian documents in the Berlin library, and there Ranke opened those investigations which he pursued at Vienna, and then more seriously at Venice and Rome. It was a new vein, and a little produce went a great way. The reports which the Venetian ambassadors made at the close of a three years' residence abroad were first brought into notice by him; but the time was not long in coming when no historian would be content without the whole of the ambassador's correspondence day by day. Thirty years ago, the use of a few unconnected reports, or a few casual instructions, implied a miracle of research. At first Ranke employed his manuscripts like his books to give point rather than solidity to his narrative. The manuscripts served him rather as a magazine of curiosities than as the essential basis of a connected history.... He set the example of that occasional miscellaneous use of unpublished materials as a subsidiary aid to history, which has been followed by the school now predominant in Belgium, Germany and France, and which has diffused much light but concentrated little.[1]

Acton tells us at a later date that from about 1840 Ranke came to the conclusion that, after the period covered by his first book—that is to say, after the year 1514—history could not be written from printed sources only.[2] The English historian has left on record also the view that Ranke's use of the Venetian *Relazioni* affected the character of the historical world which he constructed in his books. 'Of all people, the Venetians were on the governing side, and viewed the state from the point of view of the trouble and difficulty of governing.' This was Ranke's standpoint when he wrote about politics. He saw the world as it appeared through the eyes of a Venetian ambassador.[3]

The successive volumes of the *History of England* carry the story a stage further; and Acton, in his final review recognises

---

[1] *The Chronicle*, 20 July 1867, 393. Cf. Add. 4997, 259: 'Ranke's Popes long the only modern history from Mss.'

[2] 'Döllinger's Historical Work' in *History of Freedom*, 421. Cf. *Historical Essays*, 355–6.

[3] Add. 4997, 37. Cf. Gasquet, *Lord Acton and his Circle* (London, 1906), 109. Ranke's 'peculiar knowledge and views of modern history' are derived from the fact that he sees things through the eyes of Venetian ambassadors whose 'cold-blooded acuteness...suits and attracts and often misleads him'. Cf. Add. 4908, 88: 'Ranke made himself notable with Relazioni.' Add. 4931, 91: 'In the middle of the century it was much to have Relazioni.'

that in this work 'research predominates'. Now, he says, 'the sparkle is gone, but there is much more body'. It is 'no longer a history by glimpses and flashes but a patient, connected narration'. The correspondence between William III and Heinsius has only been partially used, he tells us, and 'the manuscripts in the British Museum (we suspect) rather hastily consulted'. But now, he says, Ranke 'has surpassed his predecessors in domestic politics and not only in international affairs where he is always supreme'.[1] All this belongs to the 1860's, which he regarded as a crucial period in the history of historiography; and if Ranke (who was well over seventy at the time of this review) was changing, Acton himself was undoubtedly changing still more—partly through the influence of the German scholar whom he later described as his 'master'. Henceforward he adhered to that verdict upon Ranke which he did not fail to recognise as equally valid when turned into a judgement upon himself: 'Ranke has gone along with the progress which has so vastly extended the range and influence of historians. After starting without manuscripts and then lightly skimming them, he ended by holding that it is not science to extract modern history from anything less than the entire body of written evidence.'[2]

On the other hand, Ranke never hunted the printed book and never set out to read the recondite literature in the way that Acton did; and the latter declared at the end of his life: 'I always hold up Ranke as in many ways a model student. But he was no bibliographer, no Epicurean seeker after rare works.'[3] And to the end of his life he retained his view that Ranke was no thinker. 'The dust of archives blots out ideas', he wrote. 'No great man had as few as Ranke.'[4] 'Ranke . . . never impresses with overwhelming mental power', he adds, 'as Mommsen and Treitschke [do].'[5]

Acton had a high view of the importance for the historian of a genuine catholicity of mind; and it was partly because

[1] *The Chronicle*, 20 July 1867, 394–5.   [2] *Historical Essays and Studies*, 356.
[3] Add. 4931, 33.   [4] Ibid. 15.   [5] Add. 5609, 58b.

Johann von Müller was so distinguished in this respect that he maintained his admiration for him long after he had been discredited by the critics. Acton himself showed this catholicity of mind when in his later years he discussed his differences with Ranke on the topic which he most had at heart—the question of moral judgements in history. Towards the end of his life his mind continually reverts to this theme—one upon which he radically differed also from his teacher, Döllinger, from his close friend, Gladstone, and from Bishop Creighton —one on which he said indeed that he stood alone in the world.[1] It disturbed him that Ranke refrained from any condemnation of the Inquisition.[2] And he notes that in his *History of England* Ranke devoted only eleven lines to the Bloody Assizes after Monmouth's rebellion in the West.[3] Acton tries to be scrupulously fair; he says that Ranke hides nothing of William III's responsibility for the massacre of Glencoe—indeed he has done more than anybody else to expose his guilt. Ranke, however, refrains from the actual pronouncement of a condemnation—he does not say that William III was a bad man.[4]

In the notes at the end of his life Acton seems in gentler mood, and, if he still differs from Ranke, he devotes the better part of his time and ingenuity to the exposition of Ranke's point of view. He condemns the 'exceeding vividness' of moral judgements in Macaulay and Thomas Carlyle, and in men like Michelet and Taine. Against this he speaks even somewhat nostalgically in favour of 'a little abstinence from perpetual judging'. In fact, he says, 'the best way of doing justice is a little reserve in uttering judgments—as writing for

[1] On Acton's view of moral judgements see L. Kochan, *Acton on History* (London, 1954), 68–97; 'Journal of Lord Acton: Rome 1857' in *Cambridge Historical Journal*, VIII, 3 (1946), 203–4 and n. 37; also my *Lord Acton* (Historical Association Pamphlet, 1948), 12–15, and my 'Lord Acton' in *The Cambridge Journal*, May 1953, 481–2. On the controversy with Creighton see F. E. de Jánosi, 'The Correspondence between Lord Acton and Bishop Creighton', *Cambridge Historical Journal*, vol. VI, 3 (1940), 307–21.

[2] Add. 5609, f. 56a. Acton adds: 'Palacky thought the death of his hero Hus, legitimate.'

[3] Add. 5011, 327. Add. 4997, 336.   [4] *The Chronicle*, 20 July 1867, 394.

grown-up men'.[1] He describes Ranke as in reaction against earlier historians who had been too violent in this respect. Ranke, he says, 'became the first of historians because he abstained from the cheap moralities of Spittler and Schlosser —of the ill-tempered censors'.[2] Schlosser, he says, 'took care to pronounce judgements on everybody. This helped to cool and steady the Ranke manner.'[3] Elsewhere he says: 'The secret of R[anke]'s art was to rescue his public men from the cheap judgment seat, the short shrift.'[4] Further, says Acton, Ranke

will not write up a party, like Macaulay, a country, like Thiers, a religion like Niebuhr, Droysen. But he will have a code of virtue, namely the principles which bind the historian. [The historian] is bound to be fearless, truthful, disinterested, to stretch a point in favour of those whom personally—by position or disposition—he dislikes—patient and accurate and just. He will have the best qualities of a confessor, mercifulness.[5]

Ranke wrote history, he says, without any wish whatever 'to make a point for the good cause or [to] favour those who have right on their side'. In this connection Acton even writes: 'No cause is too odious to be fairly stated.' And he adds, somewhat to our surprise, that behind Ranke's 'good-natured' system there lay 'a great truth'.[6] Again it is Acton who points out that when the conditions of the past are compared with those of the present a liberal can easily feel that there is nothing to do about bygone centuries except to scatter condemnations right and left. He notes that there is 'much more to say, than anyone now supposes, for many a lost cause. For sorcery, physiocracy, the deposing power, the dispensing power, the Ptolemaic system, the sea-serpent, the Non-jurors.'[7] He describes Ranke as a person who thinks it unwise to have people too bitter and contemptuous in their attitude to the past.[8]

It is not possible to date many of Acton's notes; but it seems likely that he still differed from Ranke on the question of moral

---

[1] Add. 4929, 182. [2] Add. 5478. [3] Add. 4929, 183.
[4] Add. 5011, 59. [5] Ibid. 326. [6] Ibid. 315.
[7] Add. 4929, 163. [8] Add. 5011, 89.

judgements in history. It was not the condemnation of acts but the condemnation of people that was in question—he wanted not merely to say that persecution was wrong but to denounce the man who had been guilty of the offence. Furthermore, he insisted that a man must be measured by the worst thing he ever did—William III by the massacre of Glencoe, the French revolutionaries by the September massacres.[1] He rejected Döllinger's suggestion that at least something like an average might be taken between a man's good actions and his crimes. If he held to his system to the very end, he is the more remarkable for his care in reconstructing and interpreting the ideas of a man with whom he differed on the issue that he regarded as the most momentous. He writes: 'Ranke would say: As to religion, politics, philosophy, literature, people differ. If we wait until all differences are reconciled, we shall wait for ever. If we try to reconcile them ourselves, we shall never get to work at our real business. There are things on which men can be made to agree; that is the domain, not of thought, but of fact.' Ranke holds that concerning the facts about Martin Luther and the figure of the man as he appears in history, there is no reason why Protestant and Catholic, conservative and liberal, should ultimately differ. The more we can rescue this realm of facts from its entanglement in jarring opinions—the more we confine ourselves to the things which must be true for the Catholic as well as the Protestant because they arise straight out of the evidence—'the more we make a science of history'.[2] Acton sees the point, therefore; but he himself has an idea of the prophetic function of the historian. This prevents his accepting a limited theory of technical history as a science which asserts only what the evidence compels one to assert—history as the laying-out of a story on which all men and all parties can form what judgements they like when they have read it.

[1] Add. 5011, 99: 'You cannot judge until you have said the worst....You must be careful to determine the very worst.' Cf. Add. 4931, 206: 'You cannot judge without low-water mark.'

[2] Cards in Add. 5011, e.g. 316, 328.

Acton notes that 'Ranke was not one of the writers of political history who, working at both demand and supply, prepared the German Empire.'[1] 'The time came', he says, 'when even men trained in Ranke's methods, skilled in all the analysis and all the austerity of the school, repudiated the aimless neutrality' which the master maintained.[2] Ranke was condemned for failing to bring history into the arena in a period which was so momentous for the destiny of the German nation. One of his chief pupils, Von Sybel, who felt himself to be a counterpart of the English Whigs, and who was to oppose Bismarck in the Prussian constitutional crisis, bitterly attacked his teacher for writing history without moral indignation. These were days in which the Habsburgs of Austria were regarded as having been the seat of evil throughout the centuries; and Von Sybel denounced them with such violence as to provoke a powerful counter-attack from their partisans. Acton's comments in one of his notes is that 'the cold politeness of Ranke would have provoked no reprisals'.[3] In fact, if you believe that Austria is the seat of all evil, you quickly make it virtue to build up by any means the power that is likely to oppose her. Some of the pupils of Ranke who quarrelled with his academic austerity as an historian are the very ones we now condemn for serving the German imperial cause. Von Sybel himself is an example of the way men came to support Bismarck when they saw him as the hammer of the wicked Habsburg power. Indeed we should probably criticise Ranke today rather for the occasions in which he lapsed from the austerity of his principles—condemn him for morally excusing or condoning on occasion, rather than for abstaining; and regret that in his history of the Reformation, he was perhaps not quite impartial enough.

[1] Add. 5011, 318. Cf. 4997, 135.   [2] Ibid. 319.   [3] Add. 4929, 176.

4. HISTORY AT THE BEGINNING OF THE
TWENTIETH CENTURY

Acton's notes on the historical movement of the nineteenth century are interspersed with general comments on the results of the whole development. These give us further evidence of the lofty conception of history held by a man who thought that 'It is the office of historical science to maintain morality as the sole impartial criterion of men and things' and that 'To develop and perfect and arm conscience is the great achievement of history'. He realised that Francis Bacon had asserted the possibility of a scientific method by means of which genuine discoveries could come within the reach of men who were not of the highest intelligence. He recognised that this applied in the field of historical research; and he saw that pupils of Ranke, though intellectually inferior to their master, were quickly able to surpass him in the development of his method. He insists, however, that all this has reference only to what he calls 'the mere grammar of the work'. And he adds: 'We want brains for the higher objects of history—the difference between knowledge of facts and the energetic understanding of their significance is so serious.'[1] For him, historical study has a peculiar relationship not only with morality but also with religion. 'History represents the spiritual part of literature....It has become what it used not to be....It is a very great infl[uence] balancing the material science. Keeping up the ideal.'[2] He tells us that the natural sciences tend to work against religion, but that, apart from sociology (which he regards as also hostile) the study of history operates in its favour.[3] 'History, moreover', he says, 'convinces more people than philosophy.'[4] And 'the lesson of modern history', he says, is 'that Religions enjoy (are endowed with) the prerogative of perpetual youth'; while philosophic systems 'seldom outlast a generation'.[5] He is not even satisfied to think that the historian's task is confined to the study of the changes that

[1] Add. 5011, 360. [2] Add. 4929, 9. [3] Add. 4931, 53. [4] Add. 5011, 20. [5] Add. 4929, 97.

take place in the world of tangible things; and, though we might be puzzled to know what, as a technical student, he has in mind, he writes on one occasion: 'The higher history is the record of the abiding.'[1]

And when he writes about the historical movement of the nineteenth century—and particularly when he puts together his final notes on the subject—it is clear that he sees the story as something more momentous than we, after a further interval of half a century, usually regard it. This is partly because he had a better knowledge of the state of human thought before the discovery of all the new implications in history. Also he stands in 1900 on the crest of what might be called a great wave of historical thinking; and perhaps it is not going too far to say that the wave has been receding ever since. In more ways than one he put the point that the historical revolution of the nineteenth century was a bigger event, a bigger change in the character of human thought, than that 'revival of learning' which we associate with the Renaissance.[2] One illustration of this we have already seen; he thought that every branch of science was now amenable to historical treatment, as well as to those procedures with which it is normally identified.[3] In the end, even when he came to the question of the philosophy of history, he said that there were many systems of such philosophy: 'Therefore we must have the history of it, not the thing itself.'[4] History, he writes,

is not only a particular branch of knowledge, but a particular mode and method of knowledge in other branches. Determines their influence on society. It embraces other sciences, records their progress and the tests by which truths have been ascertained. Historic thinking is more than historical knowledge.[5]

---

[1] Add. 5011, 21. Cf. 4948, 143.   [2] See p. 67, above.   [3] See p. 1 above.
[4] Add. 5002, 123. Cf. Add. 5011: 'Avoidance of System. History of Systems. History defeats metaphysics. April 29, 1894.' Cf. E. Kessel, 'Rankes Idee der Universalhistorie', *Historische Zeitschrift*, Oct. 1954, 285, quoting a Ranke MS. which runs: 'Verstandene Geschichte ist nach meinem Dafürhalten die wahre Philosophie der Geschichte', and p. 304, from another MS: In diesem Sinn ist die Geschichte nicht ein Gegensatz, sondern eine Erfüllung der Philosophie.'   [5] Add. 5011, 340.

And of the nineteenth century he writes: 'History went on invading other provinces, resolving system into process, and getting the better of philosophy—for a whole generation.'[1] It is not clear how this view can be squared with the notion of a 'higher history' which is 'the record of the abiding'.

One of his final notes, which may not be strictly correct, but which perhaps still has a certain validity as a token, throws further light on the change which he regards as having taken place in the structure of human thought. He asserts that

Expressions like: the growth of language, physiology of the state, national psychology, the mind of the Church, the development of Platonism, the continuity of law—questions which occupy half the mental activity of our age—were unintelligible to the eighteenth century—to Hume, Johnson, Smith, Diderot.[2]

He says somewhere that history 'is an experimental science', and it is clear that he is thinking that everything which ever happened in the past can be considered as though it had taken place in a laboratory. Therefore, he argues, we today can 'work out by induction the problem which 1789 treated deductively'—the problem, that is to say, which the French Revolution had to meet without precedents and previous experience.[3] 'History', he says, 'carries induction into sciences essentially deductive.'[4]

In all these illustrations there was something important which Acton was seeking to express. Furthermore, for him there existed a kind of historical thinking which was co-ordinate with scientific thought and capable of functioning when one's history is at various levels of generalisation. Over and above this, there were ways, no doubt, in which he gave to technical history a sovereign role which it ought not to be allowed to claim. Some might regard this as the result of theorising about history; but the person who studies the past without examining his assumptions is liable to fall into the same error through what I might call absent-mindedness.

---

[1] Add. 5011, 59.   [2] Add. 5436, 62.   [3] Add. 5478.   [4] Add. 5011, 290. Cf. 343.

In one place Acton almost seems prepared to consider the idea that the nineteenth century might have been peculiar in the favourable environment which it was able to provide for historical study. 'Renan warns us', he writes, 'that impartiality is the delicate product of certain auspicious conditions, unlikely to flourish in a later age.'[1] It has been suggested that from about 1900 the nineteenth-century rivalry between the historical and the scientific view of things was finally resolved by the victory of the scientist. If Acton's notions of the prospects and the importance of history now seem to go too far, this change in the world since 1900 may help to account for the differences between his view of the matter and ours. It may also help to explain why we have since become more the masters of things, but have not equally progressed in our attempts to deal with human relations.

[1] Add. 5011, 318.

IV

RANKE AND THE CONCEPTION OF 'GENERAL HISTORY'

I. THE UNDERLYING IDEAS

In spite of whatever over-all progress it may show at certain levels, the history of historical study often turns out to be a story of local decline. A great man arises and he may start something of a tradition, but his followers—though they claim to be wearing his mantle—easily slip into routine and miss the profundity of his basic ideas. Great historians, indeed, have to be rescued from the cages into which their immediate successors try to confine them; and here is another service that can be performed by the history of historiography. It may even happen that an initial misunderstanding about an historian will be greatly magnified through insistent reiteration and careless transmission. A paradoxical example of this is the prolonged currency in this country of the view that Ranke was an historian who had no ideas—and even disapproved of them—desiring to reproduce only 'facts', only events as they actually happened.[1]

It will be clear already that the human race, in its study of history and in its attitude to the past, has gone through a succession of varied stages and experiences. Even when these are completed and are not likely to recur they may leave a certain deposit—the world, though it may not trouble to remember them, is different because it once went through these phases. There have been times, for example, when men have found it more necessary than we should do to thresh out the question whether history is not so unreliable as to be unworthy of

---

[1] A further example would be the way in which Ranke's alleged heresies on the subject of 'the primacy of foreign policy' are often exaggerated or misunderstood. See pp. 116–25, below.

serious attention.[1] And though the controversy would not concern us now, it is possible that each of us in his individual life repeats some of those stages of experience through which mankind as a whole once passed. Each of us, therefore, may have had to face the selfsame problem at a certain stage and may feel this to have been a useful thing. The scholar, playing with his pieces of evidence, is perhaps in danger of combining these into a closed and rigid system, forgetting that there is always more evidence to come (as each new generation of research students is going to prove)—forgetting also the innumerable ways in which essential evidence may have been lost or destroyed, so that the historian may be cheated for ever and yet remain for ever unaware of the fact. We all carry some of our secrets to the grave and there is a sense in which history (and perhaps the very kind of history which the majority of people most want) is indeed an impossibility. The net result of this chapter of experience is the conclusion that historians, even when they think they possess all the evidence they require, cannot have too great flexibility of mind.

More important still, there comes a point in the history of historiography—just as there comes a point in the development of an individual student—at which nothing seems so vividly certain as the fact that every historical personage, every historical event, is unique. This view forms the basis for the case which has often been made against those who look for broad movements, general causes, lines of development and laws of history. If we misconstrue this uniqueness in personalities and events, however, or if we carry the idea too far, we make it impossible ever to reflect on human affairs. We cannot say that 'the Irish are charming' for each person is a separate creation, not comparable with another; and it is presumed that each stands solitary, fulfilling the law of his own existence. We cannot say that 'the Germans are responsible

[1] See, for example, the lists in J. G. Meusel, *Bibliotheca Historica*, I, I, pp. 13–16, 'Scriptores de fide et veritate historica et de Pyrrhonismo historico', and in J. C. Gatterer *Universalhistorie*, I, 69–70. See also A. Momigliano in 'Ancient History and the Antiquarian', *Contributo alla Storia degli Studi Classici*, 79–84, 87–9.

for the War of 1914'—for, on this view of the matter, we are only entitled to assert: 'This particular German made this particular wrong decision.' On the same argument we should be generalising too much if we even talked about 'the historical origins of the War of 1914', since certain individuals by sovereign action precipitated that war, and their responsibility cannot be transferred to predecessors who died long before. By the same rule we could not talk about the growth of toleration in western Europe; we could only say that Mary Tudor was herself responsible for being wickedly intolerant. It may be granted that there is an important aspect of truth in these *prima facie* judgments; but if we push the doctrine of the unique individual and the unique episode too far, we only end by making it impossible to reflect on the past. Statesmen could never learn anything from history, for every political episode would be a law unto itself; and human beings could never learn anything from experience. The past could only be narrated as a story of chances and changes; and indeed it would not even be a story, for between a succession of absolutely unique particles there can be no thread that would hold a narrative together. The study of history could only be a burden on the memory, and would lose most of its educational point.

Certainly each person and each historical event may stand unique and may comprise a unique combination of elements or circumstances. But in each there is something of a compound, and the parts which compose this may be grouped and compared; for these latter at least are not without parallels. We can legitimately set out to discover whether great geniuses generally have big ears or remarkable mothers, and whether a disproportionate number of painters are left-handed. We can even violate that holy of holies, the inspiration of the poet, and say that a given sonnet is unduly reminiscent of Keats. Every battle in world-history may be different from every other battle, but they must have something in common if we can group them under the term 'battle' at all. And however bad an historian I may be on grounds which pertain only to myself, I can still be given a place in a series—I exist at a certain point in the development of historical science. In other words, there is truth in both the views which we are considering and each is open to criticism chiefly in so far as it tries to exclude the other. The quality of the unique in every individual or event or moment is to be fully maintained; and yet the movements of masses and the processes of centuries can be the subject of generalisation or analysis. On the one hand we may tell a story of the things which happened to Martin Luther, or the things that he said and did; but on the other hand we can see 'the Reformation' as a great conglomerate, in which a multiplicity of particular events are compounded into one imposing shape; and then we can discuss the conditions which led to it, or the consequences it produced, or the processes within it. And history is a more difficult subject than some people realise because both these aspects of the matter have to be provided for—both have constantly to be taken into account.

It is at this point that Ranke takes up the whole problem of the nature of technical history; and the reason for his interest in the matter is worth noting. Like the Göttingen professors he had a campaign to conduct—they were all anxious to rescue what was called 'universal history', and what we should call 'general history' from the hands of the philosophers. In reality, the work of providing a rational account of man on the earth would seem to have been taken over from the theologians by the general philosophers in the eighteenth century. The need to know how mankind had come from primitive conditions to its existing state would appear to have been felt before the historians were in a condition to supply what was wanted. Man's reflections on the matter marched ahead of his researches; and it was the *philosophes*—the 'general thinkers' as we might call them—who attempted to map out the course of things in time. And this would appear to be the reason why the philosophy of history, as it was called, came to its climax before the study of history had reached its modern form. The

Göttingen school resented the facile generalisations which the men of the Enlightenment produced without research, and imposed upon human history from the outside.[1] Ranke's objections were exactly the same but they came to a point in his hostility to Hegel's philosophy of history. Both quarrelled primarily with the over-simplifications in philosophic history and with a schematisation that did not issue out of the recorded facts. In particular they set themselves against the policy of constructing the story of mankind on the basis of an assumed or presupposed doctrine of progress.

Ranke, like the men of the Göttingen school, however, is far from desiring to attack generalisations or general history. On the contrary he holds that two things are necessary for an historian. The first is a joy in detail as such, and a desire to participate in it wherever it comes—a passion for human beings in themselves, in spite of their contradictions, and a love of events in their very uniqueness. He states the case in the strongest possible manner: nothing in the world, he says, can ever be regarded as existing merely for the sake of something else. Secondly, however, he tells us that 'the historian must have an eye for generalities'—his treatment of the details must lead him to a view of the broader course of change which the world has undergone.[2] It is curious that he should

[1] See, for example, F. Rühs, *Geschichte Schwedens*, I (Halle, 1803), Vorrede, x. Cf. Rühs, *Entwurf einer Propädeutik des historischen Studiums* (Berlin, 1811), 252–3, on 'Pragmatismus'; and ibid. 30: 'In more recent times there have been two kinds of attempts to handle history philosophically; the first can be described as the French way, and it consists essentially in a vague way of reasoning about the facts of history, which instead of being treated properly, according to their individual nature and in their relations to time and place, are subjected to a criticism based on current fashionable principles or rather opinions.'

[2] For this and the following paragraphs see L. von Ranke, *Uber die Epochen der neueren Geschichte* (München und Leipzig, 1921), 15–21, together with the Introduction by Alfred Dove, ibid. 1–6. Cf. Theodore H. von Laue, *Leopold Ranke, the Formative Years*, (Princeton, N.J., 1950), 115–16: 'Ranke deeply loved the great variety of which human life was capable, and he loved it for its own sake, "as one enjoys a flower". He considered each expression of life in history as an original creation of the human spirit, without judging it or comparing it with others. His main aim was to understand it from within ...as a contemporary understanding its freedom of choice at any given moment, but as a retrospective historian also seeing the underlying necessity.... And in order to perceive the mysterious throbbings of the "idea", he strained all the faculties of his mind, reason,

ever have been charged with loving merely isolated facts; when in reality he insists on generalisations and demands only that they issue out of the facts—his great anxiety is that the facts should merge into larger shapes, and that, like the natural sciences, history should move to higher degrees of generalisation. History, he says, 'never has the unity of a philosophical system'; but it is not at all devoid of *inneren Zusammenhang*—not at all without interconnectedness. Far from repudiating general history, he said that all his mind was constantly pressing towards just that, striving to discover the connections and the continuities; and, as Edward Armstrong once said of him, 'he had much belief in the educational power of lectures covering a long period of history'.[1] Even when he was researching into some detailed episode, he was trying all the time to put that episode into its place in the whole story of the world's development. Like the Göttingen professors, he saw the map of universal history as the final objective, and, far from repudiating the idea of it, he simply claimed that it should be in the hands of historians rather than philosophers. Both he and his predecessors seem to have assumed that, if the historian himself does not undertake the task, some H. G. Wells will carry it out, and will acquire undue power over the minds of men. For our general outlook on the world is determined partly by the picture that we have made of universal history; and even the research student, except when his eye is fastened to his microscope—and perhaps even then—but certainly when his mind wanders into realms of general discussion—can hardly escape having such a picture as his constant basis of reference.

Ranke, therefore, insists on having the best of both worlds; and he boldly confronts the paradoxes. He is prepared to believe that there has been a development in the science of

emotion, and intuition. . . . Without [this] Ranke could not so successfully have dealt with Renaissance Italy, the Ottoman and Spanish empires, the Serbian revolution, and the Papacy, all subjects far removed from his own mental background.'

[1] *History of the Latin and Teutonic Nations* (revised translation in Bohn's Standard Library, London, 1909), p. xiii.

history; but he refuses to allow that anybody is a greater historian than Thucydides. He is ready to admit that in the course of time an improved moral standard may gain wider currency amongst larger classes of society; but to him there is no progress in ethics beyond the morality of the New Testament. In our time more people may benefit from the stable conditions in which it is fairly easy to live a sober and respectable life. But the present day does not excel the world of over a thousand years ago in examples of spiritual depth or in the moral strength that grapples with great difficulties and temptations.

And Ranke would not accept the view of the philosophers, that human history was moving inevitably to a predetermined consummation in this world. If on the one hand such an end were imposed on mankind from the outside, he said, it would do violence to the principle of free will. If on the other hand the inevitability came from something that is innate in human beings, this is a view that turns man into either God or nothing. In other words the free choices of free men must be regarded as having a real part in the making of the story; and this means that God has left open to the future a multiplicity of alternative possible developments. What we ourselves do here and now will make a difference to the course which the future is to take; but involved in this is a process, the laws of which are not only unknown to us, but are more secret and profound than we can understand. In a sense, says Ranke, every individual must be regarded as free; and we must assume that at any moment something original may emerge— something which comes from the primary source of historical action, inside human beings. At the same time all the parts of history are interwoven—they condition one another and have their constant repercussions on one another. In this sense, freedom and necessity, he tells us, are rubbing shoulders at every moment. We may conclude from this that on the one hand history is a story in which one never knows what is going to happen next. On the other hand it is a study of developments which become apparent and explicable when the course of things is viewed retrospectively. In this latter aspect it belongs not so much to the narrator, but rather to the expositor and the analyst.

In a parallel manner, it is necessary to avoid the temptation to regard a generation or an individual as merely a means to an end or a stepping-stone to something else. Ranke will not allow a past generation to be 'mediatised', as he calls it; as though it did not have any standing of its own in the eyes of eternity—as though only the last generation in the chain of progress was going to have the right to be considered for its own sake. If you imagine all the generations laid out before the eyes of God, it is not merely the last of them—it is every single one in the whole series—which has to be directly related to eternity. So Ranke does justice to free will and to necessity, to what is unique and what can be generalised, to personality as something always valid in itself and to the kind of movements which are supra-personal. When he comes to the marginal points at which our decisions about life affect our views concerning the structure of history, Ranke's cross-references are to that religion which he said was the primary impulse behind his study of the past. There might be faults in the edifice which came to be superimposed; there might be secularisation at certain levels of his historical thinking; but the few ideas which he laid down as fundamental are things which distinguish history as understood in a Christian world, even when that world has become secularised.[1] It is possible to imagine a strange culture which would answer the deeper problems of life and personality in a different manner. In this case historical writing might be of a different texture; or history might cease to have significance.

[1] The religious basis of this section of Ranke's thought (which has been overlooked by many people) is duly recognised, for example, by Hans Liebeschütz, *Ranke* (Historical Association Pamphlets, 1954), 4–5, 8–9.

2. THE RANGE OF GENERAL HISTORY

In all this, Ranke is affirming the possibility of what we call 'general history'—the possibility of learning new things about the past, beyond what can be discovered by merely recapitulating events or putting them under the microscope. His argument still has an important significance for us, because the problem is one which is liable to confront the student of history at the present day. We should all agree that if certain men in Europe had been wiser and better men—if they had made the different decisions which it was certainly open to them to take—the world might have been delivered from an appalling tragedy in July 1914. Is it legitimate, then, to say anything at all about the 'historical origins' of the First World War, and to trace these back to the year 1870, or earlier still—even to put part of the responsibility on certain people who were dead long before the crisis of 1914 occurred? Must we say that the men who had part in that crisis acted merely out of the uniqueness of their personalities, so that there is no point in trying to look behind the various individuals and their sovereign wills? Or, can we see these men as in any way affected, for example, by decisions which Bismarck had made nearly fifty years before—decisions about the government of Prussia, the constitution of the German Empire, and the relations between the German army and the Prussian monarchy? I cannot call to mind any practising historian who has confronted this issue as directly as Ranke, or has shown himself so determined to refer the issue back to the realm of fundamental ideas. The man who on the one hand opened in the modern field the era of scientific research is the man who on the other hand stood as the supreme apostle of 'general history'. And *ipso facto* he made out the case for the existence of a certain aspect of events which can be subjected to 'historical explanation'. He, more than anybody else, would have insisted on the interconnectedness of events and on the view that the decisions of 1866 and 1870 do in fact have relevance in July 1914. And historical study is bound to become impoverished if the world tries to retain the one half of the Ranke legacy without holding fast also to the other.

Ranke's further ideas on this subject are worthy of note, and the shape which he gave to 'general history', particularly in the modern period, is still of some significance for the world. His views have in fact provoked considerable controversy in recent years, and the twentieth century has tried to blame him for some of its own sins or mistakes. Occasionally he has been reproached as though he were responsible for developments which in reality had taken the decisive turn before he appeared on the scene. This is true to a considerable extent in respect of the problem of the scope of what we call 'modern history'— the extent of the geographical area which the general historian usually attempts to cover.

During a great part of the eighteenth century the study of the past, particularly in the universities, had been subordinate to the needs of theology, philology and law. Apart from the interest in the Bible and the cult of ancient Greece and Rome, it would appear to have been the needs of the lawyer and the political scientist, or of religious and constitutional controversy, which controlled the teaching programme at that time. Even the thing which called itself universal history had largely been confined therefore to the biblical, the classical and the European worlds. The subdivision into periods—whether one adopted the Four-Monarchy system or drew a sharp line at the fall of the Roman Empire—showed that the horizon had really been a constricted one.

The early Göttingen professors who established history as an independent teaching-subject[1] were perhaps misled by the English Universal History, which proved to be a vast collection of separate national studies. Those professors expanded the scope of their own world-history to include China, Tibet,

---

[1] Acton says, C.U.L., Add. 5011, 331, that it was Ranke who placed history on an independent footing; but here he overlooks the Göttingen school; see, for example, Wesendonck, *Begründung*, pp. ix, 142.

Japan, etc., while still striving so earnestly to achieve a unified canvas, and to work the result into an organic whole. A contraction soon occurred again, however. Johann von Müller, who was regarded by Acton as 'the first universal historian', made a remarkable advance towards the unity of an organic narrative; but he declared in the very title of his book that he was particularly concerned with the European section of the human race. Even in Göttingen, the conception of 'general history', so far as the modern period was concerned, came to be identified with that history of the modern European states-system which had already been establishing itself in German university teaching.

On this subject three significant ideas were put forward in Göttingen itself at the beginning of the nineteenth century. They were to have relevance in future generations since they helped to decide the form of what was to be regarded as 'general history'. First, it was argued that even on the widest global view the principal feature in the story of mankind since the year 1492 had been the unprecedented predominance of Europe in world-affairs. The judgement is one which I imagine we should confirm today; though we might remember that the situation would have been different if the flood of the Turks across Europe had not been checked before Vienna; if the Portuguese had not been victorious in the Asiatic waters; if the reconquest of Spain from the Moors had suffered a serious reverse; and if it had not been the Christians who had established themselves in the New World. Secondly, it was argued that the great characteristic of European history between 1492 and 1789 was the formation of the modern state and the rise of the Great Powers. Here the historian is speaking as though he has it in mind that something different might have happened, or that the order which was established on the Continent is not a thing to be taken for granted. It was held that a similar pattern had not been produced on the map, or a similar set of relationships established, on the Asiatic continent. Thirdly, these European states still formed something like a society and a unified system; for they had a common culture, a common religion, and a common moral outlook—in fact Europe was described as a single nation which was divided only in a political sense. But the Göttingen professor, Heeren, who makes out this case, adds that this fine picture no longer holds good; he writes his book, in fact, while Napoleon is overrunning the Continent. He admits that in the past there may have been vague analogies to the European system—in the city-states of ancient Greece or of fifteenth-century Italy, for example. The closest parallel in his opinion, however, would be the case of the Hellenistic monarchies which followed the break-up of the empire of Alexander the Great.[1] All the same, when he writes the history of the ancient world, this man points out that in this work he is only giving separate accounts of each separate state. His book on modern times is a more coherent treatise, because, he says, the European states can be regarded as 'a single political system'.[2] In this modern field, topics can be treated on a continental scale—the Reformation conflicts, the defence of Christendom against the Turks, the policy of mercantilism, the principle of the balance of power, for example. He insists that the expansion of Europe is one of the subjects which are capable of this general treatment; colonies and overseas trade are in fact organic to his theme. He writes during the Napoleonic era, when the European states-system seems to have collapsed, but he considers it possible that in the future a *world* states-system will emerge.

These are the ideas which Ranke inherited and made his own; and they affected the character of 'modern history' teaching down to our time. We in the twentieth century may

[1] A. H. L. Heeren, *Handbuch der Geschichte des europäischen Staatensystems und seiner Colonien, von der Entdeckung beyder Indien bis zur Errichtung des Französischen Kayserthums* (2te Ausgabe, Göttingen, 1811), Vorrede, 5 Feb. 1809, and pp. 5–6. Heeren, p. 13, makes the point that the 'balance of power' in the European states-system encourages the independent activity and increases the importance of States that are only in the second and third rank.

[2] A. H. L. Heeren, *A Manual of Ancient History*, Engl. trans. (London, 1847), p. x, Preface to 2nd German edition, 1828.

have entered upon the tradition unthinkingly, and without examining its origins; but Ranke and his predecessors thought the matter out; they began by seeing all the world as the stage and they tried to assess the importance of Europe in global history. Even when Ranke attacked the oversimplified idea of progress his charge against the mere 'philosophers' was that they built up their picture of world-history on a local view—he reminded them of what had happened to the civilisations of Asia.[1] In the opinion of Ranke, the great feature of world-history between the years 1492 and 1789 was the formation of the modern state in Europe, the rise of the Great Powers and the establishment of the states-system. If he had been indulging in wishful thinking he might have preferred the medieval world in which a Germanic monarchy had made prodigious thrusts to the west, and then the south, and then the east, and then the north. In his own day there were aggressive nationalists, already dreaming of German predominance; but he positively adhered to the idea of a multiplicity of states which should stand approximately in equilibrium with one another. He did not want unity but gloried in the variety of nations, saying that if there had existed a single European literature, instead of a multitude of national literatures, the world would have been less rich.[2] It is not clear even now that the effects of the break-up of the European states-system will not confirm his diagnosis of the importance of the development of this system down to 1789. When Ranke was asked, exactly a hundred years ago, what was the great feature of European history *after* 1789, he made the significant remark that in the nineteenth century 'all the attention which had hitherto been devoted to foreign affairs now turns to questions of internal policy'. The 'leading tendencies of our time', he said, were the conflict between monarchy and popular sovereignty, the accumulation of material power and the

[1] L. v. Ranke, *Über die Epochen der neueren Geschichte*, 16.
[2] 'Die Grossen Mächte', Engl. transl. in T. H. v. Laue, *Leopold Ranke, the Formative Years*, p. 218.

development of the natural sciences.[1] This was in 1854—well before the rise of Bismarck, which might have been calculated to alter his analysis of the nineteenth century. Therefore it was at any rate until he was sixty years of age that Ranke maintained the view which has been described—the view that from 1500 Europe lay at the centre of global history and that within Europe itself until 1789 the relations of states with one another constituted the predominant historical theme.

Indeed, in the time of Ranke it was still natural that when one moved beyond the study of one's own country, the mind should turn to a form of 'general history' which was restricted to Christendom. Even the new developments which were occurring in historical scholarship—even Ranke's separate histories of the various nations—had their principal effect in the transformation which they produced in the European story. Ranke's special interest in diplomatic documents and in the external policy of the various nations helped in fact to draw the history of the continent together. The archives which opened their doors to the research student were the ones in European capitals—in Vienna, Venice, Brussels, Paris, the Hague, London, Rome, etc. And in any case European history did in fact stand in a class by itself; and the historians formed a society—they constituted a world of scholarship that was essentially European. After the age of Gatterer and Schlözer the ordinary historian ceased to pretend to be an orientalist or a student of strange civilisations. 'General history' came to be a study which comprised in the modern period the continent of Europe and its relations with the world overseas.

Ranke, however, is charged with having narrowed the vision of the historian still more—constricting the range of European history itself, and limiting its area to the western half of the continent. His prejudices can hardly be said to have reduced the scope of 'the European states-system' as this had been envisaged and taught by his predecessors in Göttingen. But the tradition which he represented did lead to an emphasis on

[1] L. v. Ranke, *Über die Epochen der neueren Geschichte*, 139, 141.

the history of the western states, so that his teaching has proved to be vulnerable in our time. The truth is that this man, who has so often been reproached for concerning himself only with isolated facts, laid himself open to criticism because in reality he was always looking to see how the facts would congeal into massive shapes. A whole region of history or a whole period might have so much character for him that he saw it as an identifiable system—saw it as having a personality of its own. Those who study the foreign policy of Elizabeth I, the life of Mary Queen of Scots, the French wars of religion, the revolt of the Netherlands and the ambitions of Philip II of Spain, will realise how an area and an epoch may shape themselves into a unity as the historian reflects on the narratives concerned. For all these stories are interlocked and interdependent; they form a single drama, centred so to speak on the English Channel— the massacre of St Bartholomew being involved in a vast and complicated network of diplomacy, while the defeat of the Spanish Armada has its repercussions in France and the Netherlands. In addition to this, the very history which takes place in this part of Europe in the latter half of the sixteenth century possesses a recognisable character—the interplay of events produces a texture which reminds us of the novels of Dumas, and the story has a flavour all its own. Here is a considerable historical area which it is useful to envisage as a single whole.

Ranke's mind hankers to discover the places where the interconnectedness of historical events produces in this way a certain continuity of fabric, and allows us to see the past in large generalised terms. In his very first book he calls attention to an historical field in which—from a certain point of view and at a certain level of analysis—there is unity over a much larger area and a much longer period than in the countries round the English Channel in the age of Philip II. He points to the whole western half of the European continent and sees it as an historical unity for a period of well over a thousand years. Throughout this area the mingling of the Latin and the

Teutonic peoples, or the interaction between them, represents a factor that is common to all the countries concerned, so that the same pattern is repeatedly discernible, the same basic principles hold good. And, speaking of the period after Charlemagne, he says that the Hungarians and Slavonic peoples did not 'belong to the unity of our nations', and that they received only the impact of the West—they failed to exert an independent influence upon affairs.[1] I do not for a moment believe that Ranke would have denied the parallel kind of unity which Constantinople was able to give to the history of the eastern Slavs. Nor would he have denied the unity which so long existed (at a different level, and in respect of other things) over the whole continent—that is to say throughout the region which had once been regarded as 'Christendom'. Ranke himself belonged to the West, however, and he saw things most clearly, or observed them with more continuous attention, as they touched the world in which he himself lived. He gave his authority to an historical tradition which emphasised the western half of the Continent.

We might say, however, that it is natural for men to see history in concentric circles, and to deepen their interest in the innermost circles—in the regions that touch their life more closely. It is natural that a Frenchman should learn more of Europe than of Asia, should feel that the western half of Europe is more important to him than the eastern half, and should even examine his own country more intensively than that of the German or the Spaniard. Instead of setting out to disperse their interest in equal proportions over all the quarters of the globe, men legitimately intensify their focus and multiply their observations as the scene comes nearer home. Certainly it would be wrong for us today to neglect the study of the history of eastern Europe; and it is very doubtful whether, even now, our modern history curriculum has properly adjusted itself to the needs of our time. Even Ranke may be open to criticism in this respect, for it may still be true that

[1] *Latin and Teutonic Nations*, p. 6 and Vorrede to German 1824 ed.

he was content with a 'general history' which was too narrow
in its geographical range. But in these days when historians
tend to lock themselves into ever-diminishing regions of
research, which of us in fact is going to have the effrontery to
reproach Ranke with a lack of breadth? In any case Ranke
wrote the offending passage in the year 1824. And what shall
we say of the *Cambridge Modern History* and of our Modern
European History syllabus in the twentieth century? We cannot blame Ranke if a century later we were repeating his
practice without reflecting upon the terms upon which it
might be valid—without realising that a new age calls for new
assessments. It was we who, a century afterwards, still stood
where Ranke had stood, failing even so late in the day to re-
consider the framework of our general history. Even in his
first book Ranke did not forget to collate the disasters which
Venice suffered at the time of the League of Cambrai with the
blow that was given to her commerce by the contemporary
Portuguese victory in the Indian Seas.[1] And his very next
two works were devoted to Turkish and Serbian history—
fields which he entered somewhat as a pioneer.[2]

3. 'THE PRIMACY OF FOREIGN POLICY'

A more serious criticism of Ranke, and of the nineteenth-
century tradition which we inherited, has reference not merely
to the range, but rather to the form and character of the general
history which it was proposed to produce. The tendency in the
university of Göttingen, as we have seen, had at first reflected
the influence of the *philosophes* and had envisaged something
like a history of civilisation.[3] English influence, however, and

[1] L. v. Ranke, *Latin and Teutonic Nations*, Engl. transl. (London, 1909), pp. 268–78,
296–7.
[2] *Fürsten und Völker von Südeuropa, die Osmanen und die spanische Monarchie im 16
und 17 Jahrhundert* (1827), and *Die serbische Revolution* (1829).
[3] See p. 49 above. Against those who thought that the sole purpose of history, and
the sole principle upon which events should be selected, was the desire to inform and
equip people for the judgement of present-day politics, Gatterer asked whether all
readers, and indeed all students and teachers were expected to be statesmen. R. Wittram,
'Das Interesse an der Geschichte', *Die Welt als Geschichte*, XII (1952), 2.

the desire to provide an education in statesmanship, had brought the history there into closer connection with politics. Modern history, for Heeren, had become not merely a pre-dominantly European study but also a predominantly political one. Acton makes it clear that in any case the opening of the archives in the nineteenth century helped to increase the bias in favour of political history. It released a mass of documentation which, almost by definition, envisaged history in its connection with government. Acton was ready to believe that the future might have to decide whether modern history should largely remain a political study or should turn into a more general account of the development of society and culture. He himself seems to have believed and desired that political history should still prevail; for he, too, considered that the study of history had a particular relevance for an education in politics. In this connection it is curious to note that he criticised Ranke for taking, at least in one respect, too much of the statesman's point of view—thinking of events in terms of the trouble that they gave to government. Perhaps, however, it is useful—and ever more useful as the world becomes more democratic—that people should be taught to look at things as though they themselves were rulers of the state, so that they may realise the difficulties of governing. Ranke himself notes in one place that we often ascribe too much to government when the real work of history-making is being done from below. In his *History of the Popes* he repeatedly stresses the importance of public opinion, and says that we must not imagine that it only began to be operative in the nineteenth century.[1]

In recent times the followers of Ranke have been subjected to a more pointed criticism directed against their belief in 'the primacy of foreign policy'. This latter involves the thesis that external affairs are the decisive factor in the march of events, and that therefore they must form the essential framework of our general history. Some people find it easy to argue that,

[1] *History of the Popes*, Engl. transl., Bohn Library (London, 1927), I, 105, 188; II, 19.

since mankind cannot live without food, the economic side of history has the primary claim upon our attention. Others see the oppressed fighting the oppressor throughout the ages and infer that the class conflict is the infallible key to general history. In a way that is somewhat similar some men seem to think that the downfall of an order or the wiping-out of a political system may take away the whole basis of a given culture. Indeed, the belief that civilisation must collapse unless one's own state or empire prevails in international affairs is probably common to all great political organisms. It is easy to imagine that, both for the historian and the citizen, defence and foreign policy ought therefore to be the supreme concern.

From my youth I made continual protest against the kind of European history which chiefly occupies itself with the external relations of the various states; but this feature of our curriculum had little to do with Ranke—it was the result of an educational routine that had taken the line of least resistance. For my own part, I should like to cry from the housetops that the publication of Newton's *Principia* in 1687 is a turning-point in history for peoples to whom the Renaissance and Reformation can hardly mean anything at all—peoples amongst whom the battle of Waterloo would hardly be calculated to produce an echo. And, before the Scientific Revolution, the great event in our history—the big new thing which made more difference to the world than even the fall of Rome—was surely the victory of Christianity in the civilisation that surrounded the Mediterranean Sea.

But, though I differ from some of the followers of Ranke in this, I should not be disposed to treat their opinion with contempt. It is possible for us to be right in our criticism of their views, and yet more superficial than they themselves were. It is possible for us to be more slipshod in our subservience to the fashions of the mid-twentieth century than these men were in relation to the different ideas of a hundred years ago. I do not personally believe that the conflict with the world behind the Iron Curtain should be regarded as the all-important issue for the men of the West at the present time. But I am not prepared to wipe off the map as a villain or a fool the man who thinks that this issue of external relations—this conflict of alien systems for the possession of ground on the globe—should be regarded as the supreme one and as decisive for the future of civilisation. Those who look at world-history from the most comprehensive point of view cannot escape the fact that politics and the conduct of public affairs provide some of the firmest ribs in the structure that it forms. Begin by envisaging the whole of society and the march of civilisation, and you still end by discovering the startling importance of mere dynastic policy in one period, and of constitutional controversy in another period—the importance indeed of the work of government—in the shaping of history throughout the ages. A social or cultural history which fails to do justice to this aspect of the story is always a flabby and amorphous thing.

Professor Sir Charles Webster said in one of his Inaugural Lectures:

> International history does not of course deal solely with the relations of state and state. But so long as the world is organized in such a manner that the state has so great an influence in determining the nature and extent of the contacts established, such relations must always be a large part of the field of work.[1]

Having once tried to secure that questions on the history of science should replace traditional questions on the history of the art of war in certain examination papers, I find that, without altering my views on this particular matter, I wonder nowadays whether the neglect of military history and war does not have the effect of giving some people an anaemic and unreal idea of the deeper processes of mundane history. Indeed, it is possible that our conventional history-teaching underestimates the part played by war in the development of our civilisation and our economy, as well as in the rise of the modern state. It has been noted that great constitutional concessions were won

---

[1] 'The Study of International History', *History*, July 1933, 99–100.

from English kings who were unusually unsuccessful in their foreign policy; and certainly it is not easy to know what would have happened if King John or Charles I or James II had been more fortunate in this field. Ranke thought that the disgraces suffered by the French monarchy in its foreign policy had much to do with the outbreak of the Revolution; and, though it is not easy to follow him here, the problem is not so simple as it seems to be at first sight. It is more clear that two world wars in the twentieth century were largely responsible for the success of Communism over one great part of the globe, and the speeding up of egalitarianism over another great area. I remember feeling shocked when I found Ranke arguing that, in spite of Goethe, German culture and German cultural influence gained their great momentum with the rise of German power and confidence in the nineteenth century. Yet when I reflect on the cultural leadership which the United States and Russia have come to enjoy since the Second World War—and when I compare this with the situation of twenty years ago—I am staggered to see how such matters are affected by a mere redistribution of power. The Golden Age of Spain at one time, of Holland at another time, and of France in the age of Louis XIV seem to give support to the same argument.

Those who have believed in the primacy of foreign policy have even held that the constitution of a country may be seriously affected by the needs of diplomacy and war. On this argument an island state, enjoying a somewhat more sheltered existence, may be better able to devote itself to its domestic affairs, and may have a less obstructed development to constitutionalism and democracy, than a frontier-state which needs firmer governmental direction. An island-state—so long as it can enjoy the obvious benefits of its position—may not experience the grimness of some of the forces that have their part in general history. And if this is the case the members of an island-state and the members of a frontier-state may each have only a partial experience of history and so may come to have a different feeling for the texture of events. On grounds not quite the same but somewhat similar the citizens of the United States at the present day may differ at marginal points from those of Great Britain in their feeling about the nature of history and the processes of time. When such a thing happens there may be fundamental discrepancies in historiography— baffling discrepancies even between historians who are equally sincere. The reconciliation of these may be a subtle matter, but it should not be beyond the power of human thought.

When discussing the problem of the primacy of foreign policy it is useful to see the place of the doctrine in the history of historiography and to note the conditions under which it developed. It was the Göttingen school which made modern European history an essentially political affair; and if we are inclined to blame them, let us remember that they expressed their indebtedness to the English who, they said, had served the world by reviving the connection between history and politics.[1] The view that the rise of the Great Powers was the main theme in European history in the centuries before 1789 was not devised by the Prussians in their arrogance; it was promulgated in Göttingen when Germany was under the heel of Napoleon and when the Göttingen professors were coming to be internationally recognised as the leaders in the writing of history manuals. One must not overlook the further fact that, when Ranke was maturing, it was the diplomatic documents which most of all were becoming available to the student of modern times. So much was this the case that, even apart from the famous example of the Venetian ambassadors, the reports of diplomats were for a time an important source for the internal history of the countries in which these personages resided. According to Acton, it was Ranke's use of the diplomatic despatches of Brandenburg envoys in England which contributed so greatly to the success of his treatment of even the home affairs of this country under the Stuarts.[2] Partly by reason of temperament perhaps, but also by reason

[1] E.g. Schlözer, *Weltgeschichte*, I, 2 n. 4.
[2] *The Chronicle*, 20 July 1867, 394. See also Appendix VII, p. 232 below.

of opportunity, Ranke devoted much of his work to the external policy of states; but he went further perhaps than most of our general historians in his interest in the history of thought and even science. I imagine that English historians in our time who have gone far beyond Ranke in the exclusiveness of their devotion to diplomatic history would not admit the inference that they are necessarily committed to the principle of the primacy of foreign policy. Burckhardt applied himself more particularly to cultural studies, but it is not clear that in regard to the texture of general history he did not really belong in many respects to the school of his teacher, Ranke. He was more pessimistic about the future, partly because he was influenced by some ugly manifestations in the local politics of Basel, which made him distrustful of the tendencies of democracy; while Ranke in the age of Bismarck wrongly imagined that the spectre of Revolution had been conjured away.

If Ranke accepted the view that down to 1789 the essential history was that of the Great Powers, it is equally clear that his general notion of the time-process allowed him to believe that constitutionalism, the industrial revolution and the development of science were the principal features of the nineteenth century. Some of his successors seem to have exaggerated or misunderstood his ideas; and some of them overpressed the thesis concerning the primacy of foreign policy; so that his influence may have been unfortunate and yet he may not have been responsible for the aberrations that occurred. What might stand as a not uninteresting comment on the process of things in time, may become a dangerous falsity when it hardens into doctrine; and in reality Ranke was chiefly concerned to draw attention to the fact that interesting interactions constantly take place between home policy and foreign affairs. When we look at the rise of the Empire of Alexander the Great—when we consider either the development or the downfall of the Roman Empire—we can hardly deny that these vast aggregations of power are momentous things in the history of civilisation. Our own technique, however, is liable to give rise to historians' 'blind spots'; and we may overlook the still greater significance of those elements of culture which have a continuous history, irrespective of the rise and fall of empires. Those who say that the preservation of a given empire is essential to the future of civilisation are not meaning civilisation in quite the same sense—they have in mind the preservation of the civilised order which happens to be theirs and are moved no doubt by the fact that they dread even the momentary relapse which culture may suffer if that order falls. In any case, although Ranke made some interesting comments on cultural history and on the deeper processes that underlie the total history of mankind, it is not clear that during much of his life he had the materials for turning these aspects of the past into organic story.[1] It was the latter half of the nineteenth century which began to add great riches to the social and cultural side of the study, and gradually rescued this kind of history from its earlier amorphous state.

It is remarkable that those who have criticised Ranke's views on the subject of general history should have failed to consult his famous *Weltgeschichte* in which long chapters deal with the 'Athenian Democracy and its Leaders', and with 'The Antagonism and Growth of Religious Ideas in Greek Literature'. Almost at the beginning of his work he writes of ancient Judaism:

> The steps by which this religion, when it had once made itself independent, obtained the supremacy over all other forms of religious worship, and became one of the fundamental bases both of Islam and of the Christian world, form one of the most important elements in universal history.

In his Preface, however, he describes the development, and expounds his own conception, of what he calls 'universal history'. Speaking of the eighteenth century, he writes:

> Through the revolution in ideas which then took place the notion of Universal History was, as it were, secularised, a result chiefly due to

[1] See, however, the Essays on cultural history in Ranke's collected works.

the publication of a voluminous record of different nations under the title of a 'Universal History', which, appearing in England, was welcomed by German scholars and incited the latter to a display of similar industry. But it was impossible to remain content with the history of individual nations. A collection of national histories, whether on a larger or a smaller scale is not what we mean by Universal History, for in such a work the general connection of things is liable to be obscured.

In his account of his own interpretation of the theme he tells us:

But historical development does not rest on the tendency towards civilisation alone. It arises also from impulses of a very different kind, especially from the rivalry of nations engaged in conflict with each other for the possession of the soil or for political supremacy. It is in and through this conflict, affecting as it does all the domain of culture, that the great empires of history are formed. In their unceasing struggle for dominion the peculiar characteristics of each nation are modified by universal tendencies, but at the same time resist and react upon them.

Universal history would degenerate into mere theory and speculation if it were to desert the firm ground of national history, but just as little can it afford to cling to this ground alone. The history of each separate nation throws light on the history of humanity at large; but there is a general historical life, which moves progressively from one nation or group of nations to another.... We have therefore to investigate and understand not only the universal life of mankind, but the peculiarities of at any rate the more prominent nations.... Our glance must indeed be always fixed on the universal, but from false premisses only false conclusions can be drawn. Critical inquiry and intelligent generalisation are mutually indispensable...

My point of view throughout has been the following. In the course of ages the human race has won for itself a sort of heirloom in the material and social advance which it has made, but still more in its religious development. One portion of this heritage, the most precious jewel of the whole, consists of those immortal works of genius in poetry and literature, in science and art, which, while modified by the local conditions under which they were produced, yet represent what is common to all mankind. With this possession are inseparably combined the memories of events, of ancient institutions, and of great men who have passed away. One generation hands on this tradition to another, and it may from time to time be revived and recalled to the minds of men. This is the thought which gives me courage and confidence to undertake the task.[1]

Clearly it was not Ranke who turned general history into a dry account of the relations between the European states.

When I criticise Ranke I often feel myself under the difficulty into which I fall when I am trying to deal with Sir Francis Bacon. When I think that I have caught him off his guard, I often discover that in some place or other he will have anticipated my objection and provided the answer which brings me to discomfiture. If it is true that a given region or a given area of historical happening can have so much character for him that he sees it as an individual personality and conceives the whole therefore as something organic, this applies to the history of the separate nations of Europe, each of which he can envisage as a different plant or a separately-woven fabric. And, perhaps owing to some infection from Hegel, he even writes about 'nationality' sometimes in a way that leaves a bad taste in the mouth. Even in his *History of the Popes*, he repeats that inherent differences between the various nationalities have the effect of printing a peculiar pattern upon the history of each; and he goes so far as to say that a single nation, voicing the aspirations of the world, may perform a role which raises its own individual story to the rank of 'universal history' as in the case of Germany at the time of the Reformation. Yet in this book he does insist that the separate nations, though

---

[1] *Universal History. The oldest historical group of nations and the Greeks.* Engl. transl. ed. by G. W. Prothero (London, 1884), pp. xi–xiv and 2.

Since writing the above I have seen the further material adduced by E. Kessel, 'Ranke's Idee der Universalhistorie', *Historische Zeitschrift*, Oct. 1954, pp. 269–308; e.g. p. 275, Ranke's view of *Weltgeschichte*, 'die keineswegs nur politische Vorgänge, sondern "die innere Entwicklung der Nationen", den "ganzen Umfang des geistigen Daseyns" usw. umfassen soll,' and which is 'nicht anders als die Natur, insofern noch grösser und unermesslicher, als er sich noch immer durch den Gang der Begebenheiten weiterbildet'. This article prints further MS. material about Ranke's view of Universal History.

unique in a sense, have at the same time a common life—at a certain level they share a history that has a common pattern; they are not entirely locked away in their own personalities. They have part in a story which is wider than that of any single country; they are members of a universal commonwealth; and their fate is bound up with the destinies of this larger body.[1] If on occasion he wrote as though nationality were a transcendent thing and its origin a somewhat mystical affair, he was clearing away some of the mystery by the time of the *Weltgeschichte*, in the Preface of which he makes the interesting point:

Nationalities so powerful and distinct as the English or the Italian are not so much the offspring of the soil and the race as of the great events through which they have passed.[2]

It is always difficult to represent the place that power actually holds in the workings of politics and in the processes of history. Some men seem ready to speak as though power did not exist (because in their view it ought not to exist); and if others are emphatic about the reality of its presence they are assumed to be in favour of force, merely because they recognise its operation in the world. Others again assert the place of power in history, but do it with an unseemly relish, as though they would not wish the situation to be otherwise. If we reproach Ranke for his attitude to power we must not overlook the way in which he repeatedly expressed the view that brute force by itself can never achieve anything positive in history.[3] We, for our part, are inclined to believe that the victory of the democracies in two world wars has never been the victory of sheer force, and was only made possible by the collaboration of moral factors. It is a view not without its dangers and the argument can be used (and in fact was often used) in respect of the successes of Prussia and the victories of Germany in the nineteenth century. Even a Napoleon was not blind to the

---

[1] *History of the Popes*, Engl. transl., Bohn Library (London, 1927), I, 415–16.
[2] *Universal History*, p. xiii.   [3] E.g. *History of the Popes*, II, 4.

importance of the moral factor in warfare; and it is easy to blur the meanings of words—to identify 'morality' with what the army-leader understands by 'morale'. Ranke, for his part, shared the view that moral agencies must be in co-operation with power before this latter can achieve anything of consequence in the world. Like the twentieth-century democracies he held that a nation or a cause only accumulates its imposing power by virtue of the operation of moral forces. Yet when it is Ranke who holds this view, his critics are inclined to regard his whole mode of thought as a matter for reproach—they say that he is 'spiritualising' mere power. And, much as he hated even the distant smell of Communism, his view committed him—and commits its holders at the present day—to the assertion that the position of even Soviet Russia is inexplicable without the recognition of the 'moral' factor. The case of Prussia in the nineteenth century and Russia in the twentieth may make us wonder whether we ourselves have been sufficiently close in our thinking about the matter, and whether the so-called 'moral' factor is really the same thing as 'morality'. The whole view is certainly capable of serious abuse, whether it is held by a nineteenth-century German or a modern democrat; for the doctrine that 'right is might' cannot be kept separate from the doctrine that 'might is right'. Burckhardt and Acton differed from Ranke in that they were prepared to see actual evil in power as such—they were prepared to say that power tends to corrupt its possessor, for example, even when the possessor happens to be a Christian or a liberal. They were not thinking of the kind of 'power' which is possessed by the regular servants of a governmental order—the kind of power which is rather to be described as 'responsibility'. They were thinking of the actual force which prevails by its mere weight, giving its wielder the knowledge that he can do what he likes with impunity. Burckhardt and Acton were safeguarded against the dangers of Ranke's view, therefore; though all three historians agreed that, the world being constituted as it is, even power can perform a good function in society, when it imposes peace and establishes order over a wide region, thereby enabling the work of civilisation to proceed and creating a field within which men may grow in reasonableness.

Some of us may believe that in his capacity as an 'official historian' Ranke made decisions that are to be regretted, but it is a mistake to see him as a man eager to reflect the Prussian and nationalistic developments in nineteenth-century Germany. The fact that he abstracted himself from the contemporary scene was the reason why he was so greatly reproached by his fellow-countrymen; and it is the reason why so much of his thinking continues to have relevance for us, even after the nineteenth century has passed. At one moment, in order to assist in safeguarding the world against some of the dangerous tendencies of his time, he tried to frighten King Maximilian of Bavaria with two of the most dreaded bogeys of that generation. In his hostility to the idea of the absolutist state he said that if such an idea ever became realised in Germany, the result would be first of all the establishment of a republic, and then the installation of Communism.[1] By such remarks as this we can measure his animosity against any notion of absolutism.

4. THE RENAISSANCE AND THE DIVISION INTO PERIODS

The division of general history into periods had been the subject of considerable experiment and discussion in the seventeenth and eighteenth centuries, as we have already seen. Both Ranke and Acton were interested in the question as to how the various epochs were to be marked out, and how the salient tendencies in each were to be commemorated. Even after the Four-Monarchy system had been abandoned there had been particular disagreement on the subject of the point at which one ought to place the beginning of 'modern times'. The controversy was liable to be prolonged into a new era

[1] *Über die Epochen der neueren Geschichte*, 43.

since the notion of what constituted 'modernity' was itself bound to alter as one generation succeeded another. It no longer coincided with the notion that Cellarius had had in the seventeenth century; and we have seen how early there had emerged the demand for a new 'modern' period which should begin with the French Revolution.[1]

In his *Letters on History* Bolingbroke had asserted that since the close of the fifteenth century the texture of events, and the mode in which consequences proceeded out of causes, had given 'modern times' a character of their own, unlike that of the previous centuries. In his opinion the modern period was therefore more suitable for eighteenth-century study than the remoter world of the Greeks and Romans. He speaks of great changes in society at the end of the fifteenth century, yet he does this without reference to anything like a 'Renaissance'; and along with Hume and Robertson, he emphasises the importance of the modern period, having particularly in mind the kind of history which contributes to a political education. Concerning what he regards as the opening of the modern period, he writes:

I would not be understood to speak only of those great changes, that are wrought by a concurrence of extraordinary events: for instance the expulsion of one nation, the destruction of one government, and the establishment of another: but even of those that are wrought in the same governments and among the same people, slowly and almost imperceptibly, by the necessary effects of time, and flux condition of human affairs. When such changes as these happen in several states about the same time, and consequently affect other states by their vicinity, and by many different relations which they frequently bear to one another; then is one of those periods formed, at which the chain spoken of is so broken as to have little or no real or visible connexion with that which we see continue.... Such a period therefore is, in the true sense of the words, an epocha or an æra, a point of time at which you stop, or from which you reckon forward.... A new system of causes and effects, that subsists

[1] See p. 46, above.

in our time, and whereof our conduct is to be a part, arising at the last period, and all that passes in our time being dependent on what has passed since that period, or being immediately relative to it, we are extremely concerned to be well informed about those passages.[1]

The Göttingen professors in the closing decades of the eighteenth century were concerned with universal history, and when they fixed the boundaries of the great epochs they attempted to base them on a survey that should be not merely European but global. It was natural for them to take the great discoveries—and particularly the discovery of America in 1492 —as the dividing line between medieval and modern times. The same policy would not necessarily be appropriate for a form of general history that particularly envisaged the continent of Europe; and in any case the men of those days were more ready to agree that the fall of the Roman Empire signalised the end of the ancient world than to unite on the policy of beginning the modern era in the fifteenth century. Professor Heeren of Göttingen, in his book on the modern European states-system, says that there is no event which marks the end of the Middle Ages in the way that the fall of Rome marks their beginning. He suggests, however, that the invention of gunpowder and printing, and the discovery of America and of the new route to the East Indies, make the close of the fifteenth century a convenient dividing line.[2] It is clear that all the eighteenth-century propaganda in favour of the humanists and against the Middle Ages—all the talk about the 'Wiederherstellung der litterärischen Cultur' or the 'Wiederaufleben der Wissenschaften'—had not yet imprinted upon the mind of historians that strong general concept of 'the Renaissance' which left no room for doubt about the beginning of modern times.

[1] Bolingbroke, *Works* (1809), III, 440–1.
[2] Heeren, *Handbuch der Gesch. des europ. Staatensystems*, 6. Heeren, p. 17, divides modern European history into three periods: (1) 1492–1661, the era of politico-religious policy, when the 'balance of power' was being established; (2) 1661–1786, the mercantilist-military period, when the 'balance of power' was confirmed; and (3) from 1786, the revolutionary period, and the dissolution of the 'balance of power'.

The Renaissance

There had long been a view that the fifteenth century had seen a renaissance of the visual arts, but this would seem to have been understood in the way that one might talk of a renaissance of folk-dancing in the twentieth century. Similarly it had been customary to speak of a rebirth of antiquity or a renaissance of *belles lettres* or even of a 'reinstatement of the sciences' that was regarded as having taken place in the age of the humanists. The term 'Renaissance' was used in a further sense to designate a style in art and particularly in architecture—it enabled one to cover the interval between the age of Gothic and the mode of Louis XIV. It is curious to see how the Göttingen historians escape the use of 'the Renaissance' as a general term, and avoid the suggestion that the great changes of the humanist era can be englobed in a single comprehensive concept of this kind. And, though a wider notion of the Renaissance appears to be coming into currency in the 1830's and 1840's, even the writers who have an enthusiasm for the modern mind still take the revival of learning in their stride, without suggesting that the history of civilisation has come to a great dividing line. A number of historians described the progress of the twelfth and thirteenth centuries, and showed the two following centuries—particularly the fifteenth—as a period of comparative dullness or of political decline. Ranke, though he wrote so much on this early modern period, hardly seems to use the word 'Renaissance', though in 1854 he mentions it in aside as a term which other people employ. He has great enthusiasm for the art of the Renaissance; but he says in one place that the age was not glorious in literature, and in another place he takes the line that the subservience to the ancient world was not without unfortunate results. It checked originality in literature and science, he tells us, and put a brake on the discovery of new truths, and hindered the production of grand ideas.

In 1855 the French historian, Michelet, produced in his 'History of France' a volume entitled *Renaissance*. He, at any rate, clearly understands by the term something more than the reawakening of the arts and the revival of the study of classical antiquity. He envisages something like a new birth for mankind itself and finds in this epoch the genesis of the modern mentality. Even he, however, sees only decadence from the twelfth to the fifteenth centuries—that is to say, through much of the period of what we should call the Italian Renaissance. He fixes his attention on the decline of political liberty which was taking place, and he describes Italy in the fifteenth century as eating herself away, while everything was 'covered by a false peace, by tranquillity and art, and by a certain pedantesque spread of erudition'. Michelet regards the real story as beginning in 1494 when Charles VIII of France invaded Italy and 'from the resulting spark came the pillar of fire which we call the Renaissance'. It 'came out of nothing' in 1494, at a time when 'an incredible deathliness' covered the world, and it was essentially a sixteenth-century affair. Furthermore, it was not even an Italian movement. It is very significant that, for Michelet, France was 'the principal organ of the Renaissance'.[1]

In reality, then, it was the Swiss historian, Jakob Burckhardt,

[1] J. Michelet, 'Histoire de France', VII, *Renaissance* (Paris, 1855): p. ii, 'Le seizième siècle...va...de la découverte de la terre à celle du ciel. L'homme s'y est retrouvé lui-même'; p. xiii, 'L'âme...qui fit la commune du douzième siècle plus forte que Frédéric Barberousse...a...parfaitement disparu dans la bourgeoisie du quinzième'; p. lxvi, 'Dans ces ages de fer et de plomb de 1300 à 1500, la Providence prodigue les miracles, et c'est en vain. Elle secousse l'humanité et ne la réveille pas...La *Divine Comédie* passe et n'a nulle action'; p. lxvii, 'Pétrarque, bien plus populaire, échoue dans son pieux effort d'exhumer l'antiquité. Il attire les maîtres grecs, mais ils n'ont point d'écoliers'; p. lxxi, 'Qui restait pour entendre Dante? Personne...Tout fut anéanti....Il s'était fait plus que le vide, plus que le désert et la mort'; p. lxxix, 'Jamais il n'y eut un temps moins favorable à ces hautes tendances. L'Italie entrait dans une profonde prose, la matérialité violente des tyrans, des bandes mercénaires, la platitude bourgeoise des hommes de finance et d'argent'; pp. lxxxvi–lxxxvii, 'ce qui étonne le plus dans le mouvement du quinzième, c'est que l'œuvre qui fait l'admiration, la stupeur universelles, celle de Brunelleschi, a peu d'influence'; pp. xci–xcii, 'Personne ne fut plus admiré que Léonard da Vinci. Personne ne fut moins suivi....Il resta seul'; p. xciii, 'L'imprimerie...sert d'abord...à propager les ouvrages qui...ont le plus efficacement entravé la Renaissance'; p. 33, '[In Italy] Tout cela couvert d'une fausse paix, de calme et d'art, d'un certain mouvement pédantesque d'érudition'; p. 63, 'Une nation, l'organe principal de la Renaissance, se caractérise pour la première fois. Le monde apprend ici, par le bien, par le mal, ce que c'est que la France.' See also W. K. Ferguson, *The Renaissance in Historical Thought*, 173–8.

who in 1860 established the concept that has been current in our time—the idea of a Renaissance as a general movement, particularly associated with the fifteenth century, coming to its climax around the year 1500, and primarily taking place in Italy.[1] It was Burckhardt who conceived of the term Renaissance as descriptive of a whole historical period, as a great chapter in Italian history, and as a decisive stage or turning-point in the development of an entire civilisation, so that things which had hitherto been considered separate—the development of the modern state, for example—had now become enveloped by the concept too. And Burckhardt was one of the founders of what we call *Kulturgeschichte*, coming to this particular subject, indeed, with many of the prepossessions of the art-historian. Some years later, a famous book on *The Renaissance* was produced in England by Walter Pater, whom it would be proper to describe as an aesthete rather than an historian. The most considerable English history of the Italian Renaissance, which appeared in 1875–86, was written by John Addington Symonds, of whom it is perhaps not unfair to say that he was essentially a man of letters. He also produced a notable article on the subject in an edition of the *Encyclopaedia Britannica*; and this helped to give the concept its wide currency in England.

The zealous adoption by historians of this more comprehensive idea of the new birth produced, however, a certain confusion in the historical sciences. It carried the assumption that the Middle Ages had been dark and unresourceful until the clouds had finally been dispersed in the great awakening. But this view of the Middle Ages, which had been fostered by the work of the eighteenth-century *philosophes*, was beginning to be out-of-date in the very period when the new conception of the Renaissance was coming into currency. Students who

[1] In 'The Borgias and their latest Historian' (1871) in *Historical Essays and Studies*, 65–6, Acton writes: 'Burckhardt's *Cultur der Renaissance in Italien* is the most penetrating and subtle treatise on the history of civilisation that exists in literature; but its merit lies in the originality with which the author uses common books, rather than in actually new investigations.'

accustomed themselves to the idea of a fifteenth-century renaissance, had soon to face the fact that the previous ages had been by no means stagnant, in the way that had been assumed. They were compelled to carry the conception of a renaissance back to a remoter period; there appeared to be a renaissance behind the one men were looking for, and then another still further back—and so to the twelfth century, and even to the age of Charlemagne. And the mark of all these successive renaissances was the most medieval thing in the world—the further recovery or deeper appreciation of the thought of antiquity. If it were necessary to reconstruct our history in this manner, it might even be argued that the twelfth-century renaissance was a more signal and authentic example than that which took place in fifteenth-century Italy.

Lord Acton certainly shared the view which sees a great break in history at the close of the fifteenth century. He wrote:

I describe as Modern History that which begins four hundred years ago, which is marked off by an evident and intelligible line from the time immediately preceding, and displays in its course specific and distinctive characteristics of its own. The modern age did not proceed from the medieval by normal succession, with outward tokens of legitimate descent. Unheralded, it founded a new order of things, under a law of innovation, sapping the ancient reign of continuity.[1]

If the philologists and the aesthetes—as well as many other influences outside the field of technical history—had helped to establish the conception of 'the Renaissance', *tout court*, and to make the idea more radical and comprehensive than before, it is possible that the excessive significance of books for the academic historian had something to do with the establishment of a further tradition, which consecrated the eighteenth century as 'the Age of Reason'. Acton, who was himself greatly influenced by literature, was further affected—like

[1] 'The Study of History', *Lectures on Modern History*, 3.

many other historians—by the view that the French 'philo-sophic' writers had had great political importance, especially in the French Revolution. And many students may have been puzzled by the existence of another epoch which apparently claims to have seen the birth of rationalism and the genesis of the modern mentality. A deeper analysis has shown, however, that neither 'the Renaissance' nor the 'Age of Reason' enables us to put our fingers on the strategic factor behind the development of the world that we today can call 'modern'. And some things have been read backwards into the Italy of 1500, or have been transferred to the eighteenth century, which really find their roots in the Scientific Revolution of the seventeenth century. It was this, rather than the 'revival of learning' or the *philosophe* movement which brought to our civilisation something that had been unknown to Greece or Rome or India or China. On the one hand it accompanied, and on the other hand it heralded, profound changes in society and in the life of man on the earth. It would appear that from at least as early as 1400 to at least as late as 1660 there is a greater continuity in the texture of history and in the character of human thought than the nineteenth century was ready to realise. In the twentieth century it has been argued that the division of general history into ancient, medieval and modern is less adequate than the Four-Monarchy system had been at an earlier stage in the story.[1] Since so much of the Middle Ages lasted till 1660 and so many of the roots of the modern world go back behind 'the Renaissance', it might be better to say that between the fourteenth and the seventeenth centuries there shall be a new historical epoch—the post-medieval, or the pre-modern, or the early modern, or (since the ancient thought still retained its presidency) perhaps even the antique-modern. In this way we should find ourselves better able to do justice to the profounder processes of history, and we should cut deeper into the roots of the modern world than the student

[1] H. Spangenberg, 'Die Perioden der Weltgeschichte', *Historische Zeitschrift*, cxxvii (1923), 11.

of the humanists and the *philosophes* is able to do. Also we should give a more adequate place in the scheme to the Scientific Revolution as an event that was to be momentous not only for Europe—not only in the development of 'the Age of Reason' itself—but for the history of the entire globe. Perhaps it is not an accident that some of the most distinguished historians of science have joined in the criticism of the concept of 'the Renaissance', seeing the fifteenth century as rather an interval of rest between two scientific revivals, the one taking place before A.D. 1400, while the other made its appearance only some time after 1500.

The division of history into periods would hardly be important as an issue if we were not liable to become the slaves of our system, liable to forget how much of convention has entered into the dating of the epochs and the fixing of the labels. When a concept like that of the Renaissance is imposed upon the course of history it is capable of having serious consequences for the student, for the simple reason that human beings are prone to absent-mindedness. The framework that we give to the events of the past often becomes a harder form of knowledge than anything else; so that, for many people, the Renaissance becomes a 'thing' as firm as a battle or a bench, and even stands in history as the cause of causes. In these circumstances it is possible to imagine that we have explained something when we have said that it is due to the Renaissance. The history of historiography serves at least to make our concepts fluid again.

5. THE IDEA OF PROVIDENCE

Even the historian who says that he will keep himself tied to the concrete evidence can hardly do his work without sympathetic imagination. Apart from this, we must know where the concrete evidence fails; and we have only to think of the peasant, who throughout the centuries bears so much of the world's burden, to realise what gaps there are in our knowledge of the way men have thought and felt, and the way they have accepted their destiny. We have only to consider our own internal life to realise how little of the inside of men ever reaches the outside world, and how little the world can make of what it sees. The reader of technical history learns too little from it of the hopes and fears of the majority of men, too little of their joy in nature or art, their falling in love, their family affection, their spiritual questings, and their ultimate vision of things. Amid the tangles of a diplomatic story it is a rare thing if a Sir Edward Grey gives a hint that a Foreign Secretary may be watching the office-clock for the moment when he can go out to see the birds. We must wonder whether technical history can claim to give us the mirror of life any more than modern physics provides us with an actual picture of the universe.

The point becomes significant when it is so much of the spiritual life of man which, almost by the rules of the game, seems to be left to evaporate—for this is just the thing which so often must escape the technical historian's net. The history of Christianity itself easily turns into a study of institutions or of theological scholarship, of ecclesiastical statecraft or popular agitation, of professional worries here and confessional rivalries there. The history of the Reformation seems to twist in our hands, and we find ourselves studying its political implications, its educational results, and its social and economic effects. There is a sense in which the work of Acton as well as that of Ranke seems to fail us here, and disappoints us with its dryness. It is only to a certain degree that even the biographer is able to meet the case; but it is possible that biography is a necessary adjunct—indeed a necessary corrective—to technical history.

Acton said that Newman saw God working only upon the inner life of man—working therefore in biography but not in history. He himself had once believed that Providence was shown by the way in which good could come out of evil; but he passed over to the view that Providence was progress; and from this time he appears to have believed that, unless there was progress, there could be no God in history.[1] Ranke claimed that his own desire to study the past had been stimulated by a religious preoccupation. When he was charged with a lack of interest in philosophy and religion, he answered that 'it was this and this alone, which drove me to historical research'. He talked of Providence more than the technical historian would usually do at the present day; but it might be said of him that he removes Providence to the periphery of the story, ascribing to it the final combinations of events at a point where his own more mundane analysis fails. By this means, however, he is at least able to maintain the suggestion that all the activities of men are carried on next-door to a mystery. On a different type of occasion he will say, furthermore, that even in the midst of confusion there seems sometimes to exist an

---

[1] Roman Diary, C.U.L. Add. 5751, 337: 'Historians have not to point out everywhere the hand of Providence, but to find out all the natural causes of things. Enough will always remain that cannot be so explained, but we have only to indicate that such is the case, not to show it on every occasion.' This passage is transcribed into Acton's notes in Add. 4906, and is there recorded as the opinion of Döllinger. Elsewhere in Add. 4907, 273 Acton writes: 'Providence not shown by success—Examples—But by continuous extraction of good from evil.' Cf. Add. 4906: 'Providence has a large part in the things that have lasted.' Add. 5626, f. 11b: 'God overrules man in the long run. What lasts expresses God's will. Permanence is divine.' Add. 5011, 208, 24 January 1893: 'Providence means Progress...Liberty supposes progress.' Add. 5641, 55b: 'My theory is that divine gov[ern-men]t is not justified without progress. There is no *raison d'être* for the world.' Add. 4987, 55: 'Not to believe in Progress is to question the divine government.' In e.g. Add. 4987 Acton repeatedly illustrates the contrast between his own views and those of Newman, who 'discovered no progress', and saw 'no evidence of divine government in the course of things'. He adds, p. 44: 'Note that Newman denies the government of the world. Providence does not manifest itself in history.' Therefore, for Newman, 'history, apart from biography, is a world without a God'. Cf. the review of R. K. Philip, *A History of Progress in Great Britain*, Part I (London, 1858) in *The Rambler*, July 1858, pp. 63–5, in which the younger Acton attacks the current idea of progress. 'It is in reality the notion of perpetual progress which lies at the bottom of this style of historical writing. It comes from admiration of the present, not the past. The writer who brought it into vogue was Macaulay....The partisans of the theory of indefinite progress forfeit all the advantage which is to be got from the contemplation of those points on which former ages were superior to our own. Men of this school are never put to shame by the greatness of old. They generally hold it cheap....Each event and period of history must be viewed in its own native light. It is the business of historians everywhere to furnish us with this light, without which each object is distorted and discoloured. We must distrust our knowledge of every period which appears to us barbarous. For the same reason that other nations were barbarians in the eyes of the Greeks, other ages seem barbarous to us. We are unable and care not, to understand and sympathise with them. The true view of history is the reverse of this narrowness.'

occult force. It may be suspected that some of the further things which had been perhaps a mystique to Ranke—like the rise of nationality—were to prove susceptible of closer historical analysis with the further passage of time. Some have imagined that he merely made a polite but insincere and implausible bow to the deity; but it might be suggested that on this, as on other similar points, the critics of Ranke would do well to examine some of the more liberal aspects of the Protestantism of his time. The same critics would hardly be more kind to the man who arbitrarily introduces God into specific moments of history or who at every point in the story admits no explanation beyond the will of heaven. This latter attitude would seem to rule out the possibility of that 'historical thinking' which, to Ranke as well as to Acton, was so important.

The truth is that technical history is a limited and mundane realm of description and explanation, in which local and concrete things are achieved by a disciplined use of tangible evidence. I should not regard a thing as 'historically' established unless the proof were valid for the Catholic as well as the Protestant, for the Liberal as well as the Marxist. When Acton imputed to Ranke the design of laying out a demonstrable story, the facts of which were to be valid for men of all religions and parties, he may have been defining an impossible ideal, but he was defining what is really meant by technical history. Something of the same is bound to be true of the natural scientist, who must not be presumed to be an atheist merely because he keeps the rules of the game and leaves God out of the argument. It may not be possible for any historian to attain the ideal, but the cogency of a piece of history or an historical argument depends on the degree to which the ideal has been approached. When the events have been laid out by the technical historian, they can be taken over by the Catholic or Protestant or atheist—they are equally available for Whig or Tory. Each of these can add his judgements and make his evaluations; and they can at least begin by having some common ground for the great debate that still lies open to them.

Those who bring their religion to the interpretation of the story are naturally giving a new dimension to events; but they will not be less anxious than anybody else to know what can be historically established.

In other words, whenever the historical or the scientific techniques are in question, there is more than one level at which human beings can do their thinking. I may take any historical event—the fall of Rome for example—and I may deal with it as one who is living while it happens, ascribing it to men's sins and mistakes, and vindicating human responsibility and free will. If I am disposed to judge or if I am sure that in the same position I should not have been guilty of the same delinquencies, it is open to me to condemn. At this level of thought I am adopting the view that human beings make their own history. Secondly, however, I may say that there were remoter historical reasons for the fall of Rome, and I may show how for a long period the threads had been becoming desperately entangled. And here I should be resorting to historical explanation—to the study of that necessity which conditions, though it does not determine, human action. Here I am making allowance for that region of history which can conceivably be reduced to law, and I am concentrating my attention upon the kind of history-making which goes on over men's heads. Thirdly, I may say that the fall of Rome was the judgement of God on a civilisation; perhaps also it was the best thing which the wills of men allowed Providence to achieve at that moment; it was even the way to a better world, a harder and longer way because men themselves had closed up the more easy one. And here is a Providence which does not merely act (as Ranke's Providence seems to act) at marginal points or by remote control, but which touches all the details and the intimacies of life, embracing even the other things that have been mentioned, since the world of free will and the world of law both lie within it. The fact that we subject the work of Beethoven to a kind of mechanical analysis and teach composition by rules does not mean that the over-all understanding of the music depends on a knowledge of the rules—the composer does not create his music in the way that students analyse it after it has been written. And we, too, need not be the slaves of our analytical methods—we may still praise God, and not merely do honour to scientific laws, at the coming of spring; and we may thank Providence rather than Chance for those 'conjunctures' which seem to matter so much both in life and in history.

And if it is argued that it is difficult for men to do their thinking at different levels in such a manner as this, I can only reply that since the world came to its adult stage and entered the scientific era, the necessity must be accepted as the consequence of growing-up. Since man decided to make a great drive with certain techniques that were adopted for limited purposes, he must either become the slave of those techniques, or he must remember how he first came to follow them—remember that he is still able to rise above them. Having determined to restrict himself to certain kinds of tangible data, the technical historian can only expect to produce limited results that belong to a mundane and pragmatic realm. Greater degrees of certainty, more practicable forms of communicability and a wider range of unanimity can be achieved when the enquirer performs this act of self-limitation—when he asks what is the pressure of steam that a given task will require in a given engine, or enquires what was the effect of the influx of American silver on the French wars of religion in the sixteenth century. But these are not the really momentous questions upon which all human beings have to make their decision; and the technical student in any branch of science or learning is arguing in a circle if he thinks that his researches have in fact eliminated from life the things which for technical reasons he had eliminated in advance from his consideration. In reality, the poet, the prophet, the novelist and the playwright command sublimer realms than those of technical history because they reconstitute life in its wholeness. The history of historiography may help us to keep the technical historian in his place.

V

THE RECONSTRUCTION OF AN HISTORICAL EPISODE: THE HISTORY OF THE ENQUIRY INTO THE ORIGINS OF THE SEVEN YEARS WAR

For the purpose of illustrating what lies behind a piece of historical narrative—also for the purpose of exposing some of the pitfalls that beset the student and reader of history—I propose to take a definite historical episode and show how the enquiry developed, how the facts were established and how the story came to be assembled.

Desiring a convenient specimen—one which without being microscopic can be held in the palm of the hand, one also which provides us with proper names that are familiar—but possessing at the same time little to choose from, I select the series of events which immediately led to the outbreak of the Seven Years War.

The general chart of the European situation in the period concerned is supplied by three of those famous events which every schoolboy knows, and which were publicly reported and sufficiently authenticated at the time. First, in January 1756, George II of England concluded with Frederick the Great of Prussia the Convention of Westminster, guaranteeing the neutrality of Germany in an Anglo-French colonial conflict which was on the point of breaking out. Secondly, in May 1756, Maria Theresa, the Habsburg Empress-Queen, who resented Frederick's seizure of her province of Silesia, induced the French to make their sensational reversal of alliances. She secured an agreement which bound the French King, Louis XV, not to infringe the neutrality of the Austrian Netherlands in the course of his conflict with England. She herself, however, was committed to intervening in the war only if some other power should begin hostilities in Europe. Thirdly, though the treaties which have been mentioned were designed to keep the Franco-British conflict from spreading to Germany and the Low Countries so that the peace of the continent seemed all the more assured by the dispositions that had been made, Frederick the Great poured his troops into Saxony at the end of August on the ground that he had discovered an anti-Prussian conspiracy which struck at the very existence of his monarchy.

It is the accusation made by Frederick at this moment which concerns us. A concrete question was presented for historical detective-work: did any serious conspiracy exist and was Prussia provoked by a genuine threat? The confirmation of the charge made by Frederick would not necessarily justify the precise course of conduct to which he resorted in the summer of 1756. It may be of some interest to make a rapid survey of the progress of historical investigation into the validity of Frederick's claim.

I. THE PRE-COPERNICAN STAGE

The first documentary researches into the problem were carried out on the instructions of Frederick the Great himself in September 1756, immediately after Saxony had been over-run. The Dresden archives were broken into and certain documents—particularly from the correspondence with Vienna and St Petersburg—were taken away for use in a Prussian manifesto, which was called a *Mémoire Raisonné*. The documents were disappointing, however, for, in spite of some suppressions and a little doctoring by the Prussian editor, Hertzberg, they failed to justify the charge that Saxony herself had been directly implicated in any recent conspiracy against the court of Berlin.[1]

[1] Hertzberg, *Recueil des déductions, manifestes, déclarations, traités, etc., rédigés et publiés pour la cour de Prusse*, I, 2nd ed. (Berlin, 1790), 1–64. On its treatment of Saxony, see A. R. Ropes, 'Frederick the Great's Invasion of Saxony and the Prussian "Mémoire Raisonné", 1756', *Transactions of the Royal Historical Society* (N.S.), v, 157–75.

Also, they failed to support a further allegation of Frederick's, that Austria and Russia had actually signed a treaty of offensive alliance.

In fact, so far as these two points were concerned, Frederick was not only wrong but he set future historiography on the wrong track for a considerable period. We now know that he was falling into a natural error and reading the events of 1756 as though they merely continued former trends and tendencies. Piecing mere fragments of evidence together, he interpreted documents on the assumption that the various states were still maintaining the policy and general demeanour of the last ten years. In other words, he did not make allowance for the occurrence of a new thing, a surprising turn in events which should change everybody's bearings. Frederick had been disturbed by news which had come to him through leakages from the Dresden archives; but we now know that when he took his drastic decisions in the summer of 1756 he was provoked by other reports than these—other reports which were less appropriate for publication at the time. It is now clear that Saxony had not been an active partner in the conspiracy against Prussia; and, this being the case, any documents which he captured in Dresden were bound to be inadequate for the exposure of the enemy plan. Papers in the Dresden archives have revealed the fact that the chief culprits, Austria and Russia, had determined long ago not even to inform the Saxon elector of the course of their negotiations, lest the knowledge prove too dangerous for him and lay him open to a Prussian attack. Indeed the court of Vienna had long been aware that Frederick the Great was tapping the correspondence of Saxony with both Austria and Russia.[1]

Apart from the unjust charges against the court of Dresden, however, Frederick's *Mémoire Raisonné* can now be seen to be remarkable amongst war-manifestos for its extraordinary and even deliberate understatement of the Prussian case. The truth

[1] G. A. H. Stenzel, *Geschichte des preussischen Staats*, IV (Hamburg, 1851), 398 and 401, n. 3.

was that in the summer of 1756 Frederick began hostilities only against Saxony and Austria—only where attack would be useful to him—and not against Russia, though we now know that Russia was the chief culprit and the chief danger. And, in the August, as in the earlier months of the same year, he was hoaxing himself with the delusion that the British Government might succeed in keeping the Russians neutral. When he was preparing his war-manifesto, therefore, he ordered his publicists to avoid giving unnecessary offence to the court of St Petersburg; though we now know that most of the evidence which he had collected before the outbreak of war had concerned Russia, and that when he had begun to make military movements it was the Russian preparations that had given him alarm. In fact his own propagandists had to inform him even then that they could not omit all mention of Russia in their manifesto, since the name of Russia was entangled with all the evidence they found.[1] Frederick, however, even went so far as to refrain from publishing in his *Mémoire Raisonné* the bulk of what in fact was the most damaging of all the documents captured in Dresden—one which would have been clear enough in its implications even for him if his eyes had not been focused on the wrong things. To those who know the story this particular document fits into place like a piece in a jig-saw puzzle; but Frederick printed it only in the following year, in a further manifesto, after Russia had actually come into the war.[2] The truth is that Frederick never did learn the seriousness of the danger he had been in during the spring of 1756 or the magnitude of the conspiracy against him, so that he still understates the case even in his memoirs; and to a certain degree it is his gullibility throughout the story that requires to be explained. His narrative dominated the treatment of the whole theme for over a century—up to and including the work of Thomas Carlyle. Indeed he produced something like a

[1] *Politische Correspondenz Friedrich's des Grossen*, XIII, 508–9.
[2] Hertzberg, *Recueil...*I, 121–3, Prasse to Brühl, 10 May 1756. In this *Réfutation* of 1757 there is also a much fuller publication, pp. 251–5, of letters from Flemming (in Vienna) to Brühl, involving Russia, than in the *Mémoire Raisonné*.

permanent deflection of the compass, and the results are visible in the vast majority of historical writings that have been produced on this subject down to the present day. Hertzberg, who drew up the *Mémoire Raisonné* when he was thirty-one years of age, himself never learned the truth, and, when he was an old man, questioned the policy of Frederick in 1756 on grounds which show that he still lacked the most remarkable part of the evidence.[1]

In the period down to the 1860's we may tear the successive narratives and compilations to pieces; but, in spite of certain incidental information that had been brought to light, we find that for the fundamental skeleton of story historians still went on juggling with the documents which Frederick the Great had published; supplemented by one or two miscellaneous items—a few rather incriminating Austrian papers for example —that were printed in a later collection in 1841.[2] It was true that the papers of several diplomats who were active in 1756 were now printed or became available—those of the French minister in Berlin on the eve of the Seven Years War, for example, the French minister in Vienna, etc.—but the effect of these was to confuse the issue further, for the particular diplomats in question knew the real secrets neither of their own government nor of the court at which they resided; and clearly if there was a dark conspiracy against Prussia it would lie deep at the most secret level of the secret diplomacy of the time. These particular diplomats either left the impression that nothing important or sinister was taking place at this period; or they made guesses that were at cross-purposes with the real situation. Sometimes they reported that things were quiet when we know now that the most sensational transactions were being conducted in their immediate neighbourhood.

Further than this, some selections from British diplomatic documents were appearing in print in the earlier half of the

[1] Hertzberg, *Œuvres politiques* (Berlin and Paris, 1795), I, 353–5. See also Stenzel, op. cit. IV, 401, n. 2.

[2] [Graf von der Schulenberg], *Einige neue Actenstücke über die Veranlassung des siebenjährigen Krieges* (Leipzig, 1841).

nineteenth century, and these included material relating to the period and the governments with which we are concerned. In 1836, for example, Friedrich von Raumer published in German a work almost entirely composed of long extracts from the correspondence of our representatives in Berlin, St Petersburg, Vienna and Dresden—all these strung together with hardly any commentary—exactly the kind of book that would be used as a quarry by later writers.[1] All the British diplomatic documents of this period could have been published, however —and all our secrets revealed—and still the historian, far from learning the truth about the conspiracy, would have been led even further astray. Owing to the colonial conflict we had no representative in Paris at this time. Our minister in Vienna was kept in the dark while our old associate, Maria Theresa, negotiated the Diplomatic Revolution with our arch-enemy, France. All this was nothing compared with the piece of melodrama which was being enacted at St Petersburg for the precise purpose of deceiving England; for in the crucial months of spring 1756 we conducted our whole diplomacy under the influence of a hoax perpetrated by an ally who had signed a treaty with us only a few months before. In the Convention of Westminster we had joined with Prussia to guarantee the neutrality of Germany; and it was necessary for the Russians to deceive us as long as possible if they were meaning to flout this by attacking Prussia. Above all, through the false assurances which the British consequently gave to Berlin, Russia was able to secure the further object of hoaxing Frederick the Great. It was in this connection that Frederick proved so gullible; though we added to the deception by throwing in a few confident mis-statements of our own, which confirmed his view that Britain could count on the court of St Petersburg. It was not from the British diplomatic documents in 1756, therefore, that the anti-Prussian conspiracy could ever be reconstructed and the discovery be made of the way in which

[1] F. L. G. von Raumer, *Beiträge zur neueren Geschichte aus dem Britischen Museum und Reichsarchive*, 5 vols. (Leipzig, 1836–9).

the British government had been hoaxed. And perhaps this helps to explain why the British contribution to the elucidation of this particular problem has been of comparatively little importance. Furthermore, it needs an intimate knowledge of the period and quite a refined technical apparatus to interpret correctly a correspondence written under such complicated limiting conditions as that between London and St Petersburg in 1756. It was not an intelligible story that was produced when a straight digest was made of the British correspondence, or when clippings were simply cut out of it and inserted in a patchy way into the usual story.

Even in the Paris archives, which were more accessible in the time of Louis Philippe than later under Napoleon III, it was possible to examine certain diplomatic papers, but not those which related to the main negotiations of 1756. And supposing the historian were not allowed to see the papers in which the essential business was transacted—supposing he found access only to more incidental papers so that he had to try to piece out his narrative by detective-work on the revelations of men who knew nothing more than the reports that were current in the diplomatic world—then there was something to be said for an unusual study published in 1842 by a German historian called Stuhr, who had been permitted to work in Paris on the papers of the French minister at the Hague—a well-informed man in a well-informed city. The truth was that the Hague was one of those places (possibly like Lisbon in the last war if some stories are correct) which become exchanges for diplomatic news—the kind of place that seethes with the latest revelations. This kind of indirect evidence needed scientific sifting, and taken by itself it could hardly establish the central story and clinch the case. But it did bring support to the idea of an anti-Prussian conspiracy—a letter from a French diplomat in Italy who claimed to have had a 'tip' (almost, but not quite, straight from the horse's mouth), about a plan to wipe Prussia off the map; and a communication from Warsaw, where, from the couriers running hither and thither, it could safely be inferred that at any rate something unusual was afoot between Vienna and St Petersburg in the spring. It would appear that some later writers would have been saved from mistakes if this interesting study had been more widely known.[1]

Additional revelations in the 1860's brought historians further away from the truth than ever. It was useful for the cause of scientific history in nineteenth-century Germany that the country was so extensive and that regionalism had such influence—somewhere there would be a writer to challenge the Prussian or the national interpretation of events, and the intensity of conflict kept the students on their toes. The most scholarly attempts to undermine Frederick the Great's version of the origin of the Seven Years War were made in Germany itself at various periods. In the 1860's two men who hated Prussia broke with the narrative of Frederick's *Mémoire Raisonné* altogether, but, lacking any firm alternative basis, they ran into extravagances. Both writers mixed politics with their history, being deeply affected by the issues of 1866, the contest between Austria and Germany. One of them, Onno Klopp, who was in the Hanoverian service and wrote in 1860, ignored much of the available evidence and tried to solve the problem by doing a kind of detective-work on the general published writings of Frederick the Great. The other man, Count Vitzthum von Eckstädt, produced a similar attack on Frederick in 1866, and he, like Klopp, argued that there was no plot against Prussia, and that Maria Theresa in the Diplomatic Revolution—in the whole effort to win the alliance of France—had been working only for European peace. It was more easy for this latter writer to make out his case in that he confined his attention almost exclusively to the dispatches of the Saxon minister in Paris—a man who reported no sensa-

[1] P. F. Stuhr, *Forschungen und Erläuterungen über Hauptpunkte der Geschichte des siebenjährigen Krieges*, nach archivalischen Quellen (Hamburg, 1842), ch. II, e.g. pp. 42 and 48–9. On pp. 2 and 30 Stuhr discusses the limited availability of the French archives; while A. Schäfer, *Historische Zeitschrift*, xv (1866), 116, refers to the greater restrictions under Napoleon III.

tions for the simple reason that he was not admitted to the secret of what was going on even at the court to which he was attached. In any case this was the last occasion on which that particular view was possible for an historian; for in the following year, 1867, even Klopp, in a second edition of his work, corrected some of the more extravagant assertions that he had made previously; and, paradoxically enough, it was he who, after a visit to the Viennese archives, established one hard and important and relevant fact—namely, that France and Austria, after concluding their neutrality-convention and their defensive alliance on 1 May 1756, had proceeded with a secret negotiation for an offensive alliance, that is to say, were at least discussing an attack on Prussia.[1]

The attempts of Klopp and Vitzthum von Eckstädt to discredit the story of the anti-Prussian conspiracy were met in the year 1867 by the important work of Dietrich Schäfer, who was allowed to use the Prussian archives. The papers available to him confirmed the fact that Frederick the Great had received disquieting reports and had seemed to take genuine alarm; though the diplomatic documents of the Prussian government of course could not be authoritative for the conduct of Austria or Russia or France. This author, Schäfer, unlike many of his predecessors, was not satisfied to rewrite the story on the basis of the particular set of documents he had been allowed to open up. He collated these with the results of the enquiries made in the previous hundred years, and codified what had hitherto been achieved, putting the various dis-

[1] Onno Klopp, *Der König Friedrich II. von Preussen und die deutsche Nation* (Schaffhausen, 1860). For the resulting controversy with Ludwig Häusser, see Häusser's *Zur Beurtheilung Friedrichs den Grossen* (1862). Cf. O. Klopp, *Der König Friedrich und seine Politik* (Schaffhausen, 1867). [C.-F. Graf Vitzthum von Eckstädt], *Die Geheimnisse des sächsischen Cabinets* (Stuttgart, 1866). In *The Chronicle*, 5 October 1867, 668–9, [reprinted in Lord Acton, *Essays on Church and State* (ed. by D. Woodruff, 413–14)], Acton does honour to the way in which Klopp in general resisted Prussian policy, opposed the Prussian historical school and fought against the uncritical worship of Frederick the Great. 'As the impulse to expand in Germany has increased' he writes, 'the immorality of the means has become more flagrant....[Herr Klopp] is not prepared to say that [the machinery of the Prussian state] will break down under its own irremediable defects before it has accomplished the suppression of an independent Germany.'

coveries together. For instance, he found in a Belgian journal some documents reproduced from the Brussels archives, and he was able to quote a curious passage from a letter written by the Austrian Chancellor, Kaunitz, in May 1756—a passage which began: 'We have crossed the Rubicon', and which seemed to make it clear that Austria had definitely decided on war.[1] Schäfer, therefore, sums up what might be called the pre-Copernican period in the study of our problem.

2. THE OPENING OF THE ARCHIVES

A new epoch opened in 1870 when the director of the archives in Vienna, Alfred Ritter von Arneth, reached the period of the Diplomatic Revolution in volume IV of his classic life of Maria Theresa. Now at last one could see the Austrian side of the story, which indeed began to receive a more searching examination in 1871 in the work of another Austrian historian, Adolf Beer. From this date the historical reconstruction of the theme begins to be of a different order; for governments now surrender the key of the last secret drawer, and we see how their diplomacy was hammered out—we see under what persuasions or with what motives they adopted a given course of action. In 1871, again, there appeared a small but important work by Ranke on the origins of the Seven Years War; and Ranke had fuller opportunities than any man before him for using the materials in the Prussian archives on this subject.

We move away now from the romanticism of some of the earlier legends, according to which the policy of France and Russia had been determined by the anger of Mme de Pompadour and the Tsarina—both of them offended by the taunts of Frederick the Great. We move away also from some of Frederick's original mistakes—particularly the notion that the policy of states which answered to a given formula in one year, could be interpreted by reference to that formula in another year. It was now made clear that from the middle of 1755 the

[1] A. D. Schäfer, *Geschichte des siebenjährigen Krieges* (Berlin, 1867–74), I, 158.

court of Vienna, in view of the particular situation which was developing, sought to secure the help or connivance of France in a plot for the partitioning of Prussia. Henceforward it was impossible for any serious historian to question the existence of a conspiracy to make war on the Prussian king sooner or later.

Unfortunately, attention was concentrated on the problem of Austro-French relations, partly because France occupied so central a position in the diplomacy of the eighteenth century, and partly because the French 'reversal of alliances' had seemed to present the most sensational feature in the story. And all persons who today, when they think of the Seven Years War, immediately associate its origin with the so-called 'Diplomatic Revolution' between France and Austria are witnesses to the fact that this misunderstanding still persists. Though there was some difference of opinion in regard to the matter in the latter half of the 1890's, it was not possible to establish that the defensive alliance between Austria and France would ever have turned into a definitely offensive one. Certainly, it had not done so at the moment when Frederick the Great made his attack on Saxony.[1]

The twelve years from 1884 to 1896 represent the climax of historical enquiry into this problem—the German, or perhaps rather the Prussian, period in the historiography of the origins of the Seven Years War. The enterprise received a certain stimulus from the release of new material, such as the imposing publication of the *Political Correspondence of Frederick the Great*, the relevant volumes of which appeared at the opening of this period. Henceforward the Prussian confidential papers were available in great masses and in their continuity, while there was little corresponding material in print in France or England and many of the Austrian documents were available

---

[1] In France the duc de Broglie, *L'Alliance autrichienne* (Paris, 1895) tended to be anti-Prussian and doubted the offensive character of the Austro-French negotiations, while R. Waddington, *Louis XV et le Renversement des Alliances* (Paris, 1896), e.g. pp. 475–6, made the case that after the conclusion of the defensive alliance in May 1756 France was going forward to an offensive alliance. He showed that the memoirs of Cardinal Bernis, and his denial of a secret offensive intention, were not to be trusted.

for general use only in the excerpts that had been printed by Arneth. A large number of important German historians took part in this new stage of the enquiry—J. G. Droysen, Max Duncker, Reinhold Koser, Albert Naudé, Hans Delbrück, for example. The closest discussions of the subject, which are sometimes very meticulous indeed, seem to come in what sometimes are long periodical articles rather than books; and in the books of the time there was often an excessive glorification of Frederick the Great, as certain Germans themselves complained. At the same time, the learned articles present us with what we must regard as a high spot in modern German historical science, and, on our particular subject, everything that has been written since seems to represent a decline in scholarship. Some of our twentieth-century writing would have been better if it had even shown a knowledge of the work of nearly sixty years ago.

One feature of this stage in the research into the origins of the Seven Years War is the development during the years 1894–6 of the only large-scale controversy on the subject which ever seriously disturbed the learned world. It was provoked by a small book, the work of Max Lehmann, who agreed that there had been a conspiracy against Frederick, but tended to make light of it, while asserting that Frederick used it as an excuse for an aggressive policy of his own. According to Lehmann, Frederick had begun his actual war-preparations before the Austrians did, and in his *Political Testament* of 1752, as well as in writings at other periods, had stressed the importance of acquiring Saxony and West Prussia. In other words, an offensive movement in Vienna met an offensive movement in Berlin; and Frederick could not have been desperately afraid in August 1756, for he obviously thought it worth his while to go to war.[1]

---

[1] Max Lehmann, *Friedrich der Grosse und der Ursprung des siebenjährigen Krieges* (Leipzig, 1894). Cf. M. Lehmann, *Mittheilungen des Instituts für oesterreichische Geschichtsforschung*, XVI (1895), 480–91. Many writers noted the extraordinary unanimity which had prevailed for some time on the subject of the origins of the Seven Years War, until Lehmann's book appeared.

The Reconstruction of an Historical Episode

The controversy which resulted from this book was the more resounding in that Max Lehmann had made bitter attacks upon the work of other scholars, particularly Albert Naudé.[1] Not only did a host of German historians reply to his charges,[2] but—as was noted at the time—the closest Austrian and French students of this question brought evidence in favour of Frederick the Great, whose severest accuser was a German. These scholars so far made out their case that it would be difficult to deny today Frederick's general anxiety for peace during the year 1756, and impossible to deny that when he began his war-preparations he was acting under the provocation of a threat which was immediate and highly dangerous. Lehmann had produced some new evidence from the Viennese archives, but he had floundered in the great mass of material there; and perhaps the controversy would never have arisen if the Austrian documents had been published as fully as the Prussian ones. His own work had been stimulated by some hints and references in Ranke—including an allusion to the *Political Testament* of 1752—but it seems clear that he went too far in extending the implications of these.[3] And whereas Ranke had admitted that Frederick might have made territorial demands if he had been the victor in the war which his enemies had provoked, Lehmann had gone further than this and had insisted that Frederick had used the conduct of Austria as an excuse for a policy of sheer self-aggrandisement. Lehmann, furthermore, had carefully selected the documents

[1] A number of reviewers commented on Lehmann's personal animosity. On this see A. Naudé, *Deutsche Litteraturzeitung*, 1894, no. 46, cols. 1467–8. Concerning Naudé's death at the age of 38, partly the result of the strain of this controversy, see *Forschungen zur brandenburgischen und preussischen Geschichte*, IX, ii, pp. v ff. and xiii ff.

[2] Important contributors to the controversy were R. Koser, *Historische Zeitschrift*, LXXIV and LXXVII; A. Naudé, *Forschungen zur brandenburgischen und preussischen Geschichte*, VIII and IX; P. Bailleu, *Deutsche Rundschau*, Feb. 1895; E. Berner, *Mittheilungen aus der historischen Litteratur*, XXIII; W. Wiegand, *Deutsche Litteraturzeitung*, 1894, no. 51 and 1896, no. 3. The works of Arneth in Austria and Waddington in France were cited against Lehmann. For comments in foreign periodicals see M. Philippson, *Revue historique*, LX 126 f., and A. Beer in *Mittheilungen des Instituts für oesterreichische Geschichtsforschung*, XVII, 109.

[3] Ranke, *Der Ursprung des siebenjährigen Krieges* (1871), 245. Cf. M. Lehmann, *Historische Zeitschrift*, LXI (1888), 288–91.

that suited his case—occasionally omitting all reference to a paper that told the other way, though it lay in a packet that he was known to have examined. From some of the dispatches which he had quoted he had omitted passages and replaced them by dots, and sometimes it turned out that these gave an entirely different colour to the narrative. The enemies of Lehmann, who studied microscopically the day-to-day story in the relevant months of 1756, were able to justify that method against a man who, once he was seized with an hypothesis, ranged at random over Frederick's whole career to select the confirmatory pieces of evidence. Even some students who were convinced by Lehmann's argument that the Prussian war-preparations had preceded the Austrian ones, declared themselves converted again when Naudé massed the evidence on the other side. One or two historians supported Lehmann in various parts of his case, but Hans Delbrück, his main ally, differed from him in many respects—especially in his repeated assertion that Frederick the Great would have been unworthy of his place in German tradition if he had not taken the opportunity to pursue an aggressive policy. In the opinion of Delbrück, indeed, the conduct of the court of Vienna clearly justified Frederick even in such a policy.[1] For the rest, the other principal supporter of Lehmann was Onno Klopp, whom we have already met.

If we today read the literature of the 1890's on this subject a curious fact emerges. We can now see that the historians—almost unconsciously, almost as though they failed to realise what they were doing—were turning the whole face of the study in a different direction. They hardly knew what was happening, for their minds were still intent on Austro-Prussian and Austro-French relations; but we can now see that, from the vast ocean of detail which they managed to assemble, the facts which point in the direction of Russia are

---

[1] H. Delbrück, *Preussische Jahrbücher*, LXXIX, especially pp. 254–8. This and two further contributions by Delbrück, ibid. LXXXIV and LXXXVI, are conflated into a single paper in *Erinnerungen, Aufsätze und Reden*, 2nd ed. (1902), 240–69.

becoming more insistent. From the moment when Ranke began to make use of them, the Prussian papers revealed Russia as a more decisive factor in the story, though even now the truth was not squarely faced and the narrative was still kept in the old framework.

It was possible to demonstrate by various kinds of evidence that Frederick had genuinely been haunted in 1755–6 by the fear of what Russia might do; and that every significant move in his negotiations with Great Britain for the Convention of Westminster in January 1756 had had some correspondence with important pieces of news from St Petersburg. The same preoccupation governed his relations with Great Britain in the first seven months of 1756, when repeatedly he said to the British: 'Are you sure of Russia?' and repeatedly he urged that the government in London should take care to be accurately informed about the matter. Max Lehmann argued that Prussia's armaments had preceded Maria Theresa's; but, apart from other objections to this thesis, it was easy to show that Russia's preparations had been definite and threatening at an earlier period still. While the crisis was developing Frederick the Great wrote to his sister who was ill, and attempted to put on a reassuring manner—urging the lady not to worry, and talking as though he had the situation under control. But when the letter was used to support the view that he was insincere in his pretended anxieties in the middle of 1756, it was surprising to see what could be done by careful detective-work and meticulous collation of evidence to discover whether he was genuine in his anxieties or not.

It proved possible to trace in great detail how the disquieting reports trickled in to Berlin from one source after another as the year 1756 proceeded, and how Frederick reacted to each as they came. They are always reports relating to Russia, even if they also often add the information that Russia is acting in concert with the court of Vienna, so that both Frederick and the nineteenth-century historians still regarded Maria Theresa as the real source of the trouble.

Frederick himself is slow to realise the importance of the announcements, for he trusts in the assurances of Britain—trusts in the assumption that British subsidies would keep the court of St Petersburg under control. He says again to the British minister: 'Are you sure of the Russians?' and when he has reason to believe that he has been too trustful, he does not talk of invading Saxony at all at first—he talks of using the Ottoman Porte to made a diversion in the Russian rear. It affected him very much when he learned that French and Russian diplomats in European capitals had been ordered to co-operate with one another—this seemed to him like a Diplomatic Revolution with a vengeance, for it suggested that France, Russia and Austria, were now in collaboration. When he heard that the Russians had decided to stop their preparations for war for the time being, he did not realise that the postponement had been made at the request of the court of Vienna. He imagined that Russia was held back by her own difficulties and that the moment had come for him to strike Austria while she was isolated. In this way he meant to anticipate the attack which he knew the courts of Vienna and St Petersburg had postponed till 1757.

From all this it is clear to us that the anxieties of Frederick were produced by the remarkable conduct and policy of Russia in the spring of 1756. And the controversy provoked by Max Lehmann in the 1890's gave to the slight Russian material then available a strategic importance of which men were perhaps not entirely conscious at the time. Both Frederick and the nineteenth-century historians were so accustomed to regarding Maria Theresa as the real culprit that they took the hostile conduct of the court of St Petersburg as merely a by-product of her machinations—merely an incident in an essentially Austrian conspiracy. Even after the great work of the 1890's the picture was still out of focus, because the key to the whole story was still regarded as lying in Vienna.

3. THE FALLACIES OF HISTORIANS

At this point in the narrative it is the custom of the better authors to tell the reader that he now has all the clues in his hands. The investigation and the controversy up to date had been a tantalising shadow-play, as though it were necessary by the artifice of the fiction-writer and by tricks of side-stepping to postpone the *dénouement*. The culprit, so to speak, is identified now, however, and only some points of method, and the general pattern of the plot are doubtful. The final explanations could only come when a confession had been extracted, and though mere fragments of this had previously appeared[1] in the early 1870's, the full and official statement, when it finally came, was delivered after the authorities in this field had fixed a closing date for receiving new evidence. The crucial Russian documents were published in 1912, too near the First World War to have their proper effect on scholarship.[2] So far as I can discover they have not been used by any historians, even the Russian ones, for the purpose of elucidating the origins of the Seven Years War.

Apart from the deflection which Frederick the Great had given to the story in the first place, and which, as we have seen, altered the centre of gravity of the whole episode, there were many curious reasons why the attention of historians suffered a lapse in regard to those things which related to Russia. One of them is that curious and common disease which I can only call historian's blind eye; there could be a number of patent

---

[1] *Vorontsov Archives*, III (1872), prints in Russian some of the papers presented to the Russian Council (mentioned below) but not the protocols of the conferences themselves; and Alexander Brückner, writing on 'Das Archiv des Fürsten Worontsov' in *Historische Zeitschrift*, LV (1886), 207–61, called attention to the incompleteness of the documents, especially for the summer of 1756. In the *Baltische Monatschrift*, XXI (1872), Brückner had already given an account in German of the papers contained in vol. III, though with very little translation of the actual documents. He rightly showed that Russia was more eager for war than Austria (p. 318), and that one of her motives was territorial and commercial aggrandisement. On the other hand (p. 306), he clearly had not been able to gather from the *Vorontsov Archives* the real nature of the Russian Council which was involved.

[2] *Sbornik* [Russian Imperial Historical Society], CXXXVI.

facts definitely pointing to Russia, and sometimes the historian would recapitulate them like a man in a day-dream. What was necessary was that they should just be squarely faced, but the historian had his attention focused elsewhere, so that these things found themselves lodged as alien particles encumbering the very different story which the narrator had had fixed in his mind. It had always been known, for example, that there had been Russian military movements in Livonia; but these had failed to ring any bell because in previous years things that were called by the very same name had often occurred. In fact Frederick himself, a few years earlier, had said that he would treat these movements as merely Russia's way of trying to make faces at him; and on this matter he allowed himself to be deceived in 1756. It seems that one had become accustomed to hearing of Russian military movements in Livonia and to thinking that no special importance need be attached to them. In any case Frederick had felt secure that, this time, the dispositions represented nothing more than the execution of the terms of the subsidy-treaty with Great Britain.

Then again, it is a common defect of historians to poke the new evidence into the old structure of story, instead of reducing the whole narrative to its primary materials and then putting the pieces together again in a genuine work of reconstruction. A child of seven, fresh from the bosom of nature, would hardly fall into the error; but, as in the case of a rusty man-trap which I once saw on exhibition, it takes the languor and rigidity of a heavy adult to be caught in such a contraption. Because the old story has dug itself deep, and made grooves in our minds, we must always see Maria Theresa following the traditional formula—it must always be she who is pushing other governments to make war on Frederick the Great; and when the evidence is recalcitrant to this, we churn it somehow into our system, or alternatively we leave odd and unrelated facts— refractory snippets of story—hanging about the affair as loose ends. It had been known since 1841 that in a letter which to us has no ambiguity the Austrians were trying to check the

Russian preparations for war, and to postpone the attack on Frederick. The fact was used, in the work of Vitzthum von Eckstädt for example, to support the view that there was no conspiracy against Frederick and that Maria Theresa only wanted peace. Even when the significance of Russia could no longer be denied, it was just like historians, who had fixed their minds on the Austro-French reversal of alliances as the central fact, to discover a second, subsidiary Diplomatic Revolution between France and Russia, and to over-press the analogy, duplicating the pattern and organising their account of Russian policy about this incident. Much of the literature in the Russian section of the field with which we are concerned is dedicated to this view of the matter, though that literature, as well as all the new evidence that has subsequently appeared, confirms the fact that the Franco-Russian *rapprochement* was (and was always bound to be) a damp squib—the most illusory of all the diplomatic combinations of the time. And a further result of this misapprehension was that all the guns of historical science were trained on the months of May and June. Indeed throughout the history of the whole study of the origins of the Seven Years War, the period of March 1756 was the one which was most neglected—the period when the melodramatic decisions were taken in St Petersburg and the sensational turn was given to the story. Sometimes, we might feel, it would even be better if the historian could actually go to work with a mind unloaded of all hypotheses—could collect his facts and amass his microscopic details, and place everything in chronological order, until the moment comes when he can brood over the whole without any *parti pris*. It might be better if he could wait until the bubbles of mercury jump together and run into a single shape—wait until the pattern begins to stare at him from a multiplicity of facts, as his mind mixes itself into the assembled data.

Since 1900 historians have even shown a tendency to revert to routine and slip the story back into the traditional grooves. In 1923 Sir Richard Lodge, in a considerable discussion of the origins of the Seven Years War, made hardly a reference to Russia—a fact which had serious effects on the points which he was particularly discussing. Later still, a most learned and interesting book by D. B. Horn fails to emphasise the importance of the action of Russia and depends too much on the reports of a British ambassador at a time when, as we have seen, these were particularly unreliable.[1] This book did not pretend to deal with the origins of the Seven Years War, however, and was avowedly a study of the ambassador in question —it was concerned rather with Russia's part in the Diplomatic Revolution—so that the policy of its author is understandable, and it is perhaps the most important British contribution to the historiography of 1756.

In general in the twentieth century those people who did know something of the Russian half of the story failed to compare notes with those who knew the intricate narrative of Western diplomacy, so that the complete picture was still not achieved. This was true of the work of R. Nisbet Bain, who was interested only in the Russian side of the narrative and failed to see how it dovetailed into the larger European story. But there is a model specimen of the anomaly in the *Cambridge Modern History* where the subject of the origins of the Seven Years War was divided between four authors, evidently not on speaking terms with one another, and even at variance in respect of the greatest of the controversies in the 1890's— the Russian section of the narrative standing entirely on its own. What you have in such cases are two separate stories impaled and transfixed, and a trained historian could not marry the Russian story with the European one because what are omitted are just the things which provide the dovetailing and the joints between them.

We might wonder whether the world in an absent-minded way had not known all the time that Russia was the real culprit,

[1] Sir Richard Lodge, *Great Britain and Prussia in the Eighteenth Century* (Oxford, 1923); D. B. Horn, *Sir Charles Hanbury Williams and European Diplomacy, 1747–58* (London, 1930).

though failing to focus attention on this side of the problem—failing to see that the story needed to be told around Russia. The key to the riddle lies in something which Russia did, not merely as the associate or auxiliary of Maria Theresa, but of her own motion and on her own account. It is just the evidence of the Russian documents which is necessary, therefore, to enable us to see what the narrative is like when it is viewed so to speak from its own centre, and is reconstructed in its proper bearings. This evidence brings us to the heart of the particular drama that we are trying to examine. It raises the question whether, when the historian late in the day—after he has formed a certain structure of story—acquires new facts about the matter, he is justified in merely adding the new facts to the old ones, poking them into the acquired structure, pushing them into the margin of the old story, or leaving them as alien particles, only to be noticed in parenthesis. It raises the question whether when we have a chart or a diagram of European events—a view of the origin of the Seven Years War, for example—we ought not to hold it very flexibly in our minds, so that when new facts are acquired they may produce the proper displacements throughout the system. It is easy to think that we are being faithful and merely transcribing the evidence when unconsciously we are running the evidence into an ancient mould. The moulds themselves tend to become the most rigid parts of our history. It is necessary to remember that they need to be constantly re-examined.

4. THE RUSSIAN PAPERS

In St Petersburg at the opening of the year 1756 the elements of intrigue and melodrama were coming to what was perhaps their peak in respect of any time or court in the story of modern European politics, the last two decades excepted. At the heart of the sinister web was Bestuzhev, the Chancellor, who carried people with him in his first diplomatic objective, a collaboration with Austria in a war against Prussia; though he found himself challenged as the mere head of a faction in that he held an alliance with England to be the best way of effecting such a design. By a subsidy-treaty with England Russia had promised to assemble troops in Livonia so that if France attacked Hanover she could move against France's ally, Frederick the Great. Immediately after the delayed ratification of this treaty, in February 1756, however, the Russians were affronted to discover that the British king had gone behind their backs and had actually used that very treaty to bring Prussia to terms—in other words had induced Frederick to double the guarantee of Hanover and to sign the Convention of Westminster by which England and Prussia agreed to combine to prevent any foreign troops from invading Germany. The court of St Petersburg, which had accepted the English subsidy-treaty in order to have a pretext for attacking Prussia, now found that Great Britain was actually committed to assisting Prussia in just such an eventuality. The pro-French faction in St Petersburg were only too ready to assert at this moment that Bestuzhev's system was overthrown; and in their attacks upon him they were helped by the fact that the Tsarina had a sentimental attachment to France. Bestuzhev in such a predicament would seem to have been reduced to desperation-politics. It happened, moreover, that a rumour now reached St Petersburg that Russia's firm ally, the court of Vienna, had made a secret agreement with France. The report was not credited, but it was calculated to assist those enemies of Bestuzhev who, all the time, had been desirous of a French alliance, instead of an English one.

The majority of the people about the court now demanded that the wretched subsidy-treaty should be thrown back in the face of George II. Bestuzhev submitted a dissentient opinion in writing and argued that such a mode of action would proclaim to all the world the offensive intention which Russia had had in mind in the conclusion of that arrangement. The subsidy-treaty had made no actual mention of a war with Prussia, so that Great Britain, in her agreement with Frederick the Great, had not formally contravened it. Let Russia herself take advantage of the same technical point, and assemble her troops in the Baltic states—she could still claim that she was only fulfilling the terms of the subsidy-treaty with England. It was notorious that Frederick the Great's calculations rested on his conviction that the British ministers would be able to control the action of Russia by bribes and subsidies. Now, as a result of his convention with Great Britain, he was feeling secure for the first time for months. Here was the opportunity to give him a real surprise, provided one could make it appear that Russia had not broken her connection with England.[1]

At the critical moment—towards the end of March 1756—a new Council was set up in St Petersburg to deal with Russian policy as a whole. Neither contemporary diplomats nor later historians seemed able to describe this Council; though Soloviev long ago published a letter from Bestuzhev asking for such a body and calling it a Secret War Council—which was what it actually turns out to have been.[2] For a time, as we can tell from ambassadors' reports, the outside world was allowed to go on believing that it sat to discuss the question of what to do about the Anglo-Russian subsidy-treaty. From the start, however, it set out to produce a systematic plan for the reduction of the power of Prussia, and it continued in existence almost to the end of the Seven Years War, dealing with all aspects of that conflict, diplomatic, military, financial and administrative. It was a Council especially intended for the direction of what we call the Seven Years War—only it began that work in March 1756, five months before Frederick the Great attacked Saxony. The Austrian ambassador knew just enough to confirm Bestuzhev's claim that Russia at last had a

---

[1] *Sbornik*, CXXXVI, 27–9.

[2] S. M. Soloviev, *History of Russia*, published from 1859 in 29 volumes; 6-volume edition (St Petersburg, 1897), v, cols. 902–3. In this letter of 3/14 March 1756, Bestuzhev refers to a previous letter of 19/30 January on the same subject. Solovyev gives the gist of a number of documents, including the important programme elaborated by the Council at the second stage of its proceedings on 30 March/9 April 1756. Cf. F. de Martens, *Recueil des Traités...conclus par la Russie*; I (St Petersburg, 1874), 190 and IX (X) (1892), 205.

body which could produce rapid and effective decisions. A Saxon report, that came into the hands of Frederick the Great, gave the same impression—it referred to the transformation produced by a Grand Council to which the Tsarina had given unlimited power.[1]

It was the protocols of this Council, and some of the documents submitted to it or produced by it, which were published by the Russian Imperial Historical Society in 1912; and at its second day's meeting this Council worked out the whole design of an immediate attack on Prussia—if possible in the early spring—the military preparations to be entered upon straight away, so that action could start as soon as Austria gave her consent. It is curious to note that the Council anticipated a certain unwillingness on the part of Austria: and this explains a curious dispatch from the Austrian ambassador in St Petersburg which puzzled historians because it complained that Bestuzhev was too anxious for war. Bestuzhev, it declared, was constantly pressing for an immediate attack, though his other associates in the government felt that Austria would be unwilling to go to war until she was sure of France.[2] The Russian Council, however, had decided from the first that they could not fight Prussia alone, and they determined that the court of Vienna should be brought round to the idea of a joint attack. If Austria was afraid that the French might interfere against her, then the French should be caressed; and Russian ministers abroad should be instructed to collaborate with their French colleagues, while the court of Vienna should receive an explanation of this, lest they should take umbrage unnecessarily. The immediate war-preparations in Russia would act as an incentive in Vienna, it was declared, and Maria

[1] See, for example, Hertzberg, *Recueil*, I, 18; *Preussischer Jahrbücher*, XLVII (1882), 52; *Sbornik*, CXXXVI, pp. xvii–xix. In *Vorontsov Archives*, III, 356–67, are three papers on the Russian Council not printed in *Sbornik*, and referring to it as the Secret War Council.

[2] Cf. *Preussischer Jahrbücher*, XVII (1882), 562, Prasse (Polish-Saxon minister in St Petersburg) to Brühl (in Dresden), 17 May 1758, describing Bestuzhev's eagerness for a war which would make him indispensable and revive his influence after the ground he had lost through the intrigues of his enemies.

Theresa should be asked to realise that this was the moment for regaining Silesia. At a time when we now know that the court of Vienna was wondering whether Russia would contribute some 60,000 men to just such a war as this, the Council was deciding that they would offer 80,000 to see if that would encourage Austria. Almost instantly, even this offer was enlarged, and it was declared that Russia was prepared if necessary to act in this war 'with her whole strength'.

From the start, furthermore, important changes were decreed not only in the diplomatic establishment but in foreign policy generally. It was decided to replace a too Anglophile ambassador in Vienna, in the hope that a more acceptable mouthpiece and a clearer enemy of the Convention of Westminster would serve the cause with greater force. Diplomatic policy was made subservient to the plan of a war against Prussia, and it was realised that the Poles must be kept in good humour, since it was through their territory that the march into Germany would have to take place. An urgent effort was made to bring about a revival of the Russian faction in Poland, for example, and it was ordered that money should be supplied for bribes. It was equally essential that there should be no danger of an attack in the rear from the Turks; so directions were given for a change of policy that was intended to put the Ottoman Turks into a more friendly mood. There was a fortress which the Russians had been building in the Ukraine, and the Turks had been provoked by this, but, since their protests had been useless, they had even ceased to complain. It was resolved in St Petersburg that the work should be suspended. Similarly we have seen how the representatives of France in the various capitals of Europe were now to be cultivated by the Russian ministers in those same cities, though hitherto they had been treated as the agents of a hostile system.

Bestuzhev, though so discredited in his pro-English policy after the news of the Convention of Westminster had reached St Petersburg, now secured that exactly his plan should be followed, and that no break should be made with England. He even made a remarkable political exploitation of the disgrace into which he had fallen, conveying to the British ambassador the impression that he was helpless for the time being, but that if one had patience the storm would blow over and the Anglo-Russian system would recover its former position. The deception of the British ambassador was even carried to the point of pantomime. He would be told that the Empress must cajole the Austrian ambassador and 'nurse' him, since otherwise the court of Vienna might come to feel lonely and might be tempted to go over to the side of France. Similarly the Austrian ambassador was made to think it necessary that the Tsarina should cajole his English colleague; otherwise the British might feel neglected and come to suspect that a war against Prussia was being prepared. Russia's representatives in foreign capitals were ordered to explain the military movements, if explanations were called for, by saying that they were being carried out only in fulfilment of the Anglo-Russian subsidy-treaty.

Owing to a curious accident—almost owing to a kind of conjuring trick—the Russian decisions of March 1756 were overshadowed, and then lost sight of by future historians, so that a different piece of narrative came to be superimposed. The expected difficulties of the attempt to persuade Austria to agree to an attack on Prussia never materialised in fact. On the contrary what happened was that there arrived almost immediately in St Petersburg a courier from Vienna asking the self-same question—asking whether Russia would consent to act against Frederick the Great in the present year, 1756. The negotiations were immediately set on foot and a special form of oath was signed by the two empresses, committing them to a degree of secrecy beyond what was usual in diplomatic transactions.

We must not say, however, that this puts the story back into the state in which it stood before; for the papers of the Russian Council did not even mention the overture from Austria and even now that Council plunged recklessly forward on its own account as before, making both military and naval preparations, and behaving quite differently from the court of Vienna, which declared itself to be moving with the utmost caution. The fact that Russia was not in step with Austria in this matter puzzled observers a little later and led to a conjecture—one which fell into the hands of Frederick the Great—that there was a mutual agreement by which Austria was to hold back so as not to appear in any sense as an aggressor, while the Russians had been given the work of what was called 'belling the cat'.

The Russians were in fact going ahead with their scheme on their own account; and all this went on for over two months, from March to June, till the commotion reached a point at which it could be expected to deceive nobody any longer, and foreign ministers in St Petersburg were reporting that the city was ringing with the clamour of war. In April the war-manifesto was discussed with the Austrian ambassador, and after the middle of May it was realised that the secret could not be kept any longer. On 19 May Bestuzhev was being questioned by anxious foreign ministers, though not by a Prussian one, as there was no representative of the court of Berlin at St Petersburg. At the beginning of June the Council declared 'that it is to be presumed that under the present circumstances, and especially when he learns of the magnitude of the movements taking place, the Prussian King will not delay very long in at least taking measures for his own safety.'[1] The Council asked therefore that spies should be sent to Prussia to observe the military movements there. Yet more than a fortnight passed after this before Frederick the Great took alarm.

By this time the court of Vienna had been seized with fear, however, and Kaunitz, realising at last what was really happening, wrote: 'The Russians are behaving too precipitately.' It was decided to ask Russia to postpone the whole scheme until 1757. Long after this, the Russian Council were still expressing their resentment at the delay, and were saying that Frederick might now decide to attack first, in which case

[1] *Sbornik*, CXXXVI, 113.

Austria and her ally would be at a disadvantage. Frederick the Great learned of his danger astonishingly late—later than the date when the court of Vienna saw the possibility of his taking alarm, and later even than the time when the Russian Council conjectured that he must be looking out for his own safety. He was deceived because he relied for information on the British, and the British were being successfully hoaxed. When he realised the situation he related the Russian movements to those plans of a wider coalition which he had reason to know that the court of Vienna was making and which the Russians also had come to rely on by the beginning of summer —plans which included bribes for securing the collaboration of Saxony, Poland and Sweden. And when the Russians broke off their preparations he did not realise that this was at the request of the court of Vienna—did not realise that the Tsarina was still straining for the fight.

5. THE VICISSITUDES OF AN HISTORICAL THEME

We may note in conclusion that, so far as we can gather from the evidence on this particular subject, a hundred years of historical enquiry may carry students further from the truth than they were at the beginning. It may take one hundred and fifty years before the most critical problem is brought to the consciousness of historians or the most acute of the controversial issues is raised. Even if by this time sufficient clues are in the hands of scholars, further delay may arise because of the tendency to fit the new evidence into a framework that has been allowed to become too rigid. The publication of diplomatic documents fails to bring historians to the heart of the problem, and even may carry the student further away from the truth, if the secret and central documents, particularly the policy-making ones—the ones which really reveal a government's purposes—are not open to the free play of scholarship. Even now the frontiers of the enquiry have only been shifted— not removed altogether—and what we know of the conduct and policy of Bestuzhev must make us more anxious to be clear about the reasons for his actions, while the more we learn about his reasons and his motives the more we shall have to restate the policy itself. So there does not appear to be a point where the mind of the historian can safely rest. Even now we must not imagine that everything has been settled.[1]

More than once we have seen that it is possible for retrogression to take place in historical science if students lose touch with the work that their predecessors have done. The research student may miss some important opportunities if he fails to become acquainted with the history of the historiography of his subject. We may deduce further that it is wrong to assume that in a German controversy the anti-Prussian historians are always right or are necessarily more impartial than their adversaries. Finally, we may note that, even with a more limited range of materials, Ranke in 1871 had the genius to seize upon the main truths. His 'hunches' are one of the interesting features of the story. In the last resort, sheer insight is the greatest asset of all.

[1] The introduction to *Sbornik*, CXXXVI, p. xx, notes that the papers here printed are not sufficient to explain the story; and Bestuzhev's policy still requires to be explained, especially his anxiety to hasten war after the Convention of Westminster had seemed to thwart his plans and had placed him in a serious predicament. The references to the possibility that Bestuzhev as well as the court of Vienna wished to goad Prussia into making the attack—including the many references in various Saxon documents—would need a separate lecture for their discussion. The curious conduct of Bestuzhev in the summer of 1756 seems to have added to the difficulty of interpreting his policy in the spring.

VI

LORD ACTON AND THE MASSACRE
OF ST BARTHOLOMEW

I. THE BLACK LEGEND AND ITS FIRST OVERTHROW

The earliest literature on the Massacre of St Bartholomew, we are told, was dominated by the attempt of Henry, the Duke of Anjou, to secure the throne of Poland.[1] Henry needed the support of the Protestants in that country—then a more considerable body than they have ever been since; and, as he had been one of the chief culprits in the massacre, the Huguenots were determined that the world should know the magnitude of the crime. He secured his election in 1573, but, in the face of the storm which was raised against him, he was supposed to have been seized with remorse in Cracow, and to have made a confession to his doctor, Miron—a narrative which we shall have to notice later.[2]

In the subsequent periods the literature of St Bartholomew's Day still continued to be governed by polemical purposes; and when fortune smiled again upon the Huguenots—as also still later when their leader, Henry of Navarre, acquired the throne of France—it became a matter of policy to screen the monarchy a little, if only by inculpating the Church or Philip II of Spain, or the family of Guise. An extreme Protestant version of the story, packed with melodrama and premeditated treachery, was still in general currency at the beginning of the eighteenth century. In their turn, Voltaire and the Encyclopaedists set out to perpetuate this version, which provided them with so powerful a weapon against Roman Catholic bigotry; and they would deal in a summary

[1] Heinrich Wuttke, *Zur Vorgeschichte der Bartholomäusnacht* (Leipzig, 1879), 38; Anton Philipp Segesser, *Ludwig Pfyffer und seine Zeit*, II (Berne, 1881), 169.
[2] First published in *Suite des Mémoires d'éstat de Nicolas de Neufville de Villeroy* (Paris, 1623), 68–89.

manner with the documentary sources, if they conflicted with a story that seemed so self-evidently true. Then, with the coming of the French Revolution, the weapon was switched to a new purpose, and it was this whole exaggerated version which was now redirected, now turned more definitely into propaganda against the monarchy itself. Once the historiography of the subject had really reached this stage, however, we must note the significant fact that, sooner or later, the paradoxes that had long been latent in the story were bound to emerge. If the monarchy was the real culprit in the crime of St Bartholomew's Day, the traditional melodramatic Protestant narrative could not be made to hold together for very long.

Indeed, it had already been possible—by picking up the opposite end of the stick—to show that the exculpation of the Roman Catholic Church went hand in hand with the development of the case against the monarchy. A political interpretation of the massacre had made its appearance, and had challenged the religious one; but already it had produced a complete recasting of the narrative. In 1758, the Abbé Novi de Caveirac set out to show that religion had had no part in the events of St Bartholomew's Day; that the Huguenots had been attacked as a politico-military body, and as rebels; and that the decision to commit the crime had been taken at a desperate moment, only a few hours before the outrage actually occurred. Extravagant legends had been allowed to grow up, this writer said, and nobody had dared to challenge them for fear of being regarded as an actual apologist for the massacre. Caveirac himself suffered from the *philosophes* of the mid-century a scourging which exactly illustrated his point. He was not quite alone, however, for in 1767 Louis Pierre Anquetil rejected the idea of a long-prepared plan. The historian, said Anquetil, too easily turns events into an ordered sequence and then reads back into this a deliberate design.[1]

[1] [Abbé Novi de Caveirac], *Apologie de Louis XIV et de son Conseil sur la Révocation de l'Edit de Nantes...avec une Dissertation sur la journée de S. Barthélemi* (1758). Caveirac asserts that there is no firm authority for the idea of premeditation, and that the

Acton's History of the Historiography

There exists in manuscript a sketch by Lord Acton of the subsequent history of the way in which the massacre of

Memoirs of Tavannes, those of Marguerite de Valois, and the confession made by the Duc d'Anjou to Miron tell against that hypothesis.

Acton's interest in the history of the historiography of the massacre hardly seems to have extended to the eighteenth century and, though he mentions Caveirac, he does not allude to the French Jesuit, Father G. Daniel, whose *Histoire de France depuis l'Établissement de la Monarchie Françoise dans les Gaules*, originally published in 1713, had appeared in 1755, with supplementary notes and observations by Henri Griffet. Succeeding writers, including Caveirac himself and Griffet, show the significance of this republication. Daniel, though inclining to the belief in premeditation, had thrown doubts on the idea of a conspiracy at Bayonne and had said that after the attempt on Coligny 'cet emportement des chefs des huguenots, leurs assemblées...et le tumulte que cet evénément causoit...déterminèrent la reine à n'en pas demeurer là. Elle alla trouver le roi...dit qu'il s'agissait de sa couronne et de sa vie...que les huguenots se préparaient à se venger sur le duc de Guise....' Daniel's editor adds: 'Le P. Daniel paroit faire un grand fonds sur l'autorité des Mémoires de M. de Tavannes et sur l'entretien du duc d'Anjou avec Miron.' He notes that 'le nouvel éditeur du Journal de l'Étoile n'a pas fait difficulté d'avancer comme une chose certaine, que le massacre ne fut prémédité que 24 heures avant son exécution.' He asks why, if a massacre was already planned, there should have been an initial attack on Coligny alone—an attack which, if it had succeeded, would have dispersed the Huguenots then assembled in Paris.

Acton does not mention Louis-Pierre Anquetil, *L'Esprit de la Ligue ou Histoire Politique des Troubles de la France pendant les XVI & XVII siècles*, II (Paris, 1767). On p. 13 Anquetil says: 'Les Mémoires du temps, faits par les personnes les mieux instruites, tels que ceux de Brantôme, de la Reine Marguerite, de Cheverny, de Villeroy, de Castelnau, surtout de Tavannes, d'après lesquels se sont décidés Dupleix, Le Laboureur, l'auteur des Commentaires, et les meilleurs historiens, portent expressément deux choses, 1. que Charles ne se détermina au massacre qu'après la blessure de l'amiral; 2. qu'il n'eut d'abord dessein d'y comprendre que quelques chefs.'

The above authors illustrate the fact that the reliability of the chief sets of Memoirs was the main issue in the eighteenth century: and Acton was chiefly concerned with the Jesuit Father, Henri Griffet, who in his *Traité des différentes sortes de Preuves qui servent à établir la vérité de l'histoire* (Liège, 1769), 161, shows the interest which Tavannes, Marguerite de Valois and Miron must have had in promulgating a perversion of the truth. Acton regretted that this work, 'reprinted in 1838, has remained unnoticed by later historians'. Incidentally, Griffet gives a hint of the possible source of the argument of Anquetil, quoted in the text above, when he reproduces a passage from Brantôme attacking the prevalent assumption that 'les desseins des Princes sont toujours conduits de longue main, et toujours prémédités, quoi qu'ils soient souvent les effets subits d'une conjoncture tout-à-fait imprévue'.

Acton makes no mention of a curious work by Gabriel Brizard, *Du Massacre de la Saint-Barthélemi, et de l'influence des étrangers en France durant la Ligue*... (Première Partie, Paris, January 1790), which regards the crime as 'prémédité de longue main', but is concerned chiefly to show that the culprits were foreigners, while the French were only the victims. Concerning the attack on Caveirac, Brizard writes: 'Un cri général s'est élevé contre l'imprudent écrivain qui, de nos jours, a tenté, non d'en faire l'apologie, comme on l'a cru faussement, mais d'en discuter les causes....On s'est indigné qu'il n'en parlat que pour en atté\neur l'horreur....Un tel homme a été justement flétri par l'opinion publique.'

St Bartholomew had been interpreted; and this essay gives an account of the successive discoveries which in the course of a generation changed the aspect of the affair. It provides an initial summary of the melodramatic Protestant version of the story which still held the field in the first quarter of the nineteenth century. According to this version, says Acton,

the plan had been laid [in 1565 between Catherine de' Medici and the Duke of Alva] at Bayonne, [if it did not go back earlier than this to the Council of Trent] and its chief promoter was the pope. The court concluded the pacification of 1570 [with the Huguenots, at St Germain] in order to get its opportunity, but the Huguenots suspected a snare, and the match [of Catherine de' Medici's daughter, Margaret] with [the Huguenot, Henry of] Navarre was found to be the only way to lull their suspicions, and to bring them together on a spot where there was little danger of resistance or escape. The Flemish expedition [sent before the massacre, when Admiral Coligny, the Huguenot leader, had influence over Charles IX and hoped to help the Revolt of the Netherlands in its early stages] was a device to mask the real design. Lignerolles, having betrayed his knowledge of the guilty secret, was put to death. The Queen [the mother of Henry] of Navarre died [9 June 1572] by poison. The Cardinal of Lorraine, [the uncle of Henry, Duke of Guise] who wished to avoid danger, and who had stipulated the destruction of his private enemies, betook himself to Rome; and Gregory XIII, when he knew that the plot was ripe, granted the needful dispensations for the marriage [which took place on 18 August]. Coligny was made the first victim [being wounded in the attempted assassination of 22 August] because his death was likely to provoke conflict which would enable the government to involve the principal Catholics in the same fate as their enemies. In the end [24 August etc.] near 100,000 Huguenots were got rid of, and the head of their leader was sent to Rome by the Duke of Guise.[1]

[1] Cambridge University Library, Add. 4863. Amongst the other papers in this packet are a number of notes which Acton made in preparation for his short history of the historiography of the massacre. They include repeated summaries of the opinions of historians on the question of premeditation, and repeated notes or queries concerning the first appearance of particular pieces of evidence. As in many other sets of notes in the C.U.L., we also find the record (occasionally in pencil) of the way Acton was thinking out his ideas on the subject, or giving initial formulation to his arguments. Some

For seventy years, Acton tells us, scholarship on this subject had remained in the same state; and the extremist version of the massacre went on being reproduced, at any rate by the popular writers, until 1837. In Restoration France, 'those who condemned the Revolution for its excesses' would be met with the retort that the outrage, as described above, represented 'the crime of the French monarchy'. The authorities were so sensitive on this point that 'when Fragonard exhibited a picture of the bishop of Lisieux saving the Huguenots, a reference to the occasion of the scene was struck out of the catalogue'.

It was chiefly the period of reaction during the reign of Charles X that saw a change; and Acton tells us that this was begun at the same moment by the English Roman Catholic historian, Lingard, and by St Victor, a French Legitimist, who had been connected with De Maistre, Lamennais and the Jesuits. He notes somewhere, however, that Lingard's *History of England* (1823) added nothing to the arguments of Caveirac; and when Lingard in turn received his scourging from John Allen in the *Edinburgh Review* he was accused of having consulted the sources only through Caveirac.[1] A French writer, Audin, in 1826, not only denied that the massacre was premeditated but pointed to a new method of interpretation—one which was congenial to the historiography of the Romantic

---

examples are given on p. 182, n. 1, p. 183, n. 1, p. 194, n. 2, and p. 200, n. 2, below. Add. 5531 is a notebook in which Acton can be seen similarly revolving the question of Pius V and the murder of Elizabeth, reasoning out the whole case and attempting to establish his attitude to the affair. These documents throw an interesting light on the genesis and development of his historical ideas. Some of the references in Add. 4863 make it clear that these notes on the massacre of St Bartholomew, and the subsequent sketch, are later than Acton's own publications on this theme, and represent a renewed attempt to take stock of the whole subject shortly after 1873. At a later date again, as will be seen below, he re-traversed the ground and revised his view of the massacre (see p. 200 below). The Acton collection in the C.U.L. also comprises large numbers of the transcripts of documents relating to the massacre which he had procured at different times.

[1] John Lingard, *History of England*, V (1823), 334–5, 646–50, reviewed by John Allen in *Edinburgh Review*, June 1826; J. Lingard, *A Vindication of Certain Passages in the fourth and fifth volumes of the History of England* (1826); J. Allen, *Reply to Dr Lingard's Vindication in a letter to Francis Jeffray, Esq.* (2nd ed. 1827). For a survey of the controversy, see *Westminster Review*, January 1827.

movement as well as to the interest of the restored monarchy. This version was elaborated and popularised in 1829, in Mérimée's 'historical novel' on the reign of Charles IX of France; and, according to this view, it was not Catherine de' Medici who was to blame for the massacre of St Bartholomew —it was not the monarchy that was responsible—but 'a sudden and uncontrollable outburst of popular fury'. In 1834 Capefigue made this view of the matter the basis for the fullest narrative on the subject that had hitherto appeared in France.[1]

At the next stage of the story, Acton describes how new documents were brought to light, so that after 1830 the tide definitely turned against the older idea of a carefully pre-meditated conspiracy. In 1831 the German historian Raumer used the letters written by Charles IX to his representative in Rome as evidence against the existence of any long-prepared design.[2] Three years later Capefigue published the work which has already been mentioned. 'In all the manuscripts of Paris he found no trace of orders that emanated from the King; and he announced that the Simancas papers betray no secret understanding between France and Spain.' In the same year the third volume of Sir James Mackintosh's *History of England* contained extracts from the diplomatic correspondence of the Nuncio, Salviati, who had been in Paris at the time of the massacre. The despatches had been copied by Chateaubriand when the papal archives had been transferred to the French capital in the time of Napoleon;[3] and the extracts which had been supplied to Mackintosh contained 'no evidence of long preparation or of the complicity of Rome' in the affair. Acton tells us that, after this, 'Sismondi at once absolved the Nuncio;

---

[1] Jean Marie Vincent Audin, *Histoire de la Saint Barthélemy* (Paris, 1826); Baptiste Honoré Raymond Capefigue, *Histoire de la réforme, de la Ligue et du règne de Henri IV*, III (Paris, 1834), 1–272.

[2] Friedrich von Raumer, *Briefe aus Paris zur Erläuterung der Geschichte des sechzehnten und siebzehnten Jahrhunderts*, part 1 (Leipzig, 1831), 290–6.

[3] 'After the close of his public life, in 1831', says Acton in the sketch, '[Chateaubriand] advertised a volume which was to contain [the despatches], and in which he promised to vindicate Religion and Monarchy. This pledge could not be redeemed; but, at the request of Sismondi, Chateaubriand communicated to Sir James Mackintosh certain extracts.'

and Lingard, declaring that the question was now settled, suppressed his former dissertation on the massacre'. Groen van Prinsterer, using Dutch, Spanish and Austrian papers, confirmed the earlier judgement of Capefigue; that is to say, he made it clear that France was not acting in complicity with Philip II of Spain in the period in question.[1] There was now no reason for believing that the anti-Spanish policy which was being pursued by Coligny particularly in respect of the Netherlands, in the early months of 1572, was different from the policy of Charles IX, or was being undermined by any collusion between the French and Spanish courts. Next, Acton tells us that in 1838

A patriotic Italian, Alberi, encouraged by the example of Capefigue, went a step farther, and attempted to justify the Florentine Queen, compelled, in self-defence, to yield to the passions that agitated the capital. He consulted the Medicean archives and his extracts...support the same conclusion. The Tuscan envoys, with the Spaniards and the Nuncio, were added to the witnesses against premeditation. They were joined by the Venetians. The reports for the year 1572, overlooked when Tommaseo prepared his collection for the French government, were found by Ranke, and it appeared that the Venetian resident [in Paris] Cavalli believed that the resolution [i.e. to massacre the Huguenots] was unprepared.[2]

In 1843 Falloux proved forgery in the case of a document which had shown the murder of Huguenots in the provinces to have been organised many days beforehand. Another paper describing a plan of massacre dating from 1562 could not be found in the archives where it had been supposed that it existed.[3] In 1851 the publication of despatches by the Duke of

[1] Groen van Prinsterer, *Archives ou Correspondance inédite de la Maison d'Orange-Nassau*, 1st ser. III (Leydon, 1836), e.g. pp. 496–500.

[2] Eugenio Alberi, *Vita di Caterina de' Medici* (Firenze, 1838); Niccolo Tommaseo, *Relations des ambassadeurs vénitiens sur les affaires de France au XVIe siècle*, 2 vols. (Paris, 1838).

[3] Acton writes: 'Among the forgeries produced by the wish to magnify the guilt of the culprits, were three letters purporting to have been severally written by Pellevé to Lorraine, by Catharine to Strozzi, and by Thomasseau to Guise. Two of these had been long detected. But the third remained, and was, if genuine, enough to prove that the

Alva made it 'certain that no extraordinary villainy was agreed upon, or even proposed, at the interview' of Bayonne in 1565.[1] And here Acton says: 'With this discovery the evidence for the defence was closed, and the reaction came to an end.' Step by step, he tells us, in the slow lapse of years, the system which had so long prevailed had been brought to its overthrow.

Though it is against all expectation, we must note that in his sketch of the historiography of this subject Acton does less than justice to the part which German historical scholarship had been playing. Perhaps it was because of this that he found it tempting to believe that the whole development which had been taking place had been a reaction on the part of 'religious and royalist opinion' in Restoration France. Even in 1789 Spittler, in a sketch of general European history, had roundly declared that there was absolutely no basis for the idea that the massacre of St Bartholomew's Day was premeditated; and he had added that, if the attempt to shoot Coligny had succeeded as well as the poison for the Queen of Navarre had apparently done, there would have been no massacre.[2] Even in the period when Lingard was conducting his controversy—the period which Acton sees as the turning-point—the most significant event was the publication of Ludwig Wachler's *Die Pariser Bluthochzeit* (1826)—a work which seems to have had a considerable influence on the German historiography of this

murders in the provinces had been organised for many days. In 1843 Falloux demonstrated that the letter of Thomasseau is a fabrication.' See Le comte de Falloux, 'La Saint-Barthélemy' (Congrès scientifique de France à Angers, 1843) in *Études et Souvenirs* (Paris, 1885), 38 ff.

The sketch continues; 'A paper is extant which describes a plan formed by the Catholic leaders in 1562 for a more atrocious slaughter than that which was executed ten years later. Secousse, who published it in 17 , [*sic*] declined to commit his high critical reputation by declaring it genuine. A copy has been found among the papers of the duke of Guise : and Capefigue affirms that he had seen the original bearing autograph signatures. The collection designated by Capefigue has been twice examined, and his statement is not confirmed.'

[1] Louis Prosper Gachard, *Correspondance de Philippe II sur les affaires des Pays-Bas*, II (Brussels, 1851).

[2] Ludwig Timotheus, Freiherr von Spittler, *Entwurf der Geschichte der europäischen Staaten*, 2nd impression, 2 vols. (1808), 234–5.

subject.[1] According to Wachler many people might have had the wish to destroy the Huguenots at one time and another, but the actual decision must have been a sudden and desperate one. An essay by Ranke in 1835 brought out what eventually proved to be a strategic argument: namely, that a study of diplomatic relations in the period before the massacre made it impossible to think that Catherine was insincere in her support of Huguenot foreign policy, her hostility to Spain for example. The study of her hints and sayings convinced Ranke, however, that she must have been preparing at the same time to exterminate the Huguenot leaders; and he admitted that here was a deadlock—here were two approaches to the question which brought absolutely contradictory answers. He decided that history in itself could never solve the problem and that one must resort, therefore, to 'psychology'. It was Ranke's view that Catherine must have been preparing to act sincerely with the Huguenots and at the same time she must have been working out plans for their destruction. When in the long run she had to choose between the alternative courses, the decision was a sudden one, and came at a moment of desperation; but —as he shows in the *History of the Popes*—he believed that the wedding of Henry of Navarre was held in Paris in order that Catherine should be in a position to destroy the Huguenots if she desired to do so. In his *French History* (1852) Ranke gave further development to the thesis that the statesman, in his conduct of policy, may have 'two strings to his bow', and perhaps now he presented it with greater flexibility. The idea of annihilating leading Huguenots—if only half a dozen of them—was undoubtedly in the air. Catherine de' Medici gave genuine support to Coligny's anti-Spanish policy for a long time, while holding the *arrière-pensée* that the more drastic alternative measure might provide a way of escape if ever the situation became desperate.[2]

[1] On Wachler, see p. 10, above.
[2] Leopold von Ranke, *Historisch-Politische Zeitschrift*, II (1835), 581–605 (review of Capefigue, op. cit.); *Die römischen Päpste...*, II (Berlin, 1836), 6; *Französische Geschichte*, I (Hamburg, 1852), 296–333.

Acton does tell us, however, that in 1854 the German historian, Soldan, 'in an enquiry written with great moderation and fairness', worked out the standard version of the revised narrative of St Bartholomew's Day.[1] In his first printed article in 1868 Acton summarised as follows the new story that had come to hold the field:

Charles IX wished sincerely to live at peace with his Protestant subjects, and intended to cement the pacification [of 1570] by marrying his sister to the King of Navarre. A foreign war was suggested as the best means of uniting the forces which had so long contended with each other, and of diverting them from their intestine quarrels. Coligny proposed the conquest of the Spanish Netherlands, where Alva could scarcely maintain himself against the Prince of Orange. The King yielded to the ascendancy of Coligny, and entered into his scheme. Catherine and the Duke of Anjou, apprehending the ruin of their policy and the loss of their influence, hired an assassin to shoot the Admiral. When it was discovered that the wound was not mortal, and when Charles undertook to avenge it, the Queen knew that she would be found out and that the whole body of Huguenots in France would be her implacable foes. By confessing her guilt she obtained her son's consent to have the Huguenots in Paris massacred. The resolution was so suddenly taken and so quickly executed that there was not time to prepare the same thing in the provinces, where accordingly it was carried out imperfectly and indecisively.[2]

In his manuscript sketch of the history of the interpretation of the massacre, Acton adds the following note, which refers to about the middle of the 1850's:

At this point the tide reached its height. Nothing remained of the version which had been able to maintain itself until about 1837. It was so completely shattered that in 1860 H. Martin [in a new edition] modified the text of his history of France....

[1] Wilhelm Gottlieb Soldan, 'Frankreich und die Bartholomäusnacht', in *Historisches Taschenbuch*, xxv (Leipzig, 1854), 75–241.
[2] *The Chronicle*, 15 Feb. 1868, 158.

More than once, indeed, Acton points out the fact that even the French Protestants 'adopted the narrative of Soldan'.

Towards the end of the 1860's he determined to challenge the new version of the story which had come to hold the field.

2. ACTON AND THE CASE FOR PREMEDITATION

From 1864 Acton and Döllinger began their more serious manuscript work, and found materials in the Vatican archives which helped to change their attitude to the history of the Church. As their own conflict with ecclesiastical authority grew in intensity, and more particularly as the Vatican Council approached, they pursued their historical enquiries in fields that had something of a contemporary reference. Their studies were not quite insulated from polemical intent, therefore; and Acton's researches, which turned particularly to the problem of persecution, seem to have cut deep into his experience. At a later date he felt that Döllinger would not have come to diverge from him so greatly if he had not shirked this problem of persecution in just this period.[1] From 1867 Acton was more than usually interested in the massacre of St Bartholomew— interested particularly in the question whether it was premeditated or not. His manuscripts make it clear that he regarded the answer to this question as involving the further issue of the connivance or collaboration of the papal court. 'No premeditation—no complicity'—this is the burden of

---

[1] For the manuscript work of Döllinger and Acton at this time, see MS. notes in C.U.L. Add. 4903, 4905, 4909, 5609: also letters of 1866 from Acton to Simpson, now at Downside Abbey, two of which are printed in the *Cambridge Historical Journal*, 1950, pp. 99–101. Döllinger's attitude to persecution is discussed in notes in Add. 4904, 4905, 4908, 4909. In Add. 5004 Acton gives some general views of his own on the same topic. In Add. 4904 is a note: 'D[öllinger] thought persecution an evil, not a crime.' Add. 4908: 'It is more an intellectual error.' In Add. 4908 and 4909 Acton points out that Döllinger never gave his mind to the theory and history of persecution until 1864. In Add. 4904 he writes: 'D.'s scheme of writing on St Bartholomew entertained for a moment. This would have been a step beyond his study of the Inquisition [1867].' In Add. 4908 we read: 'St Bartholomew. It would have led him into new fields....He recoiled from the bloodshed.' In Add. 4909 he says: 'The decisive fact of D.'s life, separating one half from the other, was the question of forgeries. He began in 1862....'

more than one of his notes.[1] Early in 1868 he attacked in *The Chronicle* an English version of that revised narrative which Soldan had summarised so carefully. In 1869 he took up the subject again in a long article, which remained one of the most dense and heavily footnoted pieces of work that he ever produced. In 1870 the Italian translation of his own anonymous article contained further Venetian despatches, added by Tommaseo Gar, and these gave him the pretext for reasserting his case in a short review in the following year. His notes show him busily engaged on the problem—and still unconverted—in the period immediately after this. His manuscript account of the history of the historiography of the whole subject probably belongs to something like the middle of the 1870's, when he still held fast to his original arguments.[2]

It is clear from this manuscript sketch that Acton did not agree with the recent developments in historical interpretation —developments which he persisted in associating with the French Restoration. 'The religious and royalist opinion', he said, 'had triumphed over an extraordinary accumulation of error; but many of its own conclusions were based upon arguments that were illusory and unsound.' There are further signs that he regarded this new reconstruction of the story as having been over-exploited by the Ultramontane

[1] At least he imputed this way of thinking to the historians of the 'Catholic Reaction', as in the following note from Add. 4863:
'If no premeditation, no complicity.
'It became a Catholic interest to determine that it was a sudden decision.
'Not enough to show that it was not entirely decided.
'That would not show that there was no complicity.
'Therefore they were willing to show that it [the massacre] was not even discussed or proposed.'
Another note, under the heading 'Catholic Reaction', runs:
'...All turned on premeditation. If none, Rome no accomplice. Denied by Ranke, Capefigue, Audin, Lingard, Alberi, Michelet, Falloux, Soldan....'
[2] Lord Acton, review of Henry White, *The Massacre of St Bartholomew* (1868), in *The Chronicle*, 15 Feb. 1868, pp. 158–60; 'The Massacre of St Bartholomew' in *North British Review*, Oct. 1869, pp. 30–70, reprinted in *History of Freedom*, pp. 101–49; review of Tommaso Gar, *La Strage di San Bartolomeo...con introduzione ed aggiunta di documenti inediti tratti dall' archivio generale di Venezia* (Venice, 1870), in *North British Review*, 1870–1, pp. 561–2.

party.[1] Those historians who held the massacre to have been un-premeditated 'all accepted Anjou's confession', he said—that is to say the confession alleged to have been made to Miron in Cracow; therefore they believed that 'nobody had dreamed of it [the massacre] until the very last moment, on the eve of the 23rd'. But Griffet, in the eighteenth century, had proved to Acton's satisfaction that Miron's account of this conversation must be 'without authority, even if accepted as genuine'. A statement made by Anjou in Cracow in 1573 seemed to Griffet hardly calculated to contain the real truth about the affair. John Allen, in his controversy with Lingard, had given reasons for not accepting the document as the work of the doctor Miron in any case; for Allen could find no sign of it before the seventeenth century.[2] On the other hand, Chateaubriand had claimed that his transcripts of the despatches of Salviati, the papal nuncio in Paris at the time of the massacre, were sufficient to rule out the idea of premeditation. Acton, who saw all these transcripts, disagreed and said that Mackintosh had been given only carefully selected excerpts, so that Salviati's meaning had been disguised by 'the suppression of decisive letters'. Alberi, in his desire to defend a member of the Medici family, had similarly omitted significant parts of the despatches of the Florentine diplomats.

In the main published article of 1869 Acton showed how 'the doom of the Huguenots had been long expected and often foretold'. He pointed out that the infatuated Coligny, so secure in his belief that he had the King's confidence, had received warnings from men 'much oppressed with the sense of coming evil'. He described how 'for many years foreign advisers had urged Catherine to make away with' the Huguenots. He quoted reports of people who had heard Catherine de' Medici and Charles IX declare in confidence that the

---

[1] E.g. a note in Add. 4863: 'These results eagerly taken advantage of, exaggerated and caricatured in the interest of religion—of the Pope and King.'

[2] See p. 171, n. 2, above. Amongst the notes in C.U.L. Add. 4863 is a list of over twenty nineteenth-century historians who had accepted Miron. Ranke is included in the list, but he had later expressed his doubts.

reconciliation with the Huguenots in 1570 and the subsequent marriage alliance with Henry of Navarre were only the cover for a design to rid France of the Protestant menace. He found hints of the coming tragedy in despatches from the representatives of the Duke of Tuscany, and in his manuscript survey he says that these diplomats 'traced almost day by day the progress of' Catherine's 'murderous design'. As early as March 1572 the Florentine envoys had in fact been speaking of plans for the betrayal of the Huguenots. In the manuscript, however, Acton describes Salviati, the nuncio, as 'the strongest witness against the court and the Church'; and in the main published essay he claims that he has new evidence from this man, and he evidently regards this as a matter of strategic importance. In 1570 Salviati had been told that the government was making peace with the Huguenots in order to be able to lure the latter to their destruction. A few days before the massacre itself, Salviati had been informed that some kind of conspiracy was ripening, and he had written that very soon he hoped to have some good news for His Holiness. Not long after the massacre he gave an affirmative reply when Catherine de' Medici asked him to confirm her statement that she had long ago given him a hint of what had now actually taken place. Then Acton tells us that the Venetian diplomat, Contarini, had also described the French government as counting on the death of Coligny to bring about a momentous change. This man's successor Cavalli, however, ultimately came to the conclusion that a massacre so mismanaged could only have been a hasty improvisation. Acton claimed that another Venetian, Michiel, who was at Cavalli's side, was much better informed on the subject of the intrigues at the French court. Michiel later formulated his view of the whole affair, and it was his conclusion that the massacre had in reality been premeditated.

If the diplomats gave evidence in favour of Acton's case, they were supported by the Cardinal of Lorraine, who was then in Rome and who, when the news of the massacre arrived, claimed to have known all about it months beforehand.

Camillo Capilupi, a person of some consequence, supported this claim in *Lo Stratagemma di Carlo IX*, the dedication of which is dated 18 September 1572. The King's confessor a few years later, when Charles IX was dead, added his contribution to the evidence in favour of premeditation. Another witness, Cardinal Bonelli of Alessandria, had written from France on 6 March 1572 that he had some important news that was to be reserved for the Pope's private ear. Statements which were published later, with the sanction of members of his mission— two of whom were to become popes—pointed to the massacre of St Bartholomew as the very secret at which Bonelli was glancing when he made this remark. This was supported by private communications that had appeared in the after-period. Lingard had challenged this evidence in his controversy with John Allen over forty years before Acton intervened. But Acton claimed that he had found further support for the view that Cardinal Bonelli had been apprised of the massacre in advance.

Acton's main article of 1869 is written with more definite qualifications than his essay of the previous year. The court may have hinted at dark designs when making peace with the Huguenots; but he does not resurrect the story that treachery was being consistently prepared between 1570 and 1572. Cardinal Bonelli's letter of early March 1572 is clearly of some importance to him, however. It is chiefly by reason of this (together with a Florentine despatch) that he insists even now that 'by the month of February 1572 the plan [of the actual massacre] had assumed practical shape'. It is clear that he regards Charles IX as a participant in the conspiracy, and he interprets the affair by relating it to the policy of Charles himself. He admits that there is not evidence to prove—that, indeed, he has found actual evidence to disprove—the charge that the court of Rome had promoted or sanctioned the outrage; though he collects points which might suggest that the Pope had foreknowledge, and some of his arguments for premeditation rest on information alleged to have been communicated to Rome. Acton's great bugbear, Pius V, was certainly implicated to this degree if his revised version of the story was correct; for Bonelli, who had been given the information for the Pope's private ear, was at Pius's side in the weeks before his death on 1 May. Some time after the massacre, the next Pope, Gregory XIII, we are told, deplored the fact 'that the work had been but half done'. Acton does not seem to think that more than seven thousand people perished; and he sets out to show that though Catholic statesmen and ecclesiastical dignitaries rejoiced in the crime, Catholic opinion was shocked and Catholic interests were not the motive of the massacre.

3. THE CRUCIAL CONTROVERSIES

The man who is too indignant against the criminals of history is liable to fall into the error of blackening them with a redundancy of wickedness, so that villainy is carried to the point where it is purposeless. Acton's account of the massacre of St Bartholomew does not square (and did not square in 1869) with any possible diagram that could be made of the situation in France, or with any of the possible roles that could be formulated for the chief actors in the drama. Nothing could be more precise than the reasons for the massacre—and the predicament which drove Catherine de' Medici to decide upon it— as summarised by Acton himself when he described that current version of the story which he was setting out to attack. Nothing could be more blurred than his own attempt to explain the logic of the whole affair—a piece of discourse which is remarkable from the start in that it refers primarily not to Catherine de' Medici but to Charles IX. Acton writes:

> The political idea before the mind of Charles was...to repress the Protestants at home, and to encourage them abroad. No means of effectual repression was left but murder.... The Court had determined to enforce unity of faith in France. An edict of toleration was issued for the purpose of lulling the Huguenots; but it was well known that it was only a pretence.... The great object was to accom-

plish the extirpation of Protestantism in such a way as might leave intact the friendship with Protestant States....By assassinating Coligny alone it was expected that such an agitation would be provoked among his partisans as would make it appear that they were killed by the Catholics in self-defence....Zeal for religion was not the motive which inspired the chief authors of the extraordinary crime. They were trained to look on the safety of the monarchy as the sovereign law...if mere fanaticism had been the motive, the men who were most active in the massacre would not have spared so many lives.[1]

It is difficult to see how such a piece of exposition could even be brought to square with itself. If the safety of the monarchy was the matter at issue, this might conceivably have been secured at a desperate moment by the resort to a lightning atrocity; but a long-prepared plan implies a long-term calculation of interests, and could not have served either *raison d'état* or the private policies of the court. Acton, who would be fascinated by an historical riddle, had been perhaps too concerned to collect his notes around the problem of the massacre itself. He failed to grasp the internal and external situation of France, and so to discover how intimately the events of St Bartholomew's Day could be related to their context. The man who did the most to overthrow Acton's case was able to put the evidence into order because he established the whole system of relations for a considerable period before the massacre itself.[2]

In proportion as this had even been achieved before Acton wrote, it had already been possible not merely to reconstruct the story, but also to explain the discrepancies in the evidence. In respect of much of Acton's apparently imposing testimony

---

[1] Acton, *History of Freedom*, pp. 116–22.
[2] Hermann Baumgarten, *Vor der Bartholomäusnacht* (Strassburg, 1882), which on p. ix affirms 'es ist sehr viel lehrreicher, sich mit dem Kampf der Europa beherrschenden Mächte in dieser Zeit zu beschäftigen, als immer nur an dem blutigen Räthsel der Bartholomäusnacht herum zu pflücken'. On this point see also Friedrich von Bezold's review of Baumgarten in *Historische Zeitschrift*, XLVII (1882), 560. In *Historisch-Politische Zeitschrift*, II (1835), 591, Ranke had already declared that the relations between the European states in the period before the massacre were inconsistent with the old view of premeditation.

certain principles of interpretation had already been current
which served to reconcile the inconsistencies. When Coligny,
secure in the confidence of Charles IX, was conducting policy
with a high hand, it was natural that in the atmosphere of that
place and period there should be fears or rumours of possible
betrayal. One contemporary diplomat, and some later historians, however, have pointed out that if the Huguenots did
indeed have knowledge of a plan of massacre, Coligny—since
he had the means of information—must have been an 'ass' to
reject all suspicion and flout every warning.[1] And one person
who for a moment had been dismayed by such unlocated fears
was converted by Coligny to the opposite extreme of perfect
confidence. Similarly, there is no need to deny that some
Catholic leaders desired, and some foreign statesmen on
occasion advised, an extermination of the principal Huguenots. It would hardly have been the long-term policy of
Catherine and Charles IX, however—and, indeed, it was the
reverse of their policy at this period—to annihilate one of the
religious factions and thereby put themselves at the mercy of
the other. Nor would this have made possible in the reign of
Charles IX the pursuit of a Protestant foreign policy. Acton
reveals in one place his realisation of the fact that Catherine
might find it to her interest to pretend before Philip II of
Spain that she had long been cherishing the project of
massacre—long waiting for the chance to come out clearly on
the extremist Catholic side. He did not realise that Catherine
might play the same game with other people—the representatives of the Papacy, for example; and that the extremist
Catholics, including men like the Cardinal of Lorraine, might
welcome the imposture, and play up to it, in order that the
court might be irrevocably committed to their cause. From
the time when she had made peace with the Huguenots,
Catherine had had to pacify complaining extremists in the
Catholic world, and had hinted that there would be good news

[1] E.g. H. Baumgarten, op. cit. p. 255, echoing the view of the Venetian ambassador,
Cavalli.

for them at the next turn in the road. It was easy for these people to imagine after the massacre that by these dark hints they had been given the favour of some special foreknowledge of the affair. In some such way as this Acton's information was too often of the kind which had only been brought to precision after the event. This was true of the evidence furnished, for example, by Cardinal Bonelli, by the Cardinal of Lorraine, and by the King's confessor. It was true also in the case of some of the diplomats, including his favourite witness, the nuncio, Salviati.

There were other ways in which the evidence adduced by Acton came to be undermined by later criticism. He noted that the two Venetian diplomats, Cavalli and Michiel, came to opposite conclusions on the question of premeditation. He opted for Michiel, whose verdict supported his own, but both were giving reports and opinions, and both were writing after the event. It transpired later that at the time of the actual massacre these diplomats were living on terms of intimacy in the same house and were writing joint despatches to Venice. Copies of these missing despatches were discovered in the Viennese archives and were printed in 1870 at the end of the Italian translation of Acton's article. Acton, when he wrote the original article, possessed only the accounts which these diplomats produced later, at the close of their respective missions. Michiel's narrative reflects the atmosphere and talk of the autumn of 1572, when premeditation was in the air. Cavalli's account—in favour of a sudden decision—was written in 1574 and reflects the results of fuller and less fevered enquiry. The despatches of the Florentine envoys, which were quoted by Acton, proved, on the other hand, to be the work of men who knew none of the secrets and were able to catch only the flying rumours. One of the things which transpired was the fact that the evidence—especially when it was in a cryptic state—was sometimes open to alternative interpretation. Instructions concerning troop movements, which had once seemed to point to a premeditated massacre, proved equally explicable when it was admitted that the French court was preparing for hostilities against Spain. And whereas Acton accepted a report that the massacres in provincial towns had been 'staggered' according to plan, and by instructions from Paris, Henry White had already shown in 1868 that the timing of these subsidiary upheavals supported the opposite case—it answered to the period required for the news of St Bartholomew's Day to travel to the various provinces and provoke corresponding outbreaks there. Again, the scheme for the assassination of Coligny may have been prepared for more than ten days, and Acton, confronted with an oblique reference to this smaller conspiracy, was perhaps too prone to imagine that he had found an allusion to the larger plan of general massacre. He did not realize, as both earlier and later historians did, that the killing of Coligny was a pointless and hazardous move if the extermination of the leading Huguenots was also in mind. It was calculated to lead to the dispersal of the intended victims, who, on the theory of the prosecution, had needed so much artifice to bring them together in Paris. Acton possessed some if not all of the evidence that the Papacy and Spain suspected the court of Charles IX to the very last, were exasperated by its foreign policy, and were bitterly opposed to the Protestant marriage. When she was most anxious to obtain the dispensation for the marriage, Catherine de' Medici gave no hint to Gregory XIII that she was arranging it only in order to lure the Huguenots to their death. Certainly she promised benefit for the Roman Catholic Church from this marriage; but it may have been that she hoped to see Henry of Navarre ultimately converted as a result of it. In any case, the massacre might have conformed to the policy of the Duke of Guise and Philip II of Spain, but it agreed so little with the interests of the crown or of Catherine de' Medici that only the desperate necessity of the moment can account for the decision at this particular period.

Much of Acton's argument, in fact, repeats the case put forward by John Allen in his controversy with the Catholic historian, Lingard, over forty years before. It does not provide an answer to the comprehensive survey and the strong arguments already presented by Georges Gandy in a too aggressively Catholic article in the first two issues of the *Revue des Questions Historiques*, 1866.[1] Acton himself does not properly lay out his material—does not adequately reproduce even the evidence of Salviati in the way that Gandy had done—but too often purports to sum up its effect in cryptic allusions or dogmatic assertions. Cardinal Bonelli may have had a secret to communicate to Pius V in the spring of 1572; but his claim to foreknowledge seems to have resulted from reflection in a later period upon the dark hints with which Catherine sometimes liked to soothe importunate Catholics. When Acton quoted a manuscript source in support of his view he laid himself open to the criticism that he did nothing to establish either the authorship or the date of this document.[2] In fact, Lingard had been right in distrusting this whole part of the evidence; Acton was wrong in claiming—as he once did—that he had established its veracity. He had ignored arguments that had already been advanced against his view. And in respect of this, also, some subsequent writers have not spared him.

In that unfinished draft of a history of the historiography of this subject, which Acton appears to have been writing in the middle of the 1870's, he seems to put on record his failure to convince the world. 'The most unbiased critics', he writes, 'Reuss, Maury and Loiseleur continued to accept' the view that the massacre was unpremeditated. In 1879, however, Henri Bordier started up a fresh controversy by a book published in Geneva, on *La St Barthélemy et la Critique Moderne*, and he reasserted the case for the existence of a long-prepared

[1] Georges Gandy, 'La Saint-Barthélemy, ses Origines, son vrai Caractère, ses Suites'. This article makes a very considerable survey of the previous literature, discusses the value of Miron, notes the work of Griffet, and examines the evidence of Salviati.

[2] H. Baumgarten, op. cit. p. 131. Cf. Ludwig, Freiherr von Pastor, *Geschichte der Päpste seit dem Ausgang des Mittelalters*, VIII, 383 n. Bonelli had written: 'con alcuni particolari ch'io porto, dei quali ragguagliero nostro Signore a bocca, posso dire di non partirmo affato mal expedita'. On the controversy concerning these words see Pastor, op. cit. VIII, 381–6.

plot. He was a Protestant writer, avowedly polemical, and he attacked not merely the recent trends in historical interpretation but also the impartial attitude itself—the general posture of the scientific historian. In the same year, a Saxon professor, Wuttke, supported the case for premeditation in a large-scale discussion of sources, posthumously published.[1] These, together with the Italian translation of Acton's article—though Bordier was the effective influence—converted Alfred Maury, the director of the National Archives of France, who had once been designated the most reliable writer amongst the enemies of the theory of premeditation.[2] The *Revue Historique* called attention to the fact that a further historian, Wijnne, writing in the Dutch journal, *Gids*, represented still another nation that had found a spokesman on the side of the prosecution.[3] From this period the publications on the subject of the massacre of St Bartholomew came in quick succession, and between 1879 and 1882 the controversy rose to its point of maximum intensity, though Acton himself does not seem to have been an important factor in the upheaval. Loiseleur and others ably opposed the advocates of premeditation, and in 1882 Hermann Baumgarten, a Protestant (reinforced both now and later by Martin Philippson), definitely turned the balance against premeditation. Other work in the succeeding decade, such as that of La Ferrière, the editor of Catherine de' Medici's letters,

[1] Heinrich Wuttke, *Zur Vorgeschichte der Bartholomäusnacht* (Leipzig, 1879). This work also makes a full survey of the existing literature.

[2] In four articles in the *Journal des Savants*, 1871, Maury, reviewing H. White, op. cit. had admitted that the French court might have had a treacherous *arrière-pensée* in the peace of 1570, but declared that White had proved the case against premeditation in 1572, and declined to accept the essential arguments of Acton. In the same journal, March 1880, pp. 245–64, Maury, in an article entitled 'Nouvelles Recherches sur la Saint-Barthélemy', changed his opinion, however, and in particular he declared that the Miron account had lost all value since the work of Bordier. See Jules Loiseleur, 'Les Nouvelles Controverses sur la Saint-Barthélemy', *Revue Historique*, xv (1881), 82–109. Cf. Jules Loiseleur, *Trois Énigmes Historiques* (1882), p. 3. G. Bagnenault de Puchesse produced a criticism of Bordier in 'La Préméditation de la Saint-Barthélemy', *Revue des Questions Historiques* (1882), 372–9.

[3] *Revue Historique*, xv (1881), 108 n. The editors of this review declare that they do not believe in a long-prepared plan but admit 'une préméditation générale'. Also in 1879 appeared Comte Hector de la Ferrière, *Le XVI siècle et les Valois*, and Marie Camille Alfred, Vicomte de Meaux, *Les Luttes religieuses en France au 16me siècle*.

confirmed this tendency, and scholarship on this subject came to a comparatively stable condition.[1]

It was easy to pick up rumours and apparent signs of premeditation, but it is never so simple a matter to discover what the case required: namely, positive evidence for the proving of a negative. Pointers could be found, however, as in a despatch from the Venetian, Cavalli, to whom in July 1572 Catherine de' Medici asserted that the adoption of drastic measures was an impossibility in France. We should not need to believe Catherine's assertions at this point of the story, but it is striking that the suggestion of such measures provoked from her the retort that the troubles in the Netherlands were precisely due to the severities of Alva. The work of Baumgarten shows the importance of establishing the individual roles, the personal relationships and the internal and external setting of events in the years before August 1572, if the evidence is to be properly interpreted. From the 1880's, furthermore, the correspondence was recovered in greater continuity—the historian was no longer so greatly at the mercy of mere fragments and partial selections. It became apparent in this period that the diplomatic correspondence of Spain, Venice, Florence and Rome itself—even the letters of Acton's favourite witness Salviati—strengthened the overall case against premeditation. That correspondence tended to confirm the general evidence of the contemporary writers who were most in a position to disclose the truth—Marguerite de Valois, Marshal Tavannes and the writers of the alleged confession of the Duke of Anjou. The result was an explanation at least consistent with the general role that the chief actors were known to have had in the larger drama of the period.

Acton did not fail to turn a problem round and round, studying the theory of a massacre as well as the motives for it, and

[1] H. Baumgarten, op. cit.; Martin Philippson, *Westeuropa in Zeitalter von Philip II, Elizabeth und Henri IV* (Berlin, 1882), e.g. p. 268; H. de la Ferrière, *Lettres de Catherine de Médicis*, IV, 1570–4 (1891), e.g. pp. xxx–lxxviii, and *La Saint Barthélemy* (Paris, 1892); Martin Philippson, 'Die Römische Curie und die Bartholomäusnacht', *Deutsche Zeitschrift für Geschichtswissenschaft*, VII (1892), 108–37.

so rooting his history (as he always claimed to be proper) in the world of ideas. His notes as well as his published articles show his interest in this more doctrinaire side of the question; and he seems somewhat to foreshadow Platzhoff, who wrote much later on homicide in its relations with the sixteenth-century theory of state.[1] Some of this kind of reflection goes perhaps unnecessarily into regions of doctrinairism and speculation;[2] and it is not equally clear that Acton had seen the immense significance of atmosphere and tendency in that peculiar historical world in which the massacre took place. The student of these times has to remember how events had undermined the system which is necessary to procure a stable order, a world of steady expectations, and a civilised way of transacting business—all what we regard as 'normality'. In the wildest melodrama there is hardly the like of this—for both sides feel free to commit treachery and constantly expect it in return. When life is carried on under these conditions even the deeds of atrocity are by no means so numerous as the fears, the suspicions, the whisperings, the rumours of atrocity. In these circumstances the evidence of private letters and secret diplomatic correspondence may be brought to light and yet may only confront us with new pitfalls. Indeed, witnesses for a projected massacre of Huguenots can be found in 1572, but they are discoverable also in other years; and in 1567 Pope Pius V could not reconcile his conscience to the things which he had heard that the French court was planning. We can

---

[1] Walter Platzhoff, *Die Theorie von der Mordbefugnis der Obrigkeit im XVI Jahrhundert*, Historische Studien, 54 (Berlin, 1906).

[2] C.U.L. Add. 4863: 'The indifference and coldness of Europe may be partly explained.

'The barbarity and the folly of criminal jurisdiction had reached their highest point.

'Men fancied that it was their duty to punish offences against God as well as against man, and as crimes were liberally punished with death a punishment severer than death was requisite to indicate the greater atrocity of crimes against the honour of God.

'No sufferings could be too great for them and as they were defending God, they might rely that He would distinguish innocence from guilt.

'The idea on which ordeals were founded survived in the treatment of such things. And so it happened that the most frightful penalties were those which were inflicted with the least compunction and the least care.'

find evidences of premeditation in periods where no massacre occurred on which the issue of premeditation might be raised. And because there is so much evidence of so mixed a sort, any treatment of this subject must still leave one or two loose ends which are worthy of notice.

4. LOOSE ENDS

The historian who has disposed of a problem must perhaps expect a residuum of minute discrepancies, like pieces left over when a jig-saw puzzle has been completed. Alternatively, there may be anomalous fragments of evidence which have to be poked a little before they will quite fit into the final story. The result is perhaps the slightest suggestion of uneasiness—not because the mind itself has misgivings but because one writer and another still shows that he is unconvinced. The doubts on the subject of the massacre of St Bartholomew may not have affected the main stream of scholarship, but they remind us of the pieces of the puzzle that are still left over. They concern us because separate people, disturbed by separate pieces of evidence, have happened to resurrect two of Acton's witnesses, apparently without knowing of Acton's work. It is necessary, therefore, not to leave unexamined the case of Salviati and Capilupi.

Salviati—'the strongest witness against the court and the Church', as Acton once said—reported on the very day of the catastrophe that he could not believe that such a massacre would have taken place but for the failure to assassinate Coligny two days before. Acton neglected to quote this passage—which the writer repeated a little later—though he quoted another part of the same despatch, indeed from the same page in a printed book, so that he had certainly had it before his eyes.[1]

---

[1] Salviati had written: 'Se l'archibugiata ammazzava subito l'armiraglio, non mi risolvo a credere che se fussi fatto tanto a un pezzo.' Augustin Theiner, *Annales Ecclesiastici*, I (Rome, 1856), 329. Acton quotes another passage from this page and this despatch in *History of Freedom*, III, n. 3.

Yet the passage was not only to be significant in the later historiography of the subject; it had been used with considerable effect, and even italicised by more than one writer just before. It had been quoted by Henry White in the book which gave Acton the pretext for his paper in the *Chronicle* in 1868. If there were contradictions in Salviati's despatches many of these had been laid out and discussed (in a way that Acton did not condescend to do) in Gandy's article in the *Revue des Questions Historiques*, 1866. It is true that a little before St Bartholomew's Day Salviati had some warning of a conspiracy; but it is generally held that this was the conspiracy to assassinate Coligny—one which did have a short period of preparation. In subsequent weeks, however, Salviati allowed himself to be persuaded that dark hints given to him in the preceding months had really been a foreshadowing of the massacre itself. From later evidence it did seem to emerge that Salviati had convinced his court of this fact, once the massacre had actually occurred, though, as Acton realised, the Roman court believed in premeditation in any case. It is significant, however, that Salviati received from Rome the reply that since he had had this foreknowledge he ought to have communicated it at least in cipher at the time.[1] One would have said that the inconsistencies in Salviati had been sufficiently explained away; yet this diplomat was perhaps just a little firm in maintaining also his claim to foreknowledge, and he is at the same time the one person whom Catherine de' Medici declared to have been admitted to the secret in advance. Victor Martin, in *Le Gallicanisme et la Réforme Catholique* (1919), thinks that Salviati must have known of a plot which extended further than the mere assassination of Coligny; and it is this view which presents the real point of difficulty. Martin Philippson, who found more of Salviati's reports than Baumgarten had seen, put forward the suggestion that while Catherine was planning

---

[1] In Add. 5005, Acton at a later date copied out this reproof, Rusticucci to Salviati, 8 Sept. 1572, from Martin Philippson, *Deutsche Zeitschrift für Geschichtswissenschaft*, VII (1892), 132–3.

only the murder of Coligny, Salviati had learned bigger things from some of her associates of the Catholic party; and, without her knowledge, these latter had already determined to carry the design to further extremes.[1]

Lucien Romier, in the *Revue du 16me Siècle*, 1913, reproved scholars for overlooking the earliest edition of Camillo Capilupi's book, *Lo Stratagemma di Carlo IX*. As he dates the publication 18 September 1572 he seems to be referring to the edition Acton claimed to have discovered, with a dedication of the same date. Both writers claim that Capilupi is a witness of some consequence, and both are impressed by the way in which his earliest edition supports the Cardinal of Lorraine in his claim to foreknowledge of the massacre. Romier has also discovered a private letter of 5 September which shows that Capilupi was not merely putting forward this opinion for propaganda purposes. It seems that, once the news of St Bartholomew had arrived, a surprising number of people in Italy were immediately able to produce evidence that they had had letters about it in the preceding weeks, and that the Cardinal of Lorraine had foreknowledge of the event. It is the Italian writers of that time who have often been charged with the invention of the 'stratagem' version of the massacre of St Bartholomew, the version which asserts treachery and premeditation. The evidence always refers in a suspicious manner to the Cardinal (then in Rome), and nothing that has survived seems actually to reach back to an earlier date than the arrival of the news of the massacre. It is clear, however, that the Italian historians of the time were reflecting something that really existed in the background. Romier suggests that in fact from April 1572 the Guise family had been making their own plan for securing a massacre when the Huguenot leaders should be assembled for the wedding. Catherine herself was in no sense a party to the scheme, but eventually it was coupled to her own design against Coligny; and, as Ranke emphasised,

[1] Victor Martin, op. cit. pp. 105–7; M. Philippson, 'Die Römische Curie...', p. 133.

she herself did once say that she would accept responsibility for only half a dozen of the murders.[1] Something here seems to chime in with the view that emerged from the discussion of Salviati, though Romier's story is itself not without its difficulties; especially as it is not supported by evidence prior to the massacre itself, while the attack on Coligny was, in fact, a solitary attempt at assassination. Perhaps Ranke was right in a sense—though even now not sufficiently flexible—when he saw that the massacre might have been in a certain way premeditated, though in reality (and particularly so far as Catherine was concerned) it was to be regarded as a product of the sudden decision. At the same time neither Ranke nor Acton quite realized one point which may have a certain significance: namely, that if the idea of massacre had so long been in the air, this itself is to be regarded as a cause rather than as a result. In other words, it is not to be taken as evidence of long-prepared treachery, but was rather the reason why the idea itself was so handy in August 1572—why Catherine could so readily turn to it in a moment of desperation.

When all misgivings are taken into account, however, the old idea of a long period of treachery would seem to have been put out of court for ever. The peace with the Huguenots in 1570, the marriage with Henry of Navarre, and all the favours shown to Coligny, can no longer be envisaged as merely a mask for an incredibly sinister and prolonged murder-plot. Acton had been wrong in imagining that the case against premeditation had depended on Miron's account of a confession made to him by the Duke of Anjou in 1573. Bordier in 1879 persuaded some historians to reject the document, as Acton had done, and to regard it as an invention of the seventeenth century. The chief part of his argument had already appeared in the work of John Allen over fifty years before, however, and some of the developments which he gave to the thesis were later proved to be inaccurate. Acton had been wrong in thinking

---

[1] On this controversy see also L. Pastor, op. cit. IX, 359 n., and Jean-H. Mariéjol, *Catherine de Médicis*, 3rd ed. (Paris, 1922), 13 n.

that the authenticity of the document itself had merely been allowed to pass unquestioned in recent times. Historians had often said why they relied on it, and Gandy in 1866 had discussed the matter at some length, even dealing with the objections put forward by John Allen. This confession of the Duke of Anjou received further defence in French periodicals in 1880 and 1881, on the ground that it had a genuine basis, though there were signs of interpolation. In 1909 Henry Monod put forward another narrative, the *Vera et brevis Descriptio*, as the genuine confession of Anjou.[1] He showed, however, that though this might claim the greater authenticity, it was in reality less veracious than the one that had been attributed to Miron. This latter document, he insisted, must have come from an actual participant. In a sense this Miron document was vindicated in just the points at which Acton sought to assert its unreliability. Even if it is not the confession of Anjou, it is significant, because there is so much in it that is true—so much that agrees with the rest of the evidence. The case against premeditation, which in Acton's view once depended on Miron, is now the very thing which carries the case for this document and gives it a certain weight.

If the reconstruction of the narrative leaves some people wondering (as all history ought to do) and fetches perhaps the suggestion and the mere shadow of a sigh, we may note that Acton himself had no real misgivings in the long run. He accepted the general verdict of both Baumgarten and Philippson, as he admits in his *Lectures on Modern History*, which belong to the closing years of his life. He now said of the massacre: 'It is perfectly certain that it was not a thing long and carefully prepared...and those who deny premeditation in the common sense of the word are in the right.'[2] A few years later the *Cambridge Modern History* showed itself a little more Actonian on this subject than Acton himself had come to be; and resurrected the evidence of Cardinal Bonelli,

[1] *Revue Historique*, CI (1909), 316–26, Henri Monod, 'La version du duc d'Anjou sur la Saint-Barthélemy'.   [2] P. 161.

though describing him as 'Bonetti'.[1] There is a notebook of Acton's that reveals the way in which he would always think out such problems, and his pencilled arguments show how he would turn over one idea and another when he was considering such questions. He writes, for example, at this later date:

Could not be a dodge in the summer of 1572—or they [the French court] would have informed Philip II and the Pope.
They did neither.
Urging Gregory [XIII] to grant the license [for the marriage with Henry of Navarre] they say nothing about it and Philip and Alva had no idea of it.

Catherine's letters to Rome when they want to soothe the Pope say nothing of the massacre intended. This is more decisive [i.e. against the idea of premeditation] even than the Pope's resistance about the dispensation [i.e. the marriage].[2]

A new and bulky set of notes on the whole subject show Acton carefully reproducing in his immaculate handwriting the mass of evidence which had been brought forward to destroy his own case.[3] One of the pieces which he transcribed is curiously reminiscent of the passage he had omitted to quote from his favourite witness, Salviati; and he had himself possessed a transcription of it already for years, since it had been printed by Gachard in 1849 and the whole article had been copied out for him by hand. The Spanish ambassador, Zuniga—a caustic enemy of the claim that the massacre was a premeditated act of policy—wrote on 8 September 1572:

Although the French wish to make out that their King was meditating this coup ever since the peace [of 1570]...and attribute to him stratagems which would not appear to be permissible even when directed against heretics and rebels, I hold it for a certainty that if

---

[1] III, 19–20.
[2] C.U.L. Add. 5586. In Add. 4863 and Add. 5004 are further notes which show Acton working out his conclusions.
[3] C.U.L. Add. 5005.

the shooting of the Admiral was designed a few days in advance and authorised by the King, still all the rest was only precipitated by circumstances.[1]

Zuniga glanced at a truth which had already been realised by historians who wrote earlier than Acton on this subject; namely, that Catherine de' Medici was so untruthful that she is not necessarily to be believed even when she is giving evidence against herself.

[1] Transcript in Add. 4843, from *Bulletin de l'Academie de Bruxelles*, XVI (1849). In later notes of Acton, Add. 5005, the same passage is transcribed by Acton from Comte H. de la Ferrière, *Lettres de Catherine de Médicis*, IV, p. cxv.

APPENDICES

LA POPELINIÈRE'S 'HISTOIRE DES HISTOIRES'

Although he covers hundreds of pages with unconnected descriptions of successive individual historians, La Popelinière envisages the development of history from poetry to crude annals, and then to a more refined form of narrative [I, 36 ff., 158]. Apart from this, his work is governed by a thesis, for he believes 'qu'aucun de quelque temps & langue qu'il soit, n'a faict histoire telle qu'on doit & peut dresser' [I, 8]; and in his view not only were the Ancients little better than the Moderns [I, 7], but the Moderns had it in their power to excel, if they only made proper use of the advantages which they possessed over antiquity [I, 9]. He complains that even the ancient Greeks knew as little about their own earlier history as the nations of more recent times [I, 69; cf. 36]; and he will not allow that history or any of the sciences began in Greece [I, 137, 139, 149]—Enoch, for example, is in his view the first of historians and the first of authors [I, 70]. Only Thucydides seems to escape his censure [I, 167–79; II, 46, 88, 118, 174] and repeatedly he speaks of the lies of Herodotus [I, 159–63, II, 43, 48, 83] or the defamation of the Christians by Tacitus [I, 335–43; cf. II, 107–9]. Plato and Aristotle advanced themselves, he says, by burning the books of their predecessors [I, 118, 485]; while the Romans were 'Singes des Grecs en presque toutes choses' [I, 24, II, 51]. A second part of his work, on *L'idée de l'Histoire accomplie* resumes the arguments in favour of the authority of the Ancients [II, 1–2] and then attacks them at length, asserting that in any case historians pay too much respect to their predecessors [II, 197]. He asks: are we to be content with the writings of the Ancients and not write anything more? 'Si Platon, Aristote, & autres, se fussent arrestez aux escrits de leurs deuanciers, qu'elles sciences aurions nous?' [II, 282; cf. 4]. It is possible to show the weakness of the Ancients from their criticisms of one another [II, 282] though the folly of 'l'oppinion commune' now seems to insist that the Ancients 'ont...tiré l'eschelle après eux' [II, 283]. Most of the Greeks only had 'common knowledge' and the modern student has only to read their works to acquire all this while he is

Appendix I

still young [II, 286–7]. In this second part of his work La Popelinière puts forward many interesting ideas. In favour of the use of the vernacular, he asserts that the languages of his day have not yet developed all their potentialities [II, 254]. Like Machiavelli, he believes that men are always the same, and that the accidents of one age of history are repeated in another age, so that in a certain sense history is always of a similar texture [II, 38, 39, 41, 178]. He thinks that writers of the history of their own times are more worthy of credit than 'ceux qui tousiours colez sur les liures, ne s'amusant qu'à regrater les escrits de leurs deuanciers' [II, 41]. He protests against speeches in historical narratives, for these, he says, are invented by the historian, and they reflect the manners and customs of the age in which the historian, and not the supposed speaker, lived [II, 75–81]. He states the case for and against judgements (including moral judgements) on the part of the historian [II, 292 ff.], and after scoffing at the 'petis escoliers, qui sortis des Vniuersitez se hazardent de re-former les loix de Lycurgue ou de Solon ces grands politics' [II, 295], he asserts that the historian should chose a middle way [II, 309] and give 'aduis'; but in dealing with massacres, theft, adultery, etc., it is not his place to condemn or excuse—he must faithfully narrate and leave the reader to judge [II, 312]. In discussing his plan for a new history of the French [II, 330 ff.] he gives a more organised and critical account of French historiography [II, 333 ff.] and of the way in which it had been patronised by French kings [II, 372–80]. He himself wants from the king only 'permission de voir les lieux esquels ie sçay que se trouueront les plus nobles & rares choses de ce Royaume' [II, 380]. He puts forward the view that 'il n'a de sciences que par la vraye cognoissance des causes naturelles' and he applies this to history [II, 355]. Finally in his attempt to destroy the legend that the French and other European peoples were descended from Trojans who had fled at the fall of their city [II, 362; cf. I, 9] he illustrates the great ingenuity which could be displayed in the work of criticism before the birth of what we should call the scientific age.

ACTON AND ITALIAN SCHOLARSHIP

Add. 4931, 80: 'The glory departs from the French after 1712. Centres in Italy, from Muratori. The work of accumulation lasted two centuries—first, French and German and English. Then, chiefly Italian.'

Ibid. 115. 'Dec. 5 Muratori—most extensive knowledge of histories, and of History, so far as to be found in them. But only a little care, and that not the most certain. He cared so little for documents, that he never visited Rome, the home of them....'

Ibid. 174. 'Dec. 9. Italians are that part of our literature which has been most unduly neglected. Forgotten by the Germans—not referred to when giving lists of auxiliaries. Local, ecclesiastical.'

Add. 5002, 266: 'Dec. 9. From Muratori onwards Italy became the great seat of learning. A literature which was not not [*sic*] superior to the best French but more extensive, lasting to the French Revolution and even later. Not much about other countries. But Rome, the great monasteries, supplied boundless material. In our times again. We depend on Italy.'

Add. 5002, 32: 'How late Italian H[istory] dropped out of sight. Everybody knew Mabillon, Martens, Tillemont, Dugdale, Wilkins, Rymer, Goldast. But the Italians, after Maffei and Muratori, became little known beyond the Alps. Libri's Catalogue contained them nearly all. Especially ecclesiastical literature. Churches of Verona, writers of Bologna, defences of Rome, agst Giannone, Picenum.'

Add. 4929, 127: 'Immense value of Italian scholarship. It has made Mommsen so great by combining the monumental with the critical plan. Borghesi. Cavedoni. De Rossi.' Cf. *Historical Essays and Studies*, 351: 'Raumer...made it known that there was much to be learnt from the Italians.'

'Döllinger's Historical Work' in *History of Freedom*, 386–7: 'Several of his countrymen, such as Savigny and Raumer, had composed history on the shoulders of Bolognese and Lombard scholars. ...During the tranquil century before the Revolution, Italians studied the history of their country with diligence and success. Even such places as Parma, Verona, Brescia, became centres of obscure but faithful work. The story of the province of Treviso was told in twenty volumes. The antiquities of Picenum filled thirty-two folios. The best of all this national and municipal patriotism was given to the service of religion.... In this immense world of patient, accurate, devoted research, Döllinger laid the deep foundations of his historical knowledge.'

Add. 4929, 124: 'The influence of the Italians felt gradually. Sarti-Savigny. Borghesi-Mommsen. Ballerini-Maassen.'

Add. 4931, 129: 'Italian H[istory] lost sight of. Often in 10, 20 and even 30 volumes.'

Add. 4997, 223: 'Raumer knew the Italians, who were the best predecessors, quite as well as Ranke—yet they taught him nothing.'

ACTON AND DÖLLINGER

Add. 4912, 61: 'He [Döllinger] could not always account for his critical judgments. Ranke, in extreme old age, when his eyes were dim, gave an account of his critical processes. Döllinger, at last, seldom did it. He relied on the impression. The faculty developed by his incomparable practise and experience. And would say that one would assuredly see things as he sees them, if one gave a month or two to it. He should have said, if you gave half a century. As to the sincerity of a writer, the derivation of a statement, the motive of a fable, the cause of an effect.'

Add. 4912, 64: 'It is the infirmity of old men to reach their conclusions by rule of thumb, without accounting for them...they recognise types of character by a single trait, and they grievously disappoint, because their opinions, tho[ugh] probably true, have to be discarded, as unproved.'

'Döllinger's Historical Work' in *History of Freedom and Other Essays* (London, 1907), 393: 'He could impart knowledge better than the art of learning. Thousands of his pupils have...gathered... some notion of the meaning of history; but nobody ever learned from him the mechanism by which it is written.'

Add. 5609, f. 19b: '[Döllinger's] mode of work. No idea of getting things up. Mass of material already collected. Sure to supply unexpected sidelights. Read with the pen and pencil. Every striking passage noted down, marked in pencil. Paper signal. Reference in notebook. His own 30,000 volumes full of them. And a larger number of library-books. How he said they must be removed. Not copied—only the substance, not on separate sheets. In notebooks, like Darwin. Systematic indexing. No going back to the originals. Plan not sufficient. You must copy word for word. On separate papers. So as to mix as they suit. Either in boxes or in [?]S's pigeonholes—at Banbury. École des Chartes. Murray's Dictionary' [which was prepared by a similar use of slips].

ACTON'S EARLIEST ACCOUNT OF THE HISTORICAL MOVEMENT

[Written in pencil in a note-book when he was twenty-three years of age.]

[Add. 5527, 19b–21a] Monday, April 1858:

German history arose with German literature and it was very important that the men at the head of literature sh[oul]d have written history. Schelling (ac. stud.) says no country has so few historians as Germany. In the 18th century that was the case. First came Müller and had very great influence indeed, especially by the later publication of his letters. The first thing that had great influence was the Revolution. Historians awoke to the reality of history: they had seen events thro' the spectacles of mere book-learning (Gatterer...[sic]). Now these great events before them made them conscious of historical progress. Müller had some of this—Spittler. Woltmann—who is quite formed by the Revolution. Then Schiller first taught the Germans the value of form and elegance in historical writing. Till then they knew it not, and thus his bad books had great influence. Then the Freiheitskrieg awoke patriotism and the Germans looked away from the ages where they had done nothing to the M[iddle] Ages when they were so great. This new Richtung led to greater justice towards Catholicism. Müller and Niebuhr are the two chief points—Ranke, is also quite original. Nobody before him had written de l'esprit sur l'histoire. The critical tendency is due to Niebuhr entirely. It is remarkable what difference it makes even in a literary point of view to what subject this method is applied. Schwegler's Roman history is very good indeed. His Nachap-[ostolische] Zeit[alter] is as bad as possible—one could not believe they were written by the same man. He exaggerate[s] only the way of Baur.

Fairness began in Müller by real historical ability—also by patriotism anticipating 1813. Spittler was able as a political historian, but had no knowledge of religion and hated the church. Plank wrote on the pat[riotic] development pretty freely, and the dull and dismal picture he had to draw made him admire somewhat the Catholic Church when he wrote his other work. Then he wrote when the Church seemed destroyed. He was speaking of an institution gone by—which excited neither fear nor hatred more. He c[oul]d easily say how brilliant it had once been without alarm for the present as the pope was shut up, the church fallen and no bishops either in France or Germany.

The great war brought men back to olden times, and they saw that the Church had been useful then, but without any thought of her now. They could say that, tho' resolved to abide by Protest[antism] or whatever took its place for the present (Voigt). The hostility of the old rationalists (Tschimer etc.) was of a contemptuous kind. But within 1817, and the revival of the church, concordats etc.—a more bitter hatred began to develop itself (Hengstenberg). This kept pace with the progress of a more intelligent justice. Out of this again grew the fairness of Leo etc.

Contempt for Protestantism is at the bottom of much apparent impartiality of this school. Add to this old patriotism, and much is explained. But when we see men of such different tendencies and characters, opinions, countries and schools, writing with awe and respect of the Church, at a time too when many Catholics still repel them by absurd zeal, and others disgust by their lukewarmness and rationalism, as well as by inferiority in learning and ability, we must admit the great power of really profound study upon minds of the German stamp, distinguished for a disinterested and courageous love of truth.

In Plank's time the only convert was Stolberg, who was laughed at.

Philosophy did good by removing the view of history as a mere succession and heap of facts, and gave a unity to all, but it did infinite harm by leading to generalisations and [construction?] of history, which is the death of real history. Gfrörer knows only political motives and causes, but you cannot write history with one factor alone.

ACTON AND THE MIDDLE AGES

[Amongst drafts of his early publicistic programme, *c.* 1859.]

[Add. 5528, pp. 170b–173a]:

Two great principles divide the world, and contend for the mastery, antiquity and the middle ages. These are the two civilizations that have preceded us, the two elements of which our's is composed. All political as well as religious questions reduce themselves practically to this. This is the great dualism that runs through our society. In the 15th and 16th century, in the Renaissance and the Reformation which followed and agreed with it, as both were a reaction against the medieval ideas, Europe broke with the M[iddle] A[ges]. They were not misunderstood and condemned, they were forgotten and ignored. All intellectual culture was devoted to antiquity. Politics and literature were attracted exclusively by pagan antiquity, theology addicted itself almost exclusively to Christian antiquity. Both proudly and ignorantly overlooked a thousand years of Christian history. They were abandoned and abjured. In this Catholics vied with Protestants. Controversy confined itself chiefly to the early ages. To the greatest classical and ecclesiastical scholars, Protestants and Catholics, all that period was nearly a blank, to Grotius as to Bossuet. The result was Absolutism and revolution in the state; in the Church Protestantism, Gallicanism, and that aspect of religious things which belongs to the teaching of the Jesuits, which bears [?] so much contrast with the medieval habits of the Church. Indeed in literature as well as theology it has generally been the practise of the order to confine itself to ancient learning, and to pay less attention than the Benedictines for instance, to these ages in which it had no existence.

Thus it came to pass that an interest for the M[iddle] A[ges] was awakened neither among Catholics nor among Protestants, for one feared, the other hated them, but among Rationalists and infidels.

This renaissance of the Christian ages, this discovery of a palimpsest, this renewal of an interrupted continuity, is the great work of the 19th century. The epoch that was inaugurated by the Renaissance and the Reformation had reached its termination and its ruin, in the predominance of unbelief in religion, and of the revolution in politics—when a last determined effort was made to destroy every vestige of the dark, superstitious, or feudal ages, and to saw off the branch upon which all were sitting. Then it came to light that modern Europe, the world of [omission in the MS.] had pronounced judgment on itself. The nineteenth century is a period of reaction not against the 18th merely, but against all since the fifteenth. But it has this advantage over the Renaissance, that it does not exclude one world in order to adopt another. It does not reject the accumulated progress and treasures of the last 3 centuries, as of old the work of 1000 years was condemned as a failure and wholly worthless. It is not for the sake of the good which is in the M[iddle] A[ges] only, but for the sake of continuity, that we require this return—not because the Revival of paganism was wrong in its origin, but because it was wrong in its excess. . . .

In Politics we desire then the development of medieval institutions with the acquirements of modern civilisation, not the substitution of the new for the old. We wish to avoid and to repress revolution whether it come in the form of anarchy or of despotism, denying the rights of the people or the rights of the state. But we condemn equally and for the same reason the Counter-revolution. We wish, in the words of De Maistre, not the Counter-revolution, but the contrary of the revolution. The degree to which a state has preserved its early elements of govt. or its capacity to return to them, is not to be measured by its external forms. Representative govt. is the development of the medieval idea, either in a monarchy or a democracy. Absolutism is inconsistent not only with freedom but with right, and is always either a disease or a symptom of a disease. Parliamentary govt. is, in this scheme, inconsistent with monarchy.

Nor is the medieval revival of which we speak the enemy of classical culture. The classical world remains one great element of our civilisation as it was already in the M[iddle] A[ges]. It is as inconsistent with the law of continuity to dispense with the ancient as with the Medieval world. Antiquity is as indispensable to us as the M[iddle] A[ges]. But it is not our foundation in the same way, it does not influence us through the same things. It will always be at the bottom of our education. We should otherwise sink into the one-sided partiality of the M[iddle] A[ges] or into American barbarism. We should lose the memory of human virtues, and the idea of beauty in form. Classical literature will always teach men the form and method of things, not the substance. That is the error and danger of classical education. If it prevails alone, without counterpart or equipoise, we must look to it for substance as well as for form. We shall derive our ideas from it as well as our [MS. incomplete here].

The revival was fully justified against the one-sidedness of the M[iddle] A[ges] it was encouraged from the first as a new and rich element of Bildung by all the best and greatest men. But it absorbed all too soon. Long before the ref[ormation] it had caused a general apostasy. The only practical remedy ag[ains]t that was to be [found?] in the restoration of the M[iddle] A[ges].

Now M[iddle] A[ges] cannot teach us form, cannot affect us literarily. It must give us substance and facts. It must teach us history. To know ourselves we must know that [MS. incomplete here].

ACTON AND JOHANN VON MÜLLER

In the Romantic phase of nineteenth-century historiography, one of the surprises of the story is the unusual fascination which Müller exercised over a whole generation of writers, not excluding the young Ranke. It has been held with some justice that rarely has there been so great a discrepancy between contemporary reputation and genuine worth, since Müller hardly deserved to be called an historian at all.[1] Müller had been a student at Göttingen, where he had been won over to history by the influence of Schlözer, who secured that he should write on Switzerland for the German continuation of the English Universal History. By its exploitation of sentiment and local colour this work inspired much Romantic writing; but, though Müller was an omnivorous reader of sources, he compiled without critical method, reviving, for example, the legend of William Tell.[2] His public career was equally anomalous; for he once served the King of Prussia and greatly encouraged the declaration of war against France in 1806. Immediately after the defeat of Jena, however, he went over to Napoleon's side and even passed into the pay of the Bonapartes.

Certainly Acton came to see the weaknesses of Müller, and by the end of his life he says of this man's letters (of which he had once thought so highly) that they chiefly showed how history ought not to be studied.[3] It is even understandable that Acton should not have carried his narrative behind Müller, to the latter's Göttingen teachers; for, as he shows in the very first paragraph of 'German Schools of History', he was thinking in terms of good books, and—unlike Müller—the earlier Göttingen writers, though they realised the importance of style and form, were ludicrously incompetent in precisely this respect. Acton, though he knew how to tear ideas apart and trace out their independent history, makes the amiable mistake of failing to realise that generation may take place in a swamp. It did not occur to him that a new movement may take its rise in thoroughly bad books.

[1] E. Fueter, *Geschichte der Neuren Historiographie*, pp. 403–4.
[2] Ibid. 406.   [3] Add. 4912, 153.

Appendix VI

But, at the end of his life, when he is planning his Romanes lecture, the name of Müller is still the earliest of the German names in his story, and he returns to it on repeated occasions; though in a cryptic note he writes: 'Story of Göttingen', without explaining what is in his mind or expanding the note elsewhere in the way that is customary with him.[1] Müller now comes earliest for a different reason—like his teacher, Schlözer, he had produced a Universal History, but he had succeeded in achieving an even closer unity than his predecessors, as well as in producing an eminently readable book.[2] At the very end of the nineteenth century, Acton himself was preparing what he often called a 'Universal History' for the Cambridge University Press. In his notes for the Romanes lecture he repeatedly tells us that Müller was the first universal historian. At one moment, however, he seems to have had a misgiving; he asks himself whether in reality it is not Voltaire who ought to have this honour; but he dismisses the thought in a summary manner: Voltaire, he says, was 'too ignorant'.[3] After this he makes an attempt to restate his point; and he tells us now that 'Müller is the man who achieved where Voltaire attempted'.[4] He is firm about this: Müller is the 'first man to see history as a whole. Impartially studies ancient, medieval and modern'.[5] And again: 'J. Müller. Coherent. First time there has been so large an induction.'[6]

The impressions of youth are sometimes durable and certain subtle correspondences with Müller would seem to be one of the idiosyncrasies in the pattern of Acton's life. The key may lie in the fact which he himself has reported; namely that Müller had greater influence than any other German historian on Döllinger's conception of history.[7] It may be significant also that Müller, early in the day, had set out to rehabilitate the medieval papacy. Like Acton, Müller was the kind of scholar who tries to read everything and who possesses a prodigious memory. Like Acton, he tried to traverse the original sources not only for a special period but over an extended

[1] Add. 5437, 39.
[2] *24 Bücher allgemeiner Geschichten besonders der europäischen Menschheit* (Tübingen, 1811).
[3] Add. 5002, 26, 'Dec. 14'.
[4] Add. 5002, 74.   [5] Ibid. 209, 'Dec. 5'. Cf. ibid. 201, 'Dec. 7'.
[6] Ibid. 278, 'Dec. 9'. Cf. Add. 4912, 152: 'He was the most universal student of his time, and the most impartial.'
[7] Add. 4912, 152.

field of general history. It was he who called attention to the famous *Relazioni* of the Venetian ambassadors in the library at Berlin—a form of document that was to prove so useful, not only to Ranke (who hunted them out in many places) but also to succeeding historians. Like Acton, Müller used a separate sheet for each excerpt or annotation, and Acton, who informs us of this, finds it remarkable that Döllinger failed to follow his example.[1] Above all, Acton praises Müller as the universal historian who treated all ages alike, whose mind was not blocked against any religion, and who did not try to evade the discrepant detail, the inconvenient fact. Müller, he tells us, could appreciate the Catholicism of the Middle Ages, and yet do justice to Frederick the Great. He showed the ideal combination (or alternation) of sympathy and detachment; for he was able on the one hand to admire Frederick the Great, and on the other hand to avoid condoning his faults of character.[2]

One is tempted to ask whether Müller did not in a certain sense prefigure the kind of historian Acton set out to be. And here, as elsewhere, we must admire that catholicity of mind which enabled the latter to do justice to those qualities which an historian possessed even though that historian was disqualified for any serious purpose by his lack of science, and had already been brought to derision. Acton made a discriminating attack on Carlyle's *Frederick the Great* in his youth,[3] and towards the end of his life he wrote that 'the mystery of

[1] Ibid. 151: 'No religious antagonism or purpose. Always read the sources themselves. His practice, of making each extract on a separate paper, D[öllinger] did not follow.' Cf. ibid. 152: 'Of the proper use of sources he had no clear idea.'

[2] Ibid. 163: 'J. Müller began, for Germany, the practice of warm sympathy together with entire separateness. So in his enthusiasm for the papacy as warm as Comte's. He was eager about Frederic the Great but quite agreed with Gentz that he was the worst of men. He is as full of joy at the Revolution as of horror and could admire the victor of Austerlitz and Jena, without wishing to spare [him]—[without wishing] the oppressor of Germany to escape just punishment.'

[3] Review of Carlyle's *Frederick the Great*, vols. I and II (1858), in *The Rambler*, December 1858, pp. 429–31: '...There is no English historian who has a right to be judged by a higher or severer test, for no one has spoken more deeply and truly on the character and dignity of history....Of this conception of history *Past and Present* and *The French Revolution* were not entirely unworthy. The disgust which Mr Carlyle feels for the men and things of his own time seemed to give him a clearer eye for the past than most of those possess whose vision is distorted by the prejudices of their age. He showed an intelligence of things which no other English historian has understood....But he... failed even to maintain himself on the high ground he had reached....It [*Frederick the Great*] is a history made up of eccentricities....In such a book it seems hardly fair to take note of errors in matters of fact....'

investigation had not been revealed' to Carlyle when he began his *French Revolution*. But on this latter occasion he was more brave than smaller men would have dared to be, for he announced that 'we are still dependent on [Carlyle] for Cromwell, and in *Past and Present* he gave what was the most remarkable piece of historical thinking in the language'.

ACTON ON RANKE

1. ROMAN DIARY, 26 JUNE 1857

[Add. 5751, p. 218]:

Ranke's Reformation not good. He has never understood or explained the importance of the religious movement. He did not know, and he did not wish to do so. Richelieu's policy the best thing he has ever done, but he has not perceived the importance of the religious movement in France at that time which played a great part ag[ainst] Richelieu, in connexion with S. Francis, S. Vincent, Bérulle, Olier and the first Jansenists, S. Cyran etc.

2. ANOTHER EARLY VIEW

[Add. 5528, f. 69 b]:

Ranke sagt von sich: Ich gebe Geschichten, nicht die Geschichte. In preface to his first work. This predominated still when he wrote the [History of the] popes, but the Reformation was wider, and France widest of all. He admits there too that he does not look beyond the unity of Roman-German history. There is a chronological as well as a geographical limit to his knowledge and interest.

The study of the historians of about 1500 is the foundation of his learning. What he has done for the middle ages has been for an exercitation of his criticism, there so well displayed. The notion of political and religious division, begun at the time he first studied, led him naturally to all his other works—only one or two are excrescences.

This is the age to [?] which his whole character is suited to and his style of writing perfectly corresponds to a part of the character of these times.

That preface is important. He will not judge, he only relates.

He quotes p. xvii the ancients from the moderns; and has never shown a knowledge of antiquity.

There is a want of breadth in his pictures—narrative—and a want of comprehensiveness in his intelligence of history.

Leo far wider. Ranke never exhausts a subject. Epicurean.

Appendix VII

[Add. 5528, ff. 70a, b]:

A historian has no standard or organ for minds greater than his own. He reduces them to the level of his comprehension, if not of his capacity. Just as Overbeck could not draw a comic figure, just as Kaulbach would fail in a Blessed Virgin...so there are characters in history that wait long before an historian appears capable of understanding, appreciating, sympathising with them. This is why the eighteenth century, poor of character, neglected individuals and dealt with laws etc in history. Its incapacity made it make an advance in the science, as an invalid may devise ingenious contrivances etc. Richelieu is a character that just suits Ranke.

Here again sympathy, when intelligence is incomplete, misleads, only the sympathetic side is produced, but that with distinguished success, and this is valuable.

This is the great value of some partial historians—of Macaulay for instance in his William, Thiers in Napoleon, Machiavelli in [his History of Florence], Guiccardini in [his History of Italy].

Where it is not the partiality of sympathy, it may be that of passion, hatred, as the Tiberius of Tacitus.

A historian can hardly do all the things or satisfy all wants; how can the same man understand S. Francis (and do justice to) Richelieu Cromwell? Ranke thoroughly fails in the higher, simpler, religious, characters, as Bérulle.

So Gfrörer, with greater and more comprehensive talent, vaster learning, but more unsafe imagination and unsteady criticism than Ranke, degrades the men he most admires, and most expects his readers to admire, to a low level in morals, while he exalts their capacity to an extravagant degree.

3. DRAFT WRITTEN BEFORE 1864

[Add. 5528, ff. 190b–193a] Ranke's history of England:

Ranke completes in this work the circle of European states of which he has written the history during the last 30 years. Beginning with Italy, Turkey and Spain, he proceeded to write the history of the popes in the 16th and 17th century, then the history of Germany during the Reformation, and of the rise of the Prussian monarchy, finally the history of France from Francis I to the death of Lewis XIV. These two centuries are his home. For them he had brought to light much new matter from archives, and they are evidently peculiarly suited to his genius. Historians have come out of his school who have written ably and well on antiquity and the M[iddle] A[ges] but Ranke himself has never ventured on those uncongenial fields. He has never quitted the ground where his strength lies. It would be unfair to him to fail to recognise his peculiar capacity, and the limits of his powers. Ignorant of the power of religious sentiments himself, he is unable to give them their due place in the lives of others. A world entirely actuated (or primarily) by such motives is unintelligible to him. Consequently he is wholly incapable of understanding the ancient heathens or the medieval Christians, antiquity while paganism was yet powerful, or Christendom during the ages of faith. But this is not all; there is a moral defect closely connected with the religious. There is no moral warmth or zeal in his writings. This is not a consequence of the absence of religion from his soul. Tacitus was an atheist; but no historian has passed severer judgment on the morals of his age, none has a more earnest moral feeling. Nevertheless, with all these defects, it must be admitted that the period of the reformation, of the conflict of the church with Protestantism is Ranke's proper field. It must be remembered that it is as the official historiographer of Prussia that Ranke appears as a Protestant historian. This is not natural to him. Catholics ought not, he has said, to write down the Reformers and expose the errors and failings of the reformation, and the Protestants are no longer zealous in that cause. It is not the religious element of modern history that attracts him but the political. For these centuries of religious controversy were not ages of religious enthusiasm, and the wars between Protestants and Catholics had less the character of religious wars than those of the M[iddle] A[ges]. It is not from the Reformation that his studies began. He is the historian of the age not of religious zeal, but of Machiavellian politics. The history of Southern Europe during the period when absolute monarchy was founded and reduced to a system first attracted him, and this is what he has most deeply studied. His early criticism of the historians from the end of the 15th century to the middle of the 16th is a masterpiece. He is most familiar with that generation of statesman who gave Machiavelli the examples for his Prince, and who worshipped no god but fortune, and knew no merit but success. Where such men lived, Ranke is their historian. Ably he finds out the purely political element in the policy of religious nerves, and describes successfully whatever is worldly even in the church. This is his element, circumscribed in time from Lewis XI and Ferdinand the Catholic, Richard III and the Medici, to the great object of his unmixed admiration, the most Machiavellic of princes, the author of the anti-Machiavel, Frederic II; circumscribed in matter too, for his hand loses its cunning when political motives do not exist, when it has to deal with principles, or with heroes. Richelieu for instance is a man after his own heart, and his history of Richelieu is the masterpiece of his historical art, tho' he has lost sight of R[ichelieu] the churchman.

It is not therefore difficult to predict where his success will be in his new subject. It will be greater in the 16th than the 17th century, greater with the Tudors than the Stuarts, with Henry VIII and Elizabeth, with Wolsey and Cranmer, than with Laud, Cromwell.

But he will give us not history, but histories. His history is all plums and no suet. It is all garnish, but no beef. He is a great historical decorator, and avoids whatever is dull or unpleasant, whatever cannot be told in a lively way, or cannot help to his end. He is an epicure and likes only tit-bits. He is the staff officer, who leaves all the rough work to the regimental officers. He appears always in pumps and kid gloves.

This is his great art, the art of selection and of proportion and perspective. In this he is not guided by the importance of events, and here his art becomes artifice, and his ingenuity treachery. No historian has told fewer untruths, few have committed so few mistakes. None is a more unsafe guide. All that he says is often true, and yet the whole is untrue, but the element of untruth is most difficult to detect. Macaulay on the contrary invents details and imagines scenes out of very slender materials, and distorts the truth by what he adds. Ranke deceives not by additions but by selection. So an artist might make Milan Cathedral appear a Grecian edifice by giving a not unfaithful view of the façade alone. Ranke can boast of greater achievements than this.

It is therefore a consolation to know that besides this artist's account we are soon to have a fuller and more accurate and useful account of the 16th century in England. [?] Pauli's history of the later M[iddle] A[ges] is by far the fullest and most complete that exists. We have the best hopes of his treatment of the succeeding period from his criticism of Mr Froude.

He [Ranke] is a fair weather historian, of rise and progress, not of decline and fall. He carries the Prus[sian] mon[archy] to its summit, the French to the eve of its fall, the ref[ormation] to the period of its decrease, the Catholic revival to the period when it met an enemy more powerful than Prot[estantism].

[?Added later.]

Ranke on British Xty. Treatment of Macaulay and Guizot. This provokes a comparison. (Cicero on learning etc. Leo the difference of German and other historians etc).

v. [*sic*] how our political history was really determined by religious question. Errors of Ranke at the end, on history of political theories.

VII. We had a period of conquest in the M[iddle] A[ges], during which political changes were prepared that afterwards required time to develop, and this development, crossed with the Reformation, naturally occupied us a long time. Then safety from invasion, comparatively, after Scotland was reduced, prevented one incentive to external aggrandizement. The strongest instance of the predominance of political principle over ambition, is the refusal of James I to assist vigorously the Prot[estant] cause in Germany. But when our gov[ernmen]t was settled, we again had a period of conquest, out of Europe.

VIII. Theory (elsewhere) of 1688. The King did not then become subject to his par[liamen]t. That was possible only under foreign princes who received their crown from par[liamen]t. Par[liamen]t did not directly diminish the Prerogative, but having given the crown, it naturally gained influence indirectly under the foreign princes to whom it gave it. The revival of royal power was as soon as there was an English King. Even under Queen Anne intrigues of the palace determine great questions of policy as in more absolute monarchies. N.B. The Par[liamen]t not only gave the crown to Brunswick, but protected it for them, ag[ains]t the Jacobites. All this time then they owed their safety to the Par[liamen]t. When the fear of the Jacobites was over, and at the same time a popular English King appeared, these things together produced a revival of royalism.

Whilst England looked to herself, France was the most ambitious nation. Apply to it what Thuc[ydides] says of Athens.

Describe R[anke]'s general view of English history. Compare it with Gfrörer's; look to Gneist for help, in the Constitution. See also Leo's M[iddle] A[ges]. This would properly conclude the article: Ranke's general view, then our own, slightly different, set in its place.

How R[anke] does not understand the medieval element of modern history, and only the modern elements of medieval history.

After his view: This is the light in which the history of our country is viewed by the able panegyrist of the Protestant monarchy of Prussia. It is not congenial ground for him. First because Catholicism runs thro' it all. Then because in our political disputes religion was a preponderant, not a subordinate element. (Story of Joachim II as a sign of the difference.)

Somewhat different from this is the aspect in which the story of his country presents itself to a Catholic and an Englishman & [unfinished].

4. REVIEW OF 1864

A review by Acton of Ranke's *English History*, vol. IV, in *Home and Foreign Review*, April 1864, pp. 714–15, is summarised on p. 88 above. Here Acton says further that 'the author has obtained so much new matter at Paris and Oxford, in the British Museum and the Record Office, that he is entirely free from conventional influences, and presents many new points of view. There could not be a more instructive lesson in historical investigation than carefully to compare the methods used in this volume with those of Macaulay in the following reign. And yet the work has been coldly received among the writer's countrymen, and has not sustained his reputation...we feel that there is something inadequate, narrow, and unsympathising, in his treatment of the constitutional struggles and of the great political and religious parties, while his intimate knowledge of all the contemporary history of Europe is a merit not suited to his insular readers. But in all that relates to general politics, as in the Triple Alliance and the character of Clarendon, the hand of a real master is not to be mistaken.' The review is reprinted in Lord Acton, *Essays on Church and State* (ed. by D. Woodruff), 425–6.

Ranke

Within an interval of very few months Ranke has published a fifth edition of his *Popes*, a large volume on William III,[1] and the two first volumes of a revised collection of his works. All literature can show no historian whose fame rests on so many separate masterpieces. His earlier writings gave an impulse to the study of history, which has produced, in an abundance such as nobody dreamed of, information that was inaccessible when they appeared. To bring them up to the level of what is now expected would overtask the powers of a man who is past seventy. The late edition of the *Popes* was made with so little preparation that blemishes which the author's later studies must have revealed to him long ago, are left as they stood when the knowledge of the sixteenth century was in its infancy. Fifty years of unremitting labour have matured his mind, but without adding to the faculties by which the triumphs of his youth were won. Practice has taught him to rely more on his tact than on his rules; he divines much that he does not prove; and the weight of his own opinion makes him careless of his authorities. The *Popes* cannot be a classic for this age as it was for the last. Time makes its defects more glaring; and no assiduity can superadd the qualities which would now be looked for, to those original merits which gave it an influence in an important branch of learning such as no book has since acquired.

Much of the success was due to the happy choice of the subject. Definite and familiar topics cannot be profitably treated, unless the historian not only exhausts the existing knowledge, but adds to it. There are competitors to outbid; the heading of successive chapters, the authorities to be consulted, are already known to the public; and the writer has to struggle with the ballast accumulated by a hundred predecessors. The novelty which does not reside in the subject must be imported by the author. In the *Popes* the subject itself, as Ranke viewed it, was almost a discovery. The historian wandered through pleasant fields, crossing diagonally the beaten paths which others trod. It is not exactly a history of Rome, or of

---

[1] *Englische Geschichte vornehmlich im sechszehnten und siebzehnten Jahrhundert.* Von Leopold Ranke. Sechster Band. (Leipzig: Duncker und Humblot.)

Italy, or of the Church, or of modern Europe; but just so much of each as there were materials at hand for. It does not give a presentable history of a single pontificate, but fragments and illustrations of very many. The great stream is not there, but its course is marked by a string of lakes. We see a line of skirmishers, but not the chief array. In a miscellaneous subject, the books used, though common enough in their own departments, do not seem obvious, and suggest vast research. The life of Palestrina is not very recondite; but Ranke's devious method leads him to consult it for the Council of Trent, and he exults at the far-fetched prize. There is a sort of affectation with which, after a book has yielded a particular extract, it is ceremoniously dismissed as otherwise worthless. In this way Ranke treats Daru, Capefigue, and Van der Vynckt; and he has not got rid of the habit in his English history. In the second volume he uses that wonderful letter in which James I, rebuking the presumption of Somerset, lays down with force and earnestness, and almost with dignity, his theory of royal favourites. But he immediately adds that Mr Halliwell's book, in which it appeared, has nothing else to recommend it. Compared with the later performances of the author, the *Popes* was not, in truth, a book of great power or research; but it taught by its example the critical use of printed, and the value of unprinted, sources. Before Ranke appeared modern history was in the hands of Robertson and Roscoe, Coxe and Sismondi, good easy men whose merit consisted chiefly in making things more accessible which were quite well known already. But it was beginning to be understood that historical writing requires complex and methodical literary preliminaries, of which the writers on modern history knew no more than Hooke, or Hume, or Mitford. When the text of a chronicler has been ascertained, there is much remaining to be done before his statements can be accepted. His character, position, and opportunities must be investigated; his design and motives enquired into; above all, it is necessary to examine the materials of which his narrative is constructed, and to resolve it into its component parts. These principles, after having effected a revolution in the study of antiquity, had been applied by Stenzel to the Middle Ages, when Ranke adopted them in modern history. He first made himself known as a critic of published histories; and it does not appear that he was induced to resort to archives by the insufficiency of printed materials. The celebrated John

Müller, in his dreamy way, had called attention to a collection of Italian documents in the Berlin library, and there Ranke opened those investigations which he pursued at Vienna, and then more seriously at Venice and Rome. It was a new vein, and a little produce went a great way. The reports which the Venetian ambassadors made at the close of a three years' residence abroad were first brought into notice by him; but the time was not long in coming when no historian would be content without the whole of the ambassador's correspondence, day by day. Thirty years ago the use of a few unconnected reports, or a few casual instructions, implied a miracle of research. At first, Ranke employed his manuscripts like his books, to give point rather than solidity to his narrative. When he came to a well-cultivated field, the German Reformation, he found so little new matter, that Eichhorn fell into the mistake of concluding, from the poverty of his harvest, that the soil was exhausted, and that our knowledge of that eventful period was destined to have no further accessions. Ranke was not willing to admit that modern history is buried in myriads of documents yet unseen, and that the composition of books fit to live must be preceded by the underground labour of another generation. The manuscripts served him rather as a magazine of curiosities than as the essential basis of a connected history; and he has been accused of indifference to the publication of further papers, at least when they were taken from archives which he had consulted. In his *Traité de Législation*, Mably prophesied a long duration to the Swedish Constitution of 1720: before the book appeared the Constitution had been upset. Mably exclaimed:—'Le roi de Suède peut changer son pays, mais il ne changera pas mon livre.' The stories told of Ranke's impatience of the gleaners who plod after him parody that speech. Nevertheless he set the example of that occasional miscellaneous use of unpublished materials as a subsidiary aid to history, which has been followed by the school now predominant in Belgium, Germany, and France, and which has diffused much light, but concentrated little. In the *Popes* there are even portions of the text which possess nearly the value of direct original authority: such, for instance, as the description of the occupation of Ferrara by Clement VIII, which is founded on the contemporary memoirs of the Venetian Thuanus, Nicholas Contarini, which are to be found among the manuscripts of several European libraries. And the first volume of his History of the Reformation, which opens the series of his collected works, has gained notably by the researches made since its first appearance.

The new volume of the History of England is written in striking contrast to the *Popes*. The sparkle is gone, but there is much more body. The striving for effect has disappeared. Hallam's Constitutional History, or Guizot's Memoirs, are less solid and not more grave. This is not a history by glimpses and flashes, but a patient, consecutive narration, offering an unbroken chain of causes and effects, in which the relative importance of events is distinguished with a care and judgment that would be impossible in pictorial writing. Ranke has gone out of his way to avoid comparisons. The siege of Londonderry, the relief of Limerick, the victory and death of Dundee, scenes which Macaulay has made as vivid as anything in epic poetry, are described with elaborate dulness. The book suffers not only from the want of colour, but from the want of sympathy. Except William III, it has hardly any living characters. Marlborough, Seymour, Somers, Montague, and Shrewsbury are expressions standing for a certain quantity of force or talent, or a certain kind of opinion. They are effigies, but they are not men. It is hard to imagine a more remarkable position than that of Russell at La Hogue. He wished that the French might escape him, and that James might be restored, and in that frame of mind it was his fortune to crush the French fleet. Ranke knows the minutest particulars; he sees the interest of the thing; he says that it is very curious, but his account is incredibly unreal and reflected. This want of interest in his personages contributes to make him so reserved in his moral judgments. His description of the massacre of Glencoe is most exact, and betrays not the least temptation to diminish the guilt of William. Perhaps the case against him has never been put in a more damaging way. But not a word of criticism is wasted upon it. It was an action (*eine Handlung*), an incident (*eine Begebenheit*), which posterity has made a subject of reproach to the memory of King William. But to say that it was a crime would not make it more intelligible, and would not help forward the narrative. The disregard for the question which amuses ingenious boys and idle men, whether people were good or bad, extends from persons to ideas, from the question of moral virtue to the question of intellectual truth.

The problems discussed in William's reign, as to the limitation of the royal power by Parliament, and the control of Parliament by the nation, are at the root of all the political agitation of modern Europe: The debates were the nursery of political philosophy, and are as interesting as the experiments which preceded the discoveries of natural science. Ranke shows faithfully the conflict of the systems, but he does not enquire whether either of them was the right one, and does not perceive in the midst of an apparent chaos, truth fighting its way against the resisting influences of habit and of profit. He describes the proceedings at the trial: he does not say that the verdict has been long pronounced. It is as though one should write a biography of Galileo or of Harvey without admitting that anything is definitely known about the hypothesis of the movement of the earth, or of the circulation of the blood. History, in Ranke's conception, is a science complete in itself, independent, and ancillary to none, borrowing no instruments, and supplying no instruction, beyond its own domain. This dignified isolation involves a certain poverty in the reflections, a certain inadequacy of generalization. The writer seldom illustrates his facts from the state of ancient or general learning, or by the investigation of legal and constitutional problems. He does not explain the phenomena by political laws, the teaching of observation and comparison; and he has no care for literature, or for the things, apart from politics, which manifest the life and thought of nations. He is more conversant with the shifting relations of cabinets and factions than with the convictions, errors, prejudices, and passions that urge the masses of mankind and sway their rulers. He keeps these things at a distance, lest they should impede the clearness of his vision. They touch him not, and he chooses not to contemplate them. Hence his later works especially are tame and frigid compared with the books of men who have not a tenth of his learning or any conception of the disciplined and inquisitive energy which has raised him to be the Niebuhr, almost the Columbus, of modern history.

Ranke has nowhere defined what he conceives to have been the real essence of the conflict between William and James, and the cause of its importance in general history. In one or two characteristic passages he invokes the goddess Necessity, fixed fate, and unrelenting force with an awe worthy of Æschylus. But there is a hidden under-current running counter to the assumptions on which men are used to judge the great struggle, and take their side in it. The account of home politics goes to prove that William was not a friend of popular liberties; the account of foreign affairs shows that he was not the champion of the Protestant religion. Of all foreign courts the one most interested in the success of this expedition was the Court of Vienna. The Emperor had the Turkish war on his hands, while Lewis XIV was intriguing to have his son elected King of the Romans, and to obtain the succession of the Spanish Crown. The Revolution which detached Great Britain from the French alliance was an immense relief for Leopold, and he answered James's petition for assistance by telling him that he had brought his disaster on himself by his untimely zeal. The Austrian and Spanish envoys are accordingly found at once on confidential terms with the Prince of Orange, and he assured Ronquillo that he might be trusted as a good Castilian. At that time the Habsburgs represented the Catholic cause. Lewis XIV was on the point of making war on the Pope, who refused money for the support of James on the plea that all his resources were needed to protect his dominions against the French. He spoke of France as an anti-Catholic power, and armed as for a religious war. It was the first occasion since the Reformation on which by common consent Europe abandoned even the pretence of guiding policy by religion. The aid of the prince who ruled over the two great maritime States was necessary to the Catholic Powers, and their friendship was essential to the stability of his throne. In his domestic policy he was not a liberal sovereign, and the best parts of Ranke's volume are those which describe his efforts to maintain intact the power which had belonged to the Stuart kings. His countrymen in the Netherlands accused him of arbitrary acts; and the meditated treason of men like Russell was provoked by the discovery that William was a more dexterous and more formidable adversary of popular liberties than James. It was a necessity of his position to observe the capitulation of Limerick, for, until Ireland was pacified, he was robbed of much of his military power. This was prevented by the violence of the Irish Parliament, which united zeal against the Catholics with ardour against the Prerogative. The situation suggested the famous argument of Molyneux—that Ireland, being a conquered country, was subject to the royal pleasure. All these things pointed in one direction. William required all the resources of his kingdom and of his crown to carry on the war which was the object and the passion of his life. The opposition and the intolerance of Parliament were both impediments to his action. Richard Temple, one of the popular spokesmen, was the first to move the revival of the old penal laws. William's authority was as closely linked with the cause of toleration as that of James had been with the dispensing Power. He did not belong to the Established Church, in whose behalf the penal enactments were made. His doctrines were as odious to Episcopalians, and at least as much dreaded by them, as those of James. It was to exclude successors of his faith that the clause limiting the Protestant succession was inserted in the Act of 1701. He called the Anglican ceremonial a comedy. When the Scots required him to promise that he would exterminate heretics, he replied that he would not be a persecutor. In the Irish Parliament the favour which he ventured to show to Catholics was violently denounced. Ranke affirms that events had made toleration a necessity of policy, and that William bore it aloft at all times on his banner. And if his volume has any loftier theme than intrigues of ambition and trials of strength, it is the establishment of religious freedom in the country which had become the stronghold of civil freedom.

It is true that the personal position of William III and his international policy required that Catholic and Presbyterian should alike remain unmolested. But Parliament thwarted the design, and religious oppression kept pace during his reign with the increase of parliamentary influence. The power of the crown was effectually restricted, and a parliamentary power was substituted for it, equally absolute, equally ambitious, and less easy to resist. The Revolution did not establish the principles of liberty; and it is liberty acknowledged as a principle, not liberties obtained by compromise and concession, that generates toleration. The inherent connection of civil and religious freedom was not understood in England until the extinction of the Jacobite party. Somers and Locke were men of a more enlightened liberality than William, and less jealous of maintaining the State power; and they were eminently fitted to pursue a principle to its consequences. Yet they were not friendly to the liberty of conscience. Something of the same confusion which deceived those illustrious men bewilders the keen, clear, cold intellect of the great Prussian historian. During the last years of his life James and not William represented the cause of toleration. On the throne he had been animated by the desire to achieve, not liberty, but victory, for his Church—that is, by a religious, not a political or philosophical motive. He raised an issue between two religious interests, not between two principles of government, and that error cost him his throne. Some years later, when his fortune was beginning to prosper, Middleton induced him to declare that he would maintain the Test; and Ranke is persuaded that this concession would have accomplished his restoration. At the last moment James revoked the promise, and the scheme at once broke down. Now, as between those who insisted on the Test, and James who rejected it, the cause of toleration is on the side of James. On that occasion the question of the royal authority caused no difficulty. The English finally refused to have James for their king, not because of his unpopularity, or of his faith, or of his arbitrary maxims, but because he would not preserve religious disabilities. Ranke pronounces that in this matter he acted the part of a bigot. In our judgment, it is the most honourable act in the public life of James II, and gives a dignity to his exile which was wanting in the days of his greatness, and at the moment of his fall.

In this volume, as in all the works of the author, there is much new matter. He has examined in the French archives the correspondence of Marshal Tallard during his embassy to London, and the despatches of Lauzun and D'Avaux on the expedition to Ireland. Holland supplies printed as well as unprinted documents, which it is not creditable to previous writers to have overlooked. The correspondence between William and Heinsius has been partially used; but the extracts recently made known by Noorden prove that there is much more than this in the Heinsius papers, and that a vast accession of important knowledge may be expected from their publication. The manuscripts of the British Museum have been, we suspect, rather hastily consulted. Melfort's despatches from Rome would have thrown additional light on the negotiations of the banished Court. The most valuable addition has been the discovery of the correspondence of the Brandenburg envoys, extending over many years. The Elector was represented by two Swiss brothers, named Bonnet. They were well-informed and impartial; and their letters give an uninterrupted narrative of events at court and in the parliament. They enable the historian to restore lost debates; and it is due to them that Ranke has surpassed his predecessors in domestic politics, and not only in international affairs, where he is always supreme.

INDEX

Achenwall, Gottfried (1719–72), 51 nn. 2 and 5, 52 nn. 2 and 6

Acton, Lord, and archives, 78–85; on Buckle, 12 n., 66; on Burke, 68–9; on criticism, 15, 75–7; on Döllinger, 67, 68, 73 n. 3, 83 n. 2, 84, 86, 92, 94, 138 n. 1, 181, 208, 209, 216, 217; on French Revolution, 66–7, 79, 83, 135; and the German historical school, 14, 38, 63, 73–5, ch. III sect. 3, 210–11; and general history, xii, 8, 49, 50, 110, 128, 134, 139, 216–17; and 'historical thinking', 8, 96–9, 139, 218; and the history of historiography, 11, 14, 23–4, 63–6, 74–5, 97–9; on O. Klopp, 150 n. 1; and the *Liber Diurnus*, 81–2; and manuscript work, 80–5; and medieval history, 44, 69–73; and moral judgements, 71–3, 92–5; on J. v. Müller, 50, 110, 215–18; on Newman, 137; on 'periods' of history, 128, 134; on the *philosophes*, 66, 135; on power, 62 n. 1, 127; on Providence, 137–8; and Ranke, 82, 86–95, 117, 127, 139, 208, 210, 219–32; on religion, 68–9, 75–7, 96–7, 137–8; on Romanticism, 68–75; and Simancas, 81 n. 1; and Vatican archives, 80–2. *See also* Romanes Lecture *and* Middle Ages.

Alberi, Eugenio, 177, 182 n. 1, 183

Allen, John, 175, 183, 185, 190, 198–9

Alva, Duke of, 174, 177–8, 180, 193, 200

America, 22, 46, 50, 60, 81 n. 1, 120–1, 130, 213

Anjou, Henri, Duc d', 171, 172 n. 1, 180, 183, 193, 198–9

Anquetil, L'abbé Louis-Pierre (1723–1806), 172

Archives, 20, 64, 78–85, 90–1, 113, 143–51, 154–5, 181, 189

Arneth, Alfred Ritter von, 76 n. 1, 79, 151, 153, 154 n. 2

Audin, Jean Marie Vincent, 175–6, 182 n. 1

Bacon, Sir Francis, 11, 55, 96, 125

Bain, R. Nisbet, 161

Barre, Joseph (1692–1764), 43

Baumgarten, Hermann, 187 n. 2, 188 n. 1, 191 n. 2, 192–3, 196, 199

Baumgarten, Siegmund Jakob (1706–57), 47 n. 5

Bayonne, interview of, 172 n. 1, 174, 178

Beaufort, Louis de (d. 1795), 58 n. 5, 77 n. 2

Beer, Adolf (1831–1902), 151, 154 n. 2

Berlin, 67 n. 4; archives in, 84 n. 2, 150–1; court of, 143, 146–7, 153, 156

Bestuzhev, Alexis, Russian Chancellor, 162–70

Biblical scholarship, 15–16, 57–8, 75–6

Bismarck, 26, 28, 95, 108, 113, 122

Bodin, Jean, 3, 9 n. 1

Böhmer, Johann Friedrich (1785–1863), 64 n. 3, 67 n. 4, 72 n. 6, 77 n. 5

Bohun, Edmund (1645–99), 2

Bolingbroke, Henry St John, Viscount, 48, 129–30

Bonelli, Cardinal, of Alessandria, 185–6, 189, 191, 199–200

Bordier, Henri Léonard, 191–2, 198

Bossuet, 47, 66, 69, 212

Brady, Robert (1627–1700), 65

Brown, Rawdon L. (1803–83), 81

Brückner, Alexander (1834–96), 158 n. 1

Brussels, Archives in, 78, 113, 151

Buckle, Thomas, 11–12, 66

Burckhardt, Jacob (1818–97), 21–2, 122, 127–8, 132–3

Burke, Edmund, 18, 68–70

Cambridge Modern History, 24, 116, 216

Capefigue, Jean-Baptiste Honoré Raymond (1801–72), 176–7, 177 n. 3, 182 n. 1, 226

Capilupi, Camillo, 185, 195, 197

Carion, Johann (1499–1537), 45

Carlyle, Thomas, 92, 145, 217–18

Casket Letters, 65

Catherine de' Medici, ch. VI *passim*

Cavalli, Sigismondo de, 177, 184, 189, 193

Caveirac, Abbé Novi de (1713–82), 172, 175

Cellarius, Christopher (1638–1707), 35 n. 2, 45–6, 129

Charlemagne, 57 n. 1, 58, 115, 134

Charles IX of France, 172 n. 1, 174, 176–7, 180, 183, 185–6, 188, 190, 200–1

233

Index

Charles X of France, 175

Chateaubriand, François René, Vicomte de (1768–1848), 176, 183

Classical scholarship, 2, 16, 40–1, 56–7, 109

Coligny, Admiral Gaspard de, 172 n. 1, 174, 177–80, 183–4, 187–8, 190, 195–8, 201

Contemporary affairs as studied at Göttingen, 40, 51–2, 61

Creighton, Bishop Mandel, 92

Creuzer, Friedrich (1771–1858), 7 n. 2, 70 n. 1

Criticism, Historical, 9 n. 1, 15–16, 35–8, 53, 56–60, 65–6, 72, 75–7, 89, 172 n. 1, 187–9, 206, 209–10

Daniel, Father Gabriel (1649–1728), 172 n. 1

Darwin, Charles, 209

Delbrück, Hans (1848–1929), 153, 155

Diplomatic Revolution, 20, 147, 149, 151–2, 157, 160–1

Döllinger, Ignaz (1799–1890). See Acton on

Dresden, archives in, 143–5, 149

Droysen, Johann Gustav (1808–84), 76 n. 1, 78 n. 5, 93, 153

Ecclesiastical scholarship, 15–16, 56, 65–6, 76

Eckstädt, Graf Vitzthum von, 149–50, 160

Eichhorn, Karl Friedrich (1781–1854), Professor in Göttingen (1817–29), 50 n. 6, 57 n. 2, 227

Elisabeth, Tsarina, of Russia, 151, 163, 165, 167, 169

Encyclopaedists. See Enlightenment

Enlightenment, 4, 8, 16, 60, 70, 103–4, 133, 135–6, 171–2

Falloux, Alfred Frédéric Pierre, Comte de (1811–86), 177, 182 n. 1

Ferrière, Comte Hector de la, 192, 193 n. 1, 201 n. 1

Florence, archives in, 81 n. 1, 83 n. 2, 177

Foreign policy, question of the primacy of, 100 n. 1, 116–28

Forgeries, 76, 79, 177

Four-Monarchy System, 45–6, 109, 135

Frederick the Great, 142–69, 217, 222; correspondence of, 145 n. 1, 152; Political Testament of, 153–4

Frederick William IV of Prussia, 72

French Revolution, 18, 24, 27, 41, 66–8, 74, 79, 84, 94, 98, 120, 129, 135, 172, 175, 207, 210, 217 nn. 2 and 3

French wars of religion, 24, 114, 141; ch. VI passim

Gachard, Louis Prosper (1800–85), 178 n. 1, 200

Gandy, Georges, 191, 196, 199

Gar, Tommaso, 182

Gatterer, Johann Christoph, 5, 37, 42–4, 48–51, 56, 60 n. 2, 74, 101 n. 1, 113, 116 n. 3, 210

Genoa, archives in, 81 n. 1

George II, 39, 142, 163

George III, 20

German Historical School, xii, xiv–xv, 12–14, 22, 26–8, chs. II and III passim, 178–80, 207–32

Gervinus, Georg Gottfried (1805–71), 26, 76 n. 2

Gfrörer, August Friedrich (1803–61), 67 n. 4, 211, 220, 223

Giannone, Pietro (1676–1748), 55 n. 2, 207

Gibbon, E., 4, 53 n. 2, 69

Giesebrecht, Friedrich Wilhelm Benjamin (1814–89), 77 n. 5, 78 n. 5

Gladstone, William Ewart, 63 n. 1, 80, 92

Glencoe, massacre of, 92, 94, 228

Gooch, Dr G. P., 22

Göttingen, University of, 5, 7, 10, 13, 23, 39–61 passim, 74, 103–5, 109–11, 113, 116, 121, 130–1, 215–16

Gregory XIII, Pope, 174, 186, 190, 200

Grey, Sir Edward, 1st Viscount Grey of Falloden, 137

Griffet, Henri (1698–1771), 172 n. 1, 183, 191 n. 1

Guicciardini, Francesco, 220

Guise, Henri, Duc de, 172 n. 1, 174, 177 n. 3, 190

Guise, family of, 171, 197

Guizot, François Pierre Guillaume (1787–1874), 223, 228

Häberlin, Fr. D. (1720–87), 53 n. 3

Hague, The, archives at, 78, 113, 148

Hallam, Henry, 11, 65, 228

Hanover, 39–40, 163

Harnack, Adolf von (1851–1930), 64, 67

234

Index

Heeren, Arnold Hermann Ludwig (1760–1842), 10, 49 n. 1, 50 n. 5, 111, 117, 130

Hegel, 71 n. 3, 104, 125

Herder, Johann Gottfried (1744–1803), 17, 60

Herodotus, 58, 205

Hertzberg, Count Ewald Friedrich von, 143, 145 n. 2, 146, 165 n. 1

Heyne, Christian Gottlieb (1729–1812), 7 n. 2, 37 n. 1, 40–1, 47 n. 5, 59 n. 3

History, ancient, 2, 45, 48, 53, 58, 75–7, 109, 111, 205–6

History, general, xi–xii, xv, 8–10, 34, 44–50; Ranke and, 100–41

History, medieval. *See* Middle Ages

History, modern 46, 48, 110–13, 116–17, 128–36

History, national, 29–30, 38, 53, 61, 112, 124

History, technical, 94, 98, 137–41, 229

History, universal, 6–7, 37, 44–50, 103, 110, 119, 123–6, 130, 215–16

Homer, 34

Honorius I, Pope, 82

Horawitz, Adalbert Heinrich, 13

Horn, Professor D. B., 161

Hume, David, 43 *and* n. 3, 69, 98, 129, 226

Italy, 104, n. 2, 111, 132, 135, 220, 225–6; opening of the archives in, 79; historical scholarship in, 66, 207–8

James II, 80, 120, 229–31

Jesuits, 175, 212; archives of, 81 n. 1

Jörg, Josef Edmund (1819–1901), 83 n. 2, 86

Karamsin, Nikolas Mickhailovich (1765–1826), 54 n. 2

Kaunitz, Wenzel Anton, Prince von, Austrian Chancellor, 151, 168

Klopp, Onno (1822–1903), 149–50, 155

Koser, Reinhold (1852–1914), 153

Laplace, Pierre Simon Marquis de (1749–1827), 75

Lappenberg, Johann Martin (1794–1865), 69

Lasaulx, Peter Ernst (1805–61), 72 n. 6, 73

Lecky, 20 n. 2, 64

Lehmann, Max (1845–1929), 153–7

Leibniz, 64 n. 3, 69

Leipzig, 60

Leo, Heinrich (1799–1878), 86–7, 211, 223–4

Liber Diurnus, 82

Lingard, John, 175, 177–8, 182 n. 1, 183, 185, 191

Livy, 2 n. 2

Lodge, Sir Richard, 160–1

Loiseleur, Jean-Auguste-Jules (1816–1900), 191–2

Lorenz, Ottokar (1832–1904), 12, 13 n. 5, 25 n. 1

Lorraine, Cardinal of, 174, 177 n. 3, 184, 188–9, 197

Louis XIV, 78, 120, 131, 172 n. 1, 220, 230

Louis Philippe, Paris archives under, 148, 149 n. 1

Luther, Martin, 9 n. 1, 24–6, 45, 94, 103

Mabillon, Jean (1632–1707), 16 n. 1, 64 n. 3, 65, 69, 207

Mably, Gabriel Bonnot de (1709–85), 57 n. 1, 227

Macaulay, 4, 64, 88, 92–3, 138 n. 1, 220, 222–4, 228

Machiavelli, 2 n. 2, 28, 86, 89 n. 2, 206, 220–2

Mackintosh, Sir James, 78 n. 2, 176, 183

Magna Carta, 19, 25

Maistre, Joseph de (1753–1819), 175, 213

Maitland, F. W., 22

Manning, Cardinal, 80

Mantua, archives in, 81 n. 1

Maria Theresa, Empress, 67 n. 4, 79, 142, 147, 149, 151, 156–7, 160, 162, 165–6

Marie Antoinette, 79

Martin, H., 180

Martin, Victor, 196, 197 n. 1

Marx, Karl, 17

Mary, Queen of Scots, 62, 114

May, Sir Thomas Erskine, 20 n. 2

Medici, Margaret de'. *See* Valois, Marguerite de

Meinecke, Friedrich, 17 n. 1, 28, 35 n. 1

Melanchthon, 45

Mémoire Raisonné, 143–6, 149

Mérimée, Prosper (1803–70), 176

Michaelis, Johann David (1717–91), 40, 41 n. 1, 52 n. 1, 54 n. 3, 57 n. 5, 59 n. 2

Michelet, Jules (1798–1874), 78 n. 2, 92, 131–2, 182 n. 1

Michiel (Micheli), Giovanni, 184, 189

Index

Middle Ages, 13, 33, 35, 43, 45–6, 69–73, 89, 130–6, 210, 219, 222, 223, 226; Acton and, 212–14

Mignet, François Auguste Alexis (1796–1884), 78

Minghetti, Masco, 82

Miron, physician to the Duc d'Anjou, later Henri III of France, 171, 172 n. 1, 183, 191 n. 1, 192 n. 2, 198–9

Modena, Archives in, 79, 81 n. 1

Mommsen, Theodor (1817–1903), 64, 78 n. 5, 91, 207, 208

Monod, Henri, 199

Montesquieu, 9 n. 1, 41 n. 1

Monumenta Germaniae Historica, 57, 61

Moral judgements in history, 71–3, 92–6, 106, 221, 228

Mosheim, Johann Lorenz (1693–1755), 40, 69

Motley, John, 61 n. 1

Müller, Johann von (1793–1809), 9 n. 1, 50, 53, 57 n. 2, 60 n. 1, 64 n. 3, 74–5, 89, 92, 110, 210, 215–18, 227

Münchausen, Baron, 39, 55

Munich, 63, 68, 81 n. 1, 83 n. 2, 86

Münster, Count Ernst, 52 n. 6

Muratori, Lodovico Antonio (1672–1750), 64 n. 3, 69, 207

Murray, Sir James H. (1837–1915), 209

Napoleon I, 40, 111, 121, 126, 176, 215, 217 n. 2, 220

Napoleon III, French archives under, 83, 148, 149 n. 1

Naudé, Albert, 153–5

Navarre, Henry of, 171, 174, 179–80, 184, 190, 198, 200

Navarre, Queen of (Jeanne d'Albret), 174, 178

Nestor, Schlözer's edition of, 7, 36 n. 3, 55–9

Netherlands, 40, 177, 230; Revolt of the, 114, 174, 193

Newman, Cardinal, 137, 138 n. 1

Newton, Sir Isaac, 32, 118

Niebuhr, Barthold Georg (1776–1831), xiv, 32, 36, 53, 61, 64 n. 3, 67, 74–7, 89 *and* n. 2, 93, 210, 229

Orange, House of, 78, 180, 230

Paris, archives in, 81 n. 1, 83, 113, 148, 149 n. 1

Pastor, Freiherr Ludwig von, 191 n. 2, 198 n. 1

Pater, Walter (1839–94), 133

Pauli, Reinhold (1823–82), 87, 222

Periodisation, 44–6, 48, 109, 128–36

Pertz, Georg Heinrich (1795–1876), 77 n. 5

Philip II, of Spain, 78, 114, 171, 177, 188, 190, 200

Philippson, Martin (1846–1916), 154 n. 2, 192, 193 n. 1, 196–7, 199

'Philosophe' movement. *See* Enlightenment

Pius V, Pope, 174 n. 1, 186, 191, 194

Platzhoff, Walter, 194

Pliny, 59 n. 5

Popelinière, Lancelot Voisin de la (1540–1608), 2 nn. 1 *and* 2, 13 n. 4, 205–6

Positivists, 66

Prague, 42, 46, 83 n. 2

Prinsterer, Gulielmus Groen van (1801–76), 177

Providence, 136–141

Prynne, William, 86 n. 1

Puffendorf, Samuel von (1632–94), 35 n. 2

Pütter, Johann Stefan (1725–1807), 43 n. 1, 51 n. 2, 54 n. 4

Ranke, Leopold von (1795–1886), xiv–xv, 21, 23, 28, 32, 36, 43, 61, 64, 76 n. 1, 82, 208; his austerity, 95, 128; and cultural history, 120, 123–5; development of his manuscript work, 53–4, 56, 83, 88–91, 209, 226–7, 232; and the European states-system, 110–13; and general history, xv, 8, 44, 100–41 *passim*; *Latin and Teutonic Nations* (1824), 89, 104 n. 2, 220–1, 226; *History of the Popes* (1834–6), 86 n. 3, 104 n. 2, 117, 125–6, 219–20, 225–8; *History of the Reformation* (1839–47), 95, 219–21, 227–8; *History of England* (1859–68), 87–92, 94, 121, 220–32; on the massacre of St Bartholomew, 177, 179, 182 n. 1, 183 n. 2, 187 n. 2, 197–8; and the middle ages, 89; and moral judgements, 92–5, 106; and nationality, 124–6, 139; and the primacy of foreign policy, 116–25; use of *Relazioni*, 89–90, 121, 217, 227; and religion, 107, 137–9, 210, 224; and the Renaissance, 131; on the origins of

Index

Ranke, Leopold von (*cont.*)
the Seven Years War, 151, 154, 156, 170; and Western Europe, 113–16. *See also under* Acton

Rapin, Sieur de Thoyras, Paul de (1661–1725), 43

Raumer, Friedrich von (1781–1873), 66, 147, 176, 207, 208

Reason, Age of. *See* Enlightenment

Reformation, 9, 21, 25–6, 103, 111, 118, 125, 137, 212, 214, 223, 230; Acton and, 212; and historical study, 9, 45. *See also under* Ranke

Rehm, Friedrich (1792–1847), 9 n. 2, 10 n. 3, 11 n. 1, 78 n. 4

Reichstag, German, 43

Relazioni of Venetian ambassadors, 89–90, 121, 177, 217, 227

Religion and history, 31, 96, 103, 107, 137–9, 212–14, 224

Renaissance, 2, 6, 13, 17, 20–1, 24, 46, 68, 89, 97, 118, 129–36, 212–13

Renan, Ernest (1823–92), 99

Richelieu, Cardinal, 86, 219–20, 222; Political Testament of, 76 n. 1

Ritter, Gerhard, 28 n. 1

Robertson, William (1721–93), 43 n. 3, 55 n. 2, 69, 89, 129, 226

Rollin, Charles (1661–1741), 47

Roman Empire, fall of, 2 n. 2, 19, 25, 45, 109, 118, 122, 130, 140

Romanes Lecture, Acton and, 63–4, 216

Romantic Movement, 4, 18, 34–5, 60–1, 68–75, 175–6, 215

Rome, archives in, 81–3, 113, 193, 227; Acton in, 81–3; Roman Diary, 92 n. 1, 138 n. 1; Gregorovius, Roman Diary, 81 n. 1; Von Sickel, *Roman Reminiscences*, 81–2

Romier, Lucien, 197–8

Rosa, Gabriele, 14

Roscoe, William (1753–1831), 65, 89, 226

Rühs, Christian Friedrich (1781–1820), 7, 9 n. 1, 43 n. 3, 104 n. 1

Russia, 120, 127, 144–70 *passim*; historical studies in, 36, 54–5; Secret War Council, 1756, 164–5. See also under *Nestor*

Russian Imperial Historical Society, 158, 165–8

St Bartholomew, massacre of, xv, 13, 19, 65, 114, 171–201

Salviati, papal nuncio in Paris (1572), 176, 183–4, 189, 191, 193, 195–8, 200

Savigny, Karl von (1779–1861), 57 n. 2, 69 n. 1, 207, 208

Saxony, 143–5, 152–3, 157, 164–5, 169. *See also under* Dresden

Sbornik. *See under* Russian Imperial Historical Society

Schäfer, Arnold Dietrich (1819–82), 149 n. 1, 150–1

Schiller, Friedrich (1759–1805), 210

Schlosser, Friedrich Christoph (1776–1861), 57 n. 2, 93

Schlözer, August Ludwig (1735–1809), 6, 8, 36 n. 2, 37 n. 1, 41, 44 n. 2, 47 nn. 1 *and* 5, 47–60, 74, 113, 121, 215–16

Schnabel, Franz, 28 n. 1

Scientific Revolution of the seventeenth century, xiv, 39, 42, 118, 135–6

Scott, Sir Walter, 18

Second World War, 28, 40

Seeley, John Robert (1834–95), 41

Semler, Johann Salomo (1725–91), 40, 54 n. 3, 56, 77 n. 2

Seven Years War, xv, 20, 46, 142–70 *passim*

Sickel, Theodor von (1826–1908), 77, 81–2

Simancas, archives at, 81 n. 1, 176

Sismondi, Jean Charles-Léonard Simonde de (1773–1842), 89, 176, 226

Soldan, Wilhelm Gottlieb (d. 1869), 180–2

Soloviev, Sergei Mikhailovich (1620–79), 164

Spencer, Herbert, 85

Spittler, Ludwig Timotheus (1752–1810), 57 n. 2, 93, 178, 210

Stein, Heinrich Friedrich Karl Freiherr vom (1757–1831), 52 n. 6, 57 n. 2

Stenzel, Gustav Adolf Harold (1792–1854), 61, 89, 144 n. 1, 146 n. 1, 226

Stubbs, William, 23, 65

Stuhr, Peter Fedderson (1787–1851), 148–9

Sybel, Heinrich von (1817–95), 78 n. 5, 83, 95

Symonds, John Addington (1840–93), 133

Tacitus, 2 n. 2, 205, 220–1

Taine, Hippolyte (1828–93), 92

Theiner, Father Augustus, Keeper of the Papal Archives, 80, 81 n. 1, 195 n. 1

237